# Lecture Notes in Computer Science     14166

Founding Editors

Gerhard Goos
Juris Hartmanis

The series Lecture Notes in Computer Science (LNCS), including its subseries Lecture Notes in Artificial Intelligence (LNAI) and Lecture Notes in Bioinformatics (LNBI), has established itself as a medium for the publication of new developments in computer science and information technology research, teaching, and education.

LNCS enjoys close cooperation with the computer science R & D community, the series counts many renowned academics among its volume editors and paper authors, and collaborates with prestigious societies. Its mission is to serve this international community by providing an invaluable service, mainly focused on the publication of conference and workshop proceedings and postproceedings. LNCS commenced publication in 1973.

Yuhua Luo

Editor

# Cooperative Design, Visualization, and Engineering

20th International Conference on Cooperative Design,
Visualization and Engineering, CDVE 2023
Mallorca, Spain, October 1–4, 2023
Proceedings

 Springer

*Editor*
Yuhua Luo (iD)
University of Balearic Islands
Palma de Mallorca, Spain

ISSN 0302-9743            ISSN 1611-3349   (electronic)
Lecture Notes in Computer Science
ISBN 978-3-031-43814-1      ISBN 978-3-031-43815-8   (eBook)
https://doi.org/10.1007/978-3-031-43815-8

This Springer imprint is published by the registered company Springer Nature Switzerland AG
The registered company address is: Gewerbestrasse 11, 6330 Cham, Switzerland

Paper in this product is recyclable.

# Preface

The CDVE 2023 conference was held during October 1–4, 2023, in the heart of the old town of Palma de Mallorca, Spain. This was the 20th edition of the conference. The participants were happy to get together again after the pandemic and to come back to the birthplace of this very specific conference.

This volume contains the collection of the accepted papers from the 20th International Conference on Cooperative Design, Visualization and Engineering - CDVE 2023. Over a hundred authors from around 20 countries submitted papers to the conference.

The contribution in this volume reflects the research and development trends in the conference's areas of focus. An obvious trend that appears here is about the significant advantage of applying network structures in cooperative working. The network structures convincingly show the potential and power at all levels of cooperative applications, whether in the case of the well-known internet or social networks, or specific networks such as neural networks, sensor networks, or even the basic convolutional networks embedded into many basic algorithms.

One example in the volume along this direction is to use cooperating sensors in ultra-dense wireless sensor networks for monitoring such as in a vineyard. Another example is to realize the difficult challenge of wireless charging for electric vehicles on the run in an energy network. Using the same technology, a paper presents the achievement of monitoring the environment for a large coastal area.

Applying AI appears as another trend among these year's papers for a sequence of completely different cooperative applications. Among them, a paper discusses and evaluates AI-created art, which is a very timely topic in society. Papers discuss using deep learning for astronomic applications, for effective land use mapping etc. This shows that AI is already a powerful tool for many cooperative working areas.

Applying other types of AI technology such as computer vision and machine learning gives wider possibilities for cooperative user interfaces. Papers in this area include hand gesture recognition, user behavior analysis, cooperative health care, real-time human motion capturing etc.

Application of new technology means new challenges. Answering these challenges is a driving force for raising the technology to a new level. A set of papers in the volume analyzes issues that have emerged in society recently such as new forms of resource sharing and new forms of cooperative working. A paper evaluates the shared-bicycle system in big cities and how to improve the phase of reverse logistics. Another paper performs a large-scale investigation and survey for a new form of cooperative working – working at home. This is a continuous effort of our CDVE community to protect our environment and our Earth.

I would like to express my thanks to all the authors for their hard work and for submitting their papers to the CDVE 2023 conference. My thanks also go to all our volunteer reviewers, program committee members, and organization committee members for their valuable contribution. My special thanks are dedicated to my team at the University of the Balearic Islands led by our organization chairs Sebastià Galmés and Pilar Fuster. The success of the conference this year and in many other years would not have been possible without their unconditional support.

August 2023                                                              Yuhua Luo

# Organization

## Conference Chair

Yuhua Luo                              University of the Balearic Islands, Spain

## International Program Committee

### Program Chair

Thomas Tamisier                        Luxembourg Institute of Science and Technology
                                       (LIST), Luxembourg

### Members

Barbara M. Anthony              Southwestern University, USA
Jose Alfredo Costa              Federal University, UFRN, Brazil
Philipp M. Fischer              DLR (German Aerospace Center), Germany
Peter Nørkjær Gade              University College of Northern Denmark,
                                   Denmark
Sebastia Galmes                 University of the Balearic Islands, Spain
Laura Garcia                    Universidad Politécnica de Cartagena, Spain
Halin Gilles                    School of Architecture of Nancy, France
Ewa Grabska                     Jagiellonian University, Poland
Figen Gül                       Istanbul Technical University, Turkey
Shuangxi Huang                  Tsinghua University, China
Phan Duy Hung                   FPT University, Vietnam
Claudia-Lavinia Ignat           Inria, France
José Miguel Jiménez             Universitat Politècnica de València, Spain
Pierre Leclercq                 University of Liège, Belgium
Jang Ho Lee                     Hongik University, South Korea
Jaime Lloret                    Polytechnic University of Valencia, Spain
Lorena Parra                    Universitat Politècnica de València, Spain
Nobuyoshi Yabuki                Osaka University, Japan
Xinwei Yao                      Zhejiang University of Technology, China

# Organization Committee

## Chairs

Sebastià Galmés            University of the Balearic Islands, Spain
Pilar Fuster               University of the Balearic Islands, Spain

## Members

Michael Brückner           Naresuan University, Thailand
Tomeu Estrany              University of the Balearic Islands, Spain
Takayuki Fujimoto          Toyo University, Japan
Alex Garcia                University of the Balearic Islands, Spain
Juan Lladó                 University of the Balearic Islands, Spain
Guofeng Qin                Tongji University, China
Chakkrit Snae Namahoot     Naresuan University, Thailand
Linan Zhu                  Zhejiang University of Technology, China

# Contents

# Proposal and Evaluation of Collaborative Event-Triggered Algorithms in Ultra-Dense Wireless Sensor Network

Sandra Viciano-Tudela⬛, Paula Navarro-Garcia, Lorena Parra⬛, Sandra Sendra⬛, and Jaime Lloret(✉)⬛

Instituto de Investigación Para la Gestión Integrada de Zonas Costeras, Universitat Politècnica de València, C/ Paranimf, 1, Grao de Gandia, 46730 Gandia, Valencia, Spain
{svictud,sansenco}@upv.es, paunagar@alumni.upv.es, loparbo@doctor.upv.es, jlloret@dcom.upv.es

**Abstract.** Wireless sensor networks and monitoring of environmental parameters such as humidity, temperature, rainfall, and soil salinity, among others, play a crucial role in precision agriculture. Power consumption can be reduced while maintaining accuracy by using collaborative and event-triggered algorithms. In this fact, reducing the energy used by the network is possible. This paper aims to propose a set of algorithms to improve the Quality of Information and the efficiency of the data collection process in a collaborative wireless sensor network while reducing the measuring frequency. In this way, the system will only be activated when necessary, creating an alarm system that will notify the farmer of a problem. Four algorithms are compared through simulations using a cluster of 16 nodes in 41 iterations that involve the detection of events in four scenarios. The option of including broadcast or multicast in the collaborative algorithm is evaluated. The study shows that the event-driven collaborative algorithm performs equal to or better than event-driven algorithms in all tested scenarios. In Scenario 3, a collaborative-based streaming algorithm has only a 1.45% error compared to 3.20% for multicast and 5.44% for the event-driven algorithm.

**Keywords:** Precision Agriculture · Wireless Sensor Networks · Rural Environment

## 1 Introduction

The Wireless Sensor Networks (WSN) for precision agriculture are becoming an important tool for both monitoring and reacting to the variation of different sensed parameters [1]. Particularly, the sensed data is used for multiple purposes beyond the triggering of actuators. Sensed data can be used to foresee or estimate the expected harvest quantity and quality, the apparition of diseases, pests, and weeds, and the requirements of nutrients and water, among others. Thus, the sensed data must accurately reflect the sensed parameter's real value and its time evolution. The concept of Quality of Information (QoI) and Quality of Sensing (QoS) [2] provides a solid approach to evaluate the accuracy of provided data from the WSN.

© The Author(s), under exclusive license to Springer Nature Switzerland AG 2023
Y. Luo (Ed.): CDVE 2023, LNCS 14166, pp. 1–12, 2023.
https://doi.org/10.1007/978-3-031-43815-8_1

In precision agriculture, individual monitorisation of each plant is expected in order to provide accurate and tailored solutions for enhancing productivity. Some applications that require individual monitorisation might include irrigation, fertilisation, application of phytosanitary products and harvest predictions. An example in which individual monitoring might suppose a great advantage is for the vineyards, which products might have a variation in cost depending on their quality. It is precision agriculture based on remote sensing, mainly in drones; individual monitoring is common [3]. Nonetheless, the monitoring of individual plants using WSN might become problematic. Ultradense networks, a type of network with a high density of nodes [4], are required in order to achieve individual monitorisation in precision agriculture. Nevertheless, ultradense networks in agriculture are still considered a future case [5].

The particularities of the rural environments with the ultradense network and the requirement of high QoI/QoS suppose a challenge to achieve efficient and suitable WSN for precision agriculture. The high density of nodes, generally structured in a cluster topology, offers at the same time a possible solution. The collaborative algorithms might provide a solution for some of these changes. Particularly, event-triggered algorithms can help to reduce the amount of energy used for data gathering and sending. If collaborative capabilities are added to event-triggered algorithms, it might be possible to reduce the periodicity of data gathering in the nodes while maintaining a high QoI/QoS.

In this paper, we propose a series of algorithms for optimising the QoI/QoS while reducing the periodicity of data gathering in a collaborative WSN. The 4 proposed algorithms are compared in a series of simulations which includes different scenarios in which an event is detected. Among the tested algorithms, there are event-triggered algorithms and collaborative event-triggered algorithms. Four scenarios with different spatiotemporal distributions of the event are included. The distribution of nodes has been designed for vineyard monitoring. The simulation is performed in a cluster of 16 nodes and during 41 iterations. The metrics include the errors in the network, which decrease the QoI/QoS.

The rest of the paper is structured as follows; Sect. 2 outlines the related work. The proposal is described in Sect. 3. Section 4 provides the details of the performed simulations. The results are analysed in Sect. 5. Finally, Sect. 6 summarises the conclusions.

## 2   Related Work

This section summarises the current event-triggered algorithms and the collaborative algorithms in precision agriculture for enhancing the QoI.

There are previous studies that have designed wireless sensor networks for the irrigation of agricultural crops. In 2018, Jawad et al. [6] presented their proposal to reduce the energy consumption of a wireless agricultural system that is in charge of measuring air temperature, air humidity and soil humidity. Two schemes are proposed to reduce the power consumption of the sensor and router nodes. A sleep/wake scheme based on duty cycles is presented, and secondly, a sleep/wake scheme where redundant data on soil moisture are taken into account. By taking these into account, the energy consumption of the sensor node can be minimised and the data communication too. A year later,

Lozoya et al. increased the variables to be taken into account to regulate the fields [7]. Their proposal seeks to improve closed-circuit precision irrigation systems, where the switching on and off of the devices is based on soil moisture. They want to create a new algorithm where more variables are taken into account: soil, irrigation and climate, in order to obtain less water consumption and greater crop productivity.

Finally, in 2021 Lozoya et al. [8] proposed an energy-efficient communication strategy between a network of wireless sensors in charge of managing the irrigation of a plantation. In this study, the authors proposed a sensor network where the detection devices make the measurements only when is necessary. The system was implemented, messages between sensors were reduced by 85% and energy consumption was reduced by 20%. In addition, the objectives of irrigation efficiency and energy consumption were achieved.

The communication of the devices in smart agriculture can be done through different protocols, as defined in [9] by Avsar et al. In their analysis, the technical properties and practical applications of five protocols were compared: ZigBee, WiFi, Sigfox, NB-IoT, and LoRaWAN. In the end, it was concluded that the protocol that has been used the most in recent years is LoRaWAN.

There are also studies with the objective of making WSN with solar energy harvesting function more efficiently. In [10], Agrawal et al. aimed to increase the energy efficiency of a WSN for agriculture. Thus, they developed energy efficiency models and algorithms for the solar backup energy base station to maintain several sensors and gateway modules. The study evaluated the energy requirements of the base station at a random moment and how to estimate the solar energy necessary to maintain the energy neutrality of the base. An improved duty cycle algorithm was proposed using the residual power parameter. It showed an improvement in terms of average power consumption, residual power performance, performance, etc. Finally, in [11], Zou et al. sought to improve the energy efficiency in WSNs powered by solar-rechargeable batteries. They aimed to improve two aspects. Depending on solar energy for its operation, the same energy is not always available. Therefore, algorithms for the prediction of collected solar energy were proposed. And secondly, an optimisation of the grouping and routing of the nodes was proposed in order to distribute the energy obtained from the sun more efficiently. Thus, it was achieved that solar energy was present when it was necessary, making the system energy efficient.

## 3 Proposal

This section summarises the current event-triggered algorithms and the collaborative algorithms in precision agriculture for enhancing the QoI.

### 3.1 Ultra-Dense WSN

The proposed system has been designed to operate in a UDWSN deployed in a vineyard. The reason for this UDWSN is that precision agriculture requires every individual (vine) to be monitored independently. This information allows the use of individual data to predict its requirements and its future performance.

The nodes of this UDWSN are endowed with edge computing. The nodes use this edge computing to evaluate if gathered data corresponds to a normal situation or to an abnormal situation. The abnormal situations might include meteorological phenomena such as rain, hailstorm, freeze, drought, or the combination of factors which provoke the apparition of pests such as fungal diseases or insect plagues.

The topology of the network is a cluster-tree topology; see Fig. 1. The Cluster Head (CH) nodes have different characteristics than other nodes. While Cluster Nodes (CN) have WiFi connectivity, CH nodes have both WiFi and LoRa connectivity. Thus, it allows forwarding the data to the database (DB) using the different CH when necessary. In Fig. 1, the light green dots represent the CNs deployed in every vine, while dark green dots represent the CHs.

The sensor included in CH nodes could comprise the following ones: soil moisture, soil conductivity, soil temperature, humidity, air temperature, wind speed and direction, solar radiation, precipitation, dew point, and normal and infrared cameras. Meanwhile, the regular nodes only have sensors for soil moisture, soil temperature, humidity, and air temperature.

## 3.2 Collaborative Event-Triggered Algorithms

There are different evaluated algorithms. In this subsection, all used algorithms are described in details.

The proposed algorithms operate once the CH and CN nodes are aware of the network topology. Thus, the initial steps for discovering the neighbours, CHs, CNs, and network topology are not included. For all the options, the node that gathers the data determines if sensed data constitutes an event or a regular situation. If an event is detected, the nodes transmit the information about the event to the DB.

In the first option, all the nodes gather data every time slot. This algorithm ensures that the gathered information accurately reflects reality, but it supposes high energy consumption during data gathering. In the results, this algorithm is named Option 1.

Option 2 consists of an algorithm using a token to identify the node responsible for gathering data. The token is transferred from node to node sequentially according to the topology, following the same principle as Token Ring in wired networks. This option minimises the energy use for data gathering but strongly affects the accuracy of data when events occur.

The explanation of this algorithm can be seen in Fig. 2. Every turn, the node$_i$ checks if this turn has the token and has to measure. If no action has to be done because it does not have the token this turn, the node rests until the next turn. If it has to measure, the node$_i$ gathers data and, with edge computing, analyses the data to evaluate if it indicates regular conditions of an event. If an event is detected, the node$_i$ sends the information to the DB and then waits until the next turn. If data do not indicate an event, no further action is required, and the node rest until the next turn.

The third algorithm, named in the results as Option 3, this algorithm includes the generation of alarms to alert the rest of the nodes when an event is detected. This option should improve data accuracy but have a higher energy use in data gathering. This is an evet-triggered algorithm.

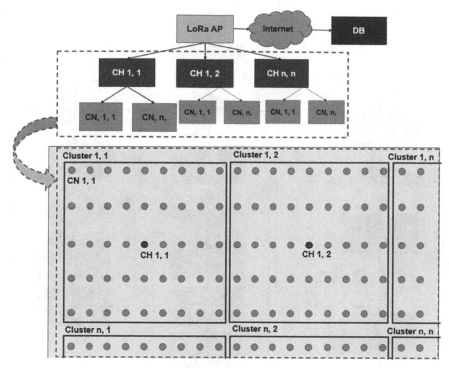

**Fig. 1.** Topology of the network.

This algorithm can be seen in Fig. 3. At every turn, the node$_i$ checks if an alarm was received. In the case that no alarm has been received, the node$_i$ have to verify if it has the token in this turn. If the node does not have the token and it should not measure, it waits until the next turn. If the node has the token, it gathers data and confirms if the data indicate an event. If data indicates an event, it sends the information to the DB and alarm to the rest of the nodes to indicate that the event has been detected. In the case that an alarm has been received, a counter of 5 turns is activated; during 5 turns the node will gather data and check if data and send it to the DB. When the counter reaches 0, the node$_i$ checks if it has or not the turn to measure as previously explained.

The last algorithm is based on the generation of a reactive alarm. The main difference with the previous algorithm is that, in this case, the alarm is verified at every turn based on the data collected by all the sensors. There are two algorithms variations according to the number of nodes that collaborate for the decision. These are collaborative event-triggered algorithms. The first variation supposes that all the CNs of the same cluster are considered for evaluating the situation and for deciding if the alarm should be maintained or not for the next turn. The second variation considers that only the adjacent nodes should be considered for the alarm.

Figure 4 shows the collaborative event-triggered algorithm for the first variation. In this case, if an alarm is received, the node$_i$ has to measure and check whether data indicates an event. If data indicates an event, it will send the event to the DB and alert all nodes of the same cluster to keep the alarm triggered. Then, it waits until the next

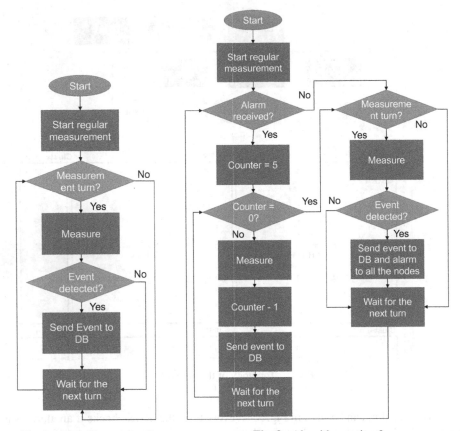

**Fig. 2.** Algorithm option 2.                    **Fig. 3.** Algorithm option 3

turn. If no alarm has been received, the node$_i$ should confirm if it has to measure in this turn. If it has to measure, the node will follow the same procedure explained above.

Finally, the variation of the collaborative event.triggered algorithm, can be seen in Fig. 5. The sole variation with regard to the algorihtm of Fig. 4 is that in this case, the node will send the alarm only to the adjacent nodes.

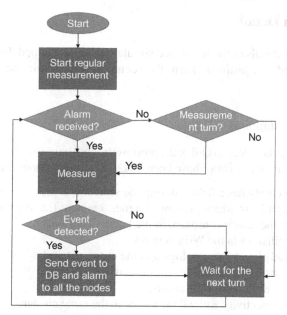

**Fig. 4.** Algorithm option 4 with broadcast.

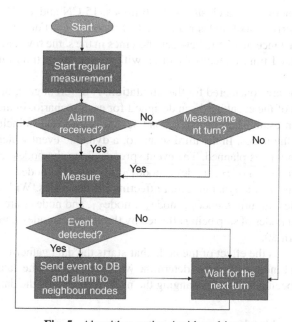

**Fig. 5.** Algorithm option 4 with multicast.

# 4  Simulation Details

In this section, the details of the performed simulations are explained. First, the assumptions are identified and justified. Then, the scenarios included in the simulations are defined (Fig. 5).

## 4.1  General Assumptions

In order to simulate the effect on QoI of the proposed algorithms, some assumptions about the sensor nodes and the network have been made. The assumptions are the following:

- No node connectivity has a failure during the simulation.
- No node has a problem which prevents the measurement (i.e. the node is stolen, the node is broken, the sensor is broken, or the battery runs out).
- There are no collisions in the WiFi network.
- The nodes already know the topology and the entire network.
- The nodes already know their turns for measuring.
- There is no false detection of the events.
- The CN have connectivity with all the nodes in the same cluster.

## 4.2  Description of Simulated Scenarios

In the simulated network is a cluster with 16 nodes, 15 CN and 1 CH. The nodes are deployed as a matrix of 4x4 nodes being the CH the $node_{2,3}$. For this specific case, a vineyard with a distance of 1.75 m between the vines in the same row and 3.5 m between rows. The simulated time includes 41 turns with a predefined time interval between turns.

Four scenarios are considered for the simulation. A different geographical and temporal distribution of the event has been designed for each scenario. In the first scenario, no event has been established. In the second scenario, an event is included in turn 9, which affects all the nodes. In the third scenario, a dynamic event which starts on turn 9 affecting the $node_{1,1}$ is planned. The event spreads along the nodes reaching the last nodes ($node_{1,4}$, $node_{2,4}$, $node_{3,4}$, $node_{4,1}$, $node_{4,2}$, $node_{4,3}$, and $node_{4,4}$) in turn 29. The last scenario starts with a dynamic event affecting all the nodes. With time, the event affects fewer nodes. In turn 9, $node_{1,1}$, $node_{2,1}$, $node_{3,1}$, and $node_{4,1}$ are not affected by the event. The last nodes of stop being affected by the event are $node_{1,4}$, $node_{2,4}$, $node_{3,4}$, and $node_{4,4}$ in turn 30.

In order to assess the effect of the node that starts the data gathering turn along the cluster, a random function is used to determine which node starts the data gathering. Six repetitions have been performed, changing the node which starts the data gathering.

## 4.3  Performance Metrics

The considered metrics to evaluate the performance of the algorithm are the following ones:

General Error of the System (GES): We will consider a GES if there is an active event and any of the nodes have noticed the event in the DB. The GES of the system is calculated as the percentage of turns over the simulation in which an event is present, and the DB is not aware.

Average Individual Error (AIE) and Maximum Individual Error (MIE). We will consider an Individual Error (IE) if there is an active event and a particular node and it has not noticed the event in the DB. The IE is calculated as the percentage of turns over the simulation in which an event is present in a certain node, and the DB is not aware. On the one hand, to compute the AIE, the average IE of all the nodes in the simulated cluster is calculated. On the other hand, the MIE is obtained by comparing the IEs of the nodes.

## 5   Results

The results are presented in this section. First, we analyse the obtained GESs for the different simulations. Then, the AIEs and MIEs are used to compare the performance.

### 5.1   Calculated GESs

In the first 2 scenarios, all options perform equally well in terms of GES; see Fig. 6. This is explained since there is no event to detect in the first case, and in the second case, the event starts in all the sensors simultaneously. Meanwhile, in the third and fourths scenario, Options 2 to 4 have some GESs. Particularly option 2 is the one that is characterised by the higher GESs, being 33.33 and 25.20% of GES in scenarios 3 and 4. In scenario 4, no GES occurred when even triggered algorithms were used. It indicates that the proposed alarms can accurately describe the remission of the event.

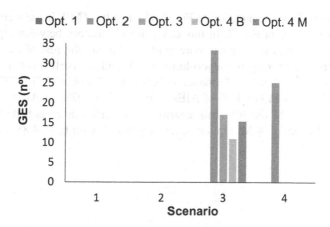

**Fig. 6.** Obtained GES of algorithms in different scenarios.

## 5.2 Calculated AIEs and MIEs

The results of obtained AIEs with the different algorithms can be seen in Fig. 7. As expected, Option 2 is the one with higher AIEs in all the cases. Among the proposed event-triggered algorithms, in scenario 2, the collaborative event-triggered algorithm using broadcast performs better in terms of AIEs than the one using multicast. Option 4 B performs equally well than Option 3. In scenario 3, the performance is better for Option 4 B (1.45% of AIEs), followed by Option 4 M (3.20% of AIEs), Option 3 (5.44% of AIEs), and Option 2 (44.77% of AIEs). Finally, in the fourth scenario, when Option 3 and Option 4 B there have no AIEs, in the case of Option 4 M, only 0.91% of cases suppose an AIE.

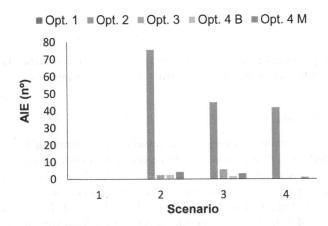

**Fig. 7.** Obtained AIE of algorithms in different scenarios.

Finally, the MIEs are summarised in Fig. 8. The results of MIE in the second scenario are similar to the AIE in Fig. 7. In this case, the differences between Option 2 and the rest of the algorithms are much more evident. Among the rest of the algorithms, the collaborative event-triggered algorithm using broadcast performs better in all the scenarios. In scenario 3, the performance is better for Option 4 B (10.98% of MIEs), followed by Option 4 M (15.45% of AIEs), Option 3 (17.07% of AIEs), and Option 2 (75.61% of AIEs). Meanwhile, in scenario 4, the performance is better for Option 4 B, followed by Option 4 M, Option 3, and Option 2, with 0, 0, 4.88, and 66.26%, respectively.

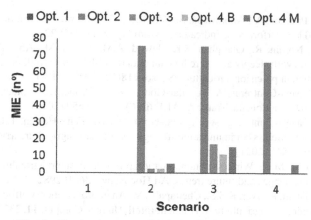

**Fig. 8.** Obtained MIE of algorithms in different scenarios.

## 6 Conclusions

In this paper, we have presented different algorithms for data gathering in WSN and analysed their impact on the QoI. The data gathering procedure's impact on energy consumption in superdense networks is a critical issue. Algorithms to reduce the data gathering times while maintaining the QoI are important. Our results indicate that the collaborative event-triggered algorithm, particularly the one that uses broadcast to alarm all the nodes, performs equally or better than event-triggered algorithms under all tested conditions.

The impact of proposed algorithms in energy will be considered in future work considering both the data-gathering procedure and the message exchange. Moreover, the algorithms will be tested with real datasets. Finally, the impact of different deployment strategies [12] in event detection will be evaluated.

**Acknowledgements.** This work has been funded by the "Ministerio de Ciencia e Innovación" through the Project PID2020-114467RRC33/AEI/10.13039/501100011033 and by the "Ministerio de Economía y Competitividad" through the Project TED2021-131040BC31.

## References

1. García, L., et al.: Deployment strategies of soil monitoring WSN for precision agriculture irrigation scheduling in rural areas. Sensors **21**(5), 1693 (2021)
2. Katona, R., Cionca, V., O'Shea, D., Pesch, D.: Virtual network embedding for wireless sensor networks time-efficient QoS/QoI-aware approach. IEEE Internet Things J. **8**(2), 916–926 (2020)
3. Ampatzidis, Y., Partel, V., Costa, L.: Agroview: cloud-based application to process, analyse and visualise UAV-collected data for precision agriculture applications utilising artificial intelligence. Comput. Electron. Agric. **174**, 105457 (2020)
4. Kamel, M., Hamouda, W., Youssef, A.: Ultra-dense networks: a survey. IEEE Communications surveys & tutorials **18**(4), 2522–2545 (2016)

5. Stoynov, V., Poulkov, V., Valkova-Jarvis, Z., Iliev, G., Koleva, P.: ultra-dense networks: taxonomy and key performance indicators. Symmetry **15**(1), 2 (2022)
6. Jawad, H.M., Nordin, R., Gharghan, S.K., Jawad, A.M., Ismail, M., Abu-AlShaeer, M.J.: Power reduction with sleep/wake on redundant data (SWORD) in a wireless sen-sor network for energy-efficient precision agriculture. Sensors **18**(10), 3450 (2018)
7. Lozoya, C., Favela-Contreras, A., Aguilar-Gonzalez, A., Orona, L.: A precision Irrigation model using hybrid automata. Trans. ASABE **62**(6), 1639–1650 (2019)
8. Lozoya, C., Favela-Contreras, A., Aguilar-Gonzalez, A., Félix-Herrán, L.C., Orona, L.: Energy-efficient wireless communication strategy for precision agriculture irrigation control. Sensors **21**(16), 5541 (2021)
9. Avşar, E., Mowla, M.N.: Wireless communication protocols in smart agriculture: a review on applications, challenges and future trends. Ad Hoc Netw. **136**, 102982 (2022)
10. Agrawal, H., Dhall, R., Iyer, K.S.S., Chetlapalli, V.: An improved energy effi-cient system for IoT enabled precision agriculture. J. Ambient Intell. Human. Comput. **11**, 2337–2348 (2020)
11. Zou, T., Lin, S., Feng, Q., Chen, Y.: Energy-efficient control with harvesting pre-dictions for solar-powered wireless sensor networks. Sensors **16**(1), 53 (2016)
12. Garcia, M., Bri, D., Sendra, S., Lloret, J.: Practical deployments of wireless sensor networks: a survey. Int. J. Adv. Netw. Serv **3**(1/2), 163–178 (2010)

# A Cooperative Protocol for Wireless Energy Networks

Juan Lladó[1] and Sebastià Galmés[1,2]

[1] Universitat de les Illes Balears, 07122 Palma, Spain
jllmartorell@gmail.com, sebastia.galmes@uib.es
[2] Institut d'Investigació Sanitária Illes Balears, 07120 Palma, Spain

**Abstract.** The recent revival of Tesla's original idea of transferring power without the use of wires has led to the conception of a wireless energy network as a new networking paradigm. Starting from the bases established in a previous article, this paper proposes a protocol to regulate the interaction between energy users and energy providers. Specifically, in that earlier publication, two categories of energy providers were introduced, namely a primary source and multiple secondary sources. The proposed protocol promotes cooperation between primary and secondary sources to save as much energy as possible in the process of supplying energy to users.

**Keywords:** Communication protocol · Internet of Things · RF energy harvesting · Wireless propagation model

## 1 Introduction

Recent advances in low-power integrated circuits and wireless technologies, the growing number of IoT (Internet of Things) applications, and a better understanding of propagation phenomena, have motivated researchers to revisit Tesla's initial idea about transferring energy without wires [1]. This idea is now seen as a promising solution to overcome the limitations of conventional power supply methods, such as batteries or wired connections to fixed power grids, or even the limitations of more recent alternatives based on the use of renewable sources. Given the large number of nodes that are expected to be part of future IoT and 5G scenarios, the benefits of Radio Frequency Energy Harvesting (RF-EH) in terms of operating cost savings and self-sustainability are undoubted. Whether based on RF-EH alone or combined with other renewable sources (solar radiation, mechanical vibration, airflow, etc.), the panacea for perpetual wireless device operation is closer today. For an overview of current state of the art on RF energy harvesting, see [2–7].

A user device can opportunistically harvest energy from the electromagnetic environment, simply by taking advantage of the multiple transmitters in its

Supported by Universitat de les Illes Balears.

Y. Luo (Ed.): CDVE 2023, LNCS 14166, pp. 13–18, 2023.
https://doi.org/10.1007/978-3-031-43815-8_2

surrounding area. This alternative, called ambient energy harvesting, does not require any infrastructure, but the amount of energy that can be obtained in a given period is small and unpredictable. A more efficient alternative is based on the use of dedicated power sources. This entails a new cooperative scenario in which such power sources play the role of energy servers, while low-power devices act as energy clients. In [8], energy servers were classified in two categories, namely primary and secondary sources. A primary source is connected to the power grid; in contrast, a secondary source is not equipped with such connection and its role is to extend the coverage of the primary source. It is precisely the primary source that supplies RF energy to any secondary source within its coverage. The primary source, the set of secondary sources under the coverage of the primary source, and the set of user devices under the coverage of at least one of the sources, constitute the basic service area of a wireless energy network (WEN). In the general case of a user requesting energy within the coverage area of the primary and several secondary sources, some form of cooperation is required between them in order to decide which one will finally fulfill the energy demand. The present paper focuses on the characterization of the protocol that will support this cooperation. Unless other criteria are explicitly stated, we will assume that cooperation between sources is aimed at minimizing total energy consumption.

The rest of the paper is organized as follows. Section 2 describes the basic architecture of a WEN and lists the initial assumptions that we have adopted in the design of the protocol. In Sect. 3 we provide the details of the proposed protocol and we characterize it by means of a state diagram. Finally, in Sect. 4, we draw the main conclusions and suggest some ideas for future research.

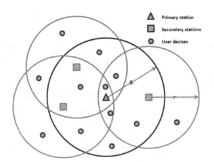

**Fig. 1.** Basic architecture of a WEN.

## 2    System Model and Assumptions

Figure 1 shows the basic architecture of a WEN. The core operation of the system obeys the client-server model, though implemented via three types of elements:

- Primary station (P). This station is supposed to be connected to the power grid and thus it can always supply power on demand. It plays the role of energy server. The energy consumed by the entire system is the energy consumed by this station.
- Secondary stations (S). Secondary stations extend the coverage of the primary station, but they are not connected to the power grid. They can act as both client and server. As clients, secondary stations request energy from the primary one; as servers, they supply energy in response to user demands.
- User devices (U). User devices are the final clients of the overall system. In principle, they can be served by any source or set of sources (though this paper will only consider the former case).

In the design of the protocol, we have adopted the following assumptions (future work will consider the relaxation of some of them):

- As stated above, user devices are static. The same happens with the primary and secondary stations.
- The primary station knows the location of all secondary ones within its range.
- The user device is equipped with a local or global self-positioning system (like GPS).
- A user device can only be served by a single source, which can be any station within its range, be it the primary or any secondary.

## 3    Cooperative Protocol

The objective of the proposed protocol is to support the necessary cooperation between energy sources in order to determine the optimal provider for a given user demand. It should be noticed that, if $\Delta E$ is the amount of energy requested by a user device, the amount of energy wasted by the system to satisfy this demand is larger than $\Delta E$. Here, the performance of the propagation channel plays a determinant role. Let us consider the case of a user device located in the coverage area of the primary station and at least one of the secondary stations. Also, let $E_P$ denote the energy wasted by the primary station and, similarly, let $E_{Si}, i = 1...n$ denote the energy wasted by any of the involved secondary stations ($n$ represents the total number of secondary stations). Finally, let $h_{P,U}$ and $h_{Si,U}$ denote, respectively, the channel coefficient between the primary station and the user device ($U$), on one hand, and the secondary station $Si$ and the user device, on the other one. The channel coefficient is a complex number that depends on many factors, among them the antenna heights and gains, the distance between transmitter and receiver, the presence of obstacles (shadowing) and multi-path effects. The energy wasted by the primary station to directly supply an amount of energy $\Delta E$ to the user device can be formulated as follows:

$$E_P = \frac{\Delta E}{\|h_{P,U}\|^2} \tag{1}$$

Here, $\| \cdot \|$ denotes the module of a complex number. On the other hand, the energy wasted by the primary station when the user demand is satisfied by a secondary station $Si$ is given by:

$$E_P = \frac{\frac{\Delta E}{\|h_{Si,U}\|^2}}{\|h_{P,Si}\|^2} = \frac{\Delta E}{\|h_{Si,U}\|^2 \cdot \|h_{P,Si}\|^2} \tag{2}$$

Equation (2) takes two facts into account: (1) all the energy consumed by the system takes place in the primary station, which is the only one connected to the power grid, and (2) the primary station has to feed the secondary station for the amount of energy consumed by the latter to restore the energy demanded by the user device. It is not evident which expression, either (1) or (2) for any of the involved secondary stations, is larger. Accordingly, the purpose of the proposed protocol is to support the exchange of control messages between the primary station and the involved secondary ones in order to select the best alternative in terms of energy consumption. Such optimization problem is highlighted in Fig. 2, for a scenario where the user device is located in the intersection region between the coverage areas of the primary and three secondary stations.

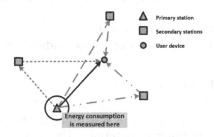

**Fig. 2.** Potential energy flows for a user device in the intersection area between the primary and three secondary stations.

At this point, we formulate the following additional assumptions:

- There is channel side information at the energy sources, which means that $h_{P,Si}$ and $h_{P,U}$ are known to the primary station, and $h_{Si,U}$ is known to the secondary station $Si$. Moreover, the secondary station $Si$ can communicate the value of $h_{Si,U}$ to the primary station. Therefore, either directly or indirectly, the primary stations knows all channel coefficients.
- The processing of Eqs. (1) and (2), as well as the selection of the best alternative, take place in the primary station.

Under these assumptions and the ones stated in Sect. 2, Fig. 3 shows the state transition diagram of the proposed protocol for both, user devices and energy sources. From the point of view of user devices, the diagram is valid for any combination of energy sources, including or not the primary station. Two types of transitions are shown: state transitions, represented by solid arrows, and control messages, represented by dashed arrows. Next, a more detailed description of the involved messages is provided:

- *beacon* message. This message announces the presence of a potential energy server. It identifies the sending station, either containing a PID (Primary IDentifier) or a SID (Secondary IDentifier).
- *energy_request* message. By means of this message, a user device announces its energy demand. The arguments of this message include a self-identification via a UID (User IDentifier), its location (GPS position, for example) and the amount of energy requested ($\Delta E$).
- *energy_response* message. This message is the response to the *energy_request* message. It contains the identity of the designated energy provider, which is also the sender of such message.
- *energy_provider* message. By means of this message, the primary station broadcasts the identity of the station that has been designated as energy provider. Thus, only a secondary station can wait for this message.
- *redirect* message. This message is addressed to the primary station and can only be sent by a secondary one. By means of this message, a secondary station forwards the contents of a received *energy_request* to the primary station, including also its own identity (SID).
- *ready* message. As stated above, this message indicates the readiness of its sender (user device) to start the energy restoration process. The destination of this message is the designated energy provider.
- *end* message. This message signals the end of the energy restoration operation. The energy provider returns to its initial state (waiting for new energy requests) and the user device resumes its communication activity (WIT state).

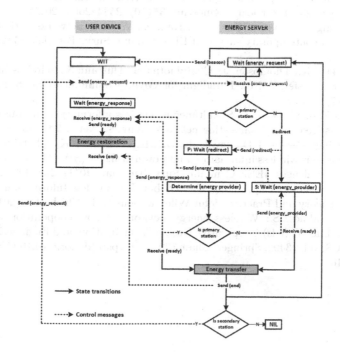

**Fig. 3.** State diagram for the proposed protocol.

An additional operation is pending, only if the designated energy provider was a secondary station. This station needs to recover the energy wasted to feed the user device, for which reason it starts a new energy transfer process exclusively with the primary station. In this case, the secondary station switches its role from server to customer.

## 4   Conclusions

In this paper, we have proposed a protocol to support cooperation between energy servers in a wireless energy network context. The protocol aims to minimize the amount of energy consumption to meet the energy demands emitted by user devices. Future research may focus on various aspects, such as the queuing problem that arises when multiple user devices request energy from the same provider, the joint optimization of energy consumption and other performance metrics, or the case where a user device can be powered simultaneously by multiple servers.

## References

1. Tesla, N.: Apparatus for transmitting electrical energy. US1119732A US Patent (1902)
2. Fan, X., Mo, X., Zhang, X.: Research status and application of wireless power transmission technology. Zhongguo Dianji Gongcheng Xuebao/Proceedings of the Chinese Society of Electrical Engineering 35(10), 2584–2600 (2015)
3. Lu, X., Wang, P., Niyato, Kim, D. I., Han, Z.: Wireless networks with RF energy harvesting: a contemporary survey. IEEE Commun. Surv. Tutorials 17(2), 757–789 (2015)
4. Jakayodi, D.N.K., Thompson, J., Chatzinotas, S., Durrani, S.: Wireless Information and Power Transfer: A New Paradigm for Green Communications. Springer, New York (2017)
5. Huang, S., Yao, Y., Feng, Z.: Simultaneous wireless information and power transfer for relay assisted energy harvesting network. Wireless Netw. 24, 453–462 (2018)
6. Ponnimbaduge Perera, T.D., Jayakody, D.N.K., Sharma, S.K., Chatzinotas, S., Li, J.: Simultaneous wireless information and power transfer (SWIPT): recent advances and future challenges. IEEE Commun. Surv. Tutorials 20(1), 264–302 (2018)
7. Ng, D.W.K., Duong, T.Q., Zhong, C., Schober, R.: Wireless Information and Power Transfer: Theory and Practice. John Wiley & Sons Ltd., Chichester (2019)
8. Lladó, J., Galmés, S.: Wireless energy networks - how cooperation extends to energy. In: Luo, Y. (eds) Cooperative Design, Visualization, and Engineering. CDVE 2022. LNCS, vol. 13492. Springer, Cham (2022). https://doi.org/10.1007/978-3-031-16538-2_10

# Dynamic Secure Mesh for Collaborative Nodes of IoT Devices

Sylvia Encheva[1(✉)] and Sharil Tumin[2]

[1] Western Norway University of Applied Sciences, Inndalsveien 28, Post box 7030,
5020 Bergen, Norway
sbe@hvl.no
[2] Trimensity IoT, Inger Bang Lunds vei 17, 5059 Bergen, Norway
sharil@trimensity.eu

**Abstract.** The *ESP-NOW* protocol on ESP32 MCUs with MicroPython firmware can create a system of smart IoT nodes based on dynamic secure mesh networks. Collaboration between static and mobile nodes is achieved through connectionless communication. A layered IoT architecture helps model, design, and implement the system. The mesh is secured by node authentication mechanism. Brokerless publish/subscribe message passing is used for message exchange. A mesh-to-cloud setup using UART communication between two nodes is proposed. The dynamic mesh network together with dynamic scripting can create an environment for smart IoT AI-enabled systems that is reliable, efficient, maintainable, and cost-effective.

**Keywords:** Secure Mesh · ESP-NOW Protocol · Network Security ·
Dynamic Routing · Smart IoT · ESP32 MCU · MicroPython

## 1 Introduction

A dynamic secure mesh for collaborative nodes is a network infrastructure that enables secure and efficient communication and coordination among multiple Internet of Things (IoT) devices. It usually entails the use of mesh networking technology, which allows devices to communicate directly with one another, forming a self-configuring network [3,4], and [5].

Some important aspects of such a system are: 1) mesh networking, 2) collaborative nodes, 3) dynamic configuration, 4) security, 5) resource efficiency, and 6) scalability. Only IoT devices consisting of tiny microcontrollers with radio capabilities, limited random-access memory (RAM), flash memory, and processing resources are considered.

The network is automatically and dynamically set up as a mesh network, with each device acting as a node capable of sending and receiving data from other nodes on the network. Because nodes can relay data to reach distant nodes, this decentralized structure provides better coverage and resilience.

The nodes are sensors and actuators. Sensors collect data from their surroundings, such as temperature, humidity, or motion, whereas actuators are

Y. Luo (Ed.): CDVE 2023, LNCS 14166, pp. 19–30, 2023.
https://doi.org/10.1007/978-3-031-43815-8_3

devices that can perform actions based on the data they receive. Motors, valves, and lights are examples of actuators. Some devices will only serve as data collectors. Data collected by these devices from remote sensors will be uploaded to the IT cloud via mesh to cloud gateways.

The network can dynamically configure itself as devices join and leave the network. When a new device is added, it can automatically detect and connect to nearby nodes. Similarly, if a node goes down or leaves the network, the remaining nodes can adjust their routing paths accordingly.

To ensure efficient operation, the network optimizes the utilization of available resources such as bandwidth and energy. Nodes can work together to save energy by utilizing sleep modes or adjusting transmission power levels based on network conditions. The network should be scalable in order to support a large number of nodes. As the number of devices grows, the network must be able to handle the increased traffic while maintaining reliable communication.

The *ESP-NOW* communication protocol [6] was developed by Espressif Systems, the company that created the ESP8266 and ESP32 microcontroller platforms. It enables direct communication between devices at the data link level, eliminating the need for network, transport, session, and presentation layer implementations.

*ESP-NOW* is energy-efficient, making it suitable for battery-powered devices or applications where power consumption is an issue [7]. Low-power sleep modes are supported by the protocol, allowing devices to conserve energy when not actively transmitting or receiving data. *ESP-NOW* is intended to be lightweight and simple to use. It offers a straightforward API (Application Programming Interface) for sending and receiving data packets between devices, making it simple to integrate into ESP32 based applications [8,9].

Both one-to-one and one-to-many communication models are supported by *ESP-NOW*. Two ESP nodes establish a direct communication link in a one-to-one scenario. A single ESP device can send data to multiple recipient nodes at the same time in a one-to-many scenario.

MicroPython is a software implementation of the Python 3 programming language designed for microcontrollers and embedded systems. It offers a lightweight and efficient Python interpreter that can run on low-resource devices, making it ideal for projects that require microcontrollers with limited memory and processing power, such as ESP32-based boards [10,11], and [12].

MicroPython is highly extensible, allowing developers to add custom modules and libraries tailored to their specific application requirements. This adaptability allows users to customize MicroPython to their specific needs and integrate it with existing hardware and software components.

## 2   IoT Architecture

The IoT architecture for a Secure Dynamic Mesh network with both fixed and roaming nodes typically includes multiple layers and components to enable secure and reliable communication between devices. We will introduce a five-layer architecture [2] and briefly describe each one below:

1. Device Layer: Fixed and roaming nodes comprise the device layer. Fixed nodes are stationary network devices such as sensors, actuators, gateways, or control units. They are in charge of data collection, local processing, and interaction with the mesh network. Roaming nodes are transient or mobile devices that move around the network. Examples include mobile sensors, robots, and drones. Roaming nodes can join and leave the network and communicate with other nodes on the fly.

2. Communication Layer: Mesh networks are made up of interconnected nodes that can relay data to one another. It creates a self-configuring and self-healing network with multiple data transmission paths, ensuring reliability and robustness. To manage the mesh network and determine the best paths for data transmission, a routing protocol is used. The protocol should support dynamic node addition and removal, as well as effectively handle node mobility. The *ESP-NOW* protocol can be used to communicate efficiently between ESP32-based devices in a mesh network. It transmits data in a low-power, low-latency, and reliable manner.

3. Security Layer: To establish trust and prevent unauthorized access, network nodes authenticate themselves. This can be accomplished using methods such as shared keys, and secure protocols. To ensure the confidentiality and integrity of data exchanged between nodes, it is encrypted. A simple encryption algorithms and protocols can be used. Firmwares and scripts include protection mechanisms to prevent unauthorized changes or tampering.

4. Application Layer: Fixed nodes process sensor data, perform local computations, and generate meaningful insights or control commands. Gateways act as bridges between the mesh network and external networks or cloud platforms. They collect data, translate protocols, and connect to external systems. Based on system requirements, application-specific functionalities support features such as real-time monitoring, automation, remote control, and data analytics.

5. Cloud/Server Layer: Data from the IoT network can be sent to cloud platforms for storage, analysis, and remote access. Cloud services offer scalability, data processing capabilities, and remote management. To visualize and interact with data collected from the IoT network, a user interface or dashboard can be implemented. This allows users to monitor and control the system.

## 3   Mesh Network

A mesh network is a type of node network. It is special in that each node in a mesh is linked to other nodes, either directly or indirectly.

A **path** has a direction; if $A$ and $B$ are nodes, $A \succ B \neq B \succ A$. The two paths $A \succ B$ and $B \succ A$ can be combined to form $A \prec\succ B$.

A **link** between $A$ and $B$ is defined as $A|B$. A minimal direct link between $A$ and $B$ is the shortest paths between these two nodes, which is $A \prec\succ B$. A path from $A$ to $B$ and a path from $B$ to $A$ must both exist for these two nodes to be linked.

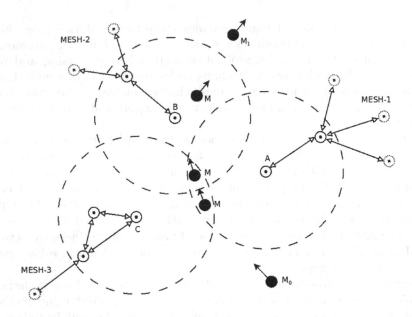

**Fig. 1.** Mobile node moving between meshes making bridges

Assume four nodes, $A$, $B$, $C$, and $D$. If $A \succ B \succ D$ and $D \succ C \succ A$ existed, the indirect link $A|D$ would exist. The links $A|D$ and $D|A$ are interchangeable.

$M_{min} = [\{A,B\}, \{A \prec\succ B\}]$ denotes a minimal mesh.
$M_1 = [\{A,B\}, \{A \prec\succ B\}] \oplus M_2 = [\{B,C\}, \{B \prec\succ C\}]$
$\quad = M_{12} = [\{A,B,C\}, \{A \prec\succ B, B \prec\succ C, A \succ B \succ C, C \succ B \succ A\}]$
$\quad = M_{12} = [\{A,B,C\}, \{A|B, B|C, A|C\}]$

Similarly, two meshes with at least one comment node can be combined to form a larger mesh.

$M_{12} = [\{A,B,C\}, \{A|B, B|C, A|C\}] \oplus M_3 = [\{C,D\}, \{C \prec\succ D\}]$
$\quad = M_{123} = [\{A,B,C,D\}, \{A|B, B|C, A|C, C|D, B|D, A|D\}]$

Within a certain range, the *ESP-NOW* broadcasting protocol will generate a full mesh network topology, with each node directly connected to all other nodes. In practice however, only partial mesh topology is possible. At any time, one or more nodes can be removed from a mesh. To reach another node, a massage from one node must pass through another intermediate node. This is not a problem as long as a path exists from one node to all other nodes. A message may require multiple hops to reach other nodes.

A bridge node located between overlapping radio signal ranges will connect two or more established meshes by linking to bordering nodes of these meshes. Massages from one mesh will be routed to nodes in the other mesh via the bridge node.

The Fig. 1 depicts how a mobile node moves and forms bridges between meshes. The mobile node $M$ journey begins at $M_0$ and ends at $M_1$. $M$ becomes a bridge node to *MESH-1* and *MESH-3*, as well as to *MESH-1*, *MESH-2*, and *MESH-3* at the two intervening locations. The first bridge is formed when $M$ is linked to $A$ and $B$. When $M$ is linked to $A$, $B$, and $C$, the second bridge is established. *MESH-1*, *MESH-2*, and *MESH-3* border nodes are $A$, $B$, and $C$, respectively. Before leaving the mesh cluster, the mobile node $M$ is only a member of *MESH-3*. At $M_0$ and $M_1$, the mobile node is outside of the mesh cluster's signal range and is not connected to any mesh.

# 4   Implementation

The implementation process is logically divided into five steps in relation to the IoT Architecture mentioned earlier. The goal is to set up a base system to test the feasibility of using *ESP-NOW* to create a dynamic secure mesh network of collaborative nodes.

## 4.1   Device

The Espressif Systems in Shanghai, China, was first known in the West by its ESP8266 is a low-cost WiFi microchip. A development board based on ESP8266 named ESP-01 became popular in August 2014 to western maker community and engineers. In 2020, Espressif announced a new chip ESP32-C3, which is pin-compatible with ESP8266 and will serve as its replacement.

Only the ESP32 SoC (System on a Chip) is considered in this paper. Different third party manufacturers produce different development boards based on different types of ESP32 SoC. Table 1 summarizes some important features of the various ESP32 SoCs. These third-party OEMs (Original Equipment Manufacturers) add components to the ESP32 SoC such as quartz, LED (Light Emitting Diode), sensors, flash memory, GPIO (General Purpose Input/Output) breakout pins, among others, to create PCBs (Printed Circuit Boards) with easy access to the ESP32 SoC functionality.

The development boards that were used in the experiment are shown in Fig. 2. Each has a different amount of flash memory. Typically, 4MB of flash memory is provided. A 4 MB flash memory is sufficient to hold a normal size MicroPython firmware and a small size file system for the storage of application scripts. The limiting factor of an application is the amount of RAM (Random Access Memory) available at run time. Some boards add PSRAM (pseudostatic random access memory) to increase the amount of RAM available.

**Table 1.** ESP32 Chipsets

| Soc | MCU | Speed | Memory (KB) | | | GPIO | Radio Chip | |
|-----|-----|-------|-----|-----|-----|------|------------|---|
| | 32Bits Core | MHz | RAM | RTC | ROM | Pins | WiFi | Bluetooth |
| ESP32 | 2 Xtensa LX6 | 240 | 448 | 16 | 448 | 34 | 2.4 GHz | Classic, BLE |
| ESP32-C3 | 1 RISC-V | 160 | 400 | 8 | 384 | 22 | 2.4 GHz | BLE5 |
| ESP32-S2 | 1 Xtensa LX7 | 240 | 320 | 16 | 128 | 43 | 2.4 GHz | - |
| ESP32-S3 | 2 Xtensa LX7 | 240 | 512 | 16 | 384 | 45 | 2.4 GHz | BLE5 |

**Fig. 2.** ESP32 variants: (left to right) esp32, esp32-c3, esp32-s2, esp32-s3

IoT and embedded applications are developed and deployed using the Python programming language. The MicroPython firmware acts as an operating system (OS), managing hardware and software resources and interfacing high-level user scripts with low-level microcontroller hardware components. Custom firmware can be used to reduce the size of MicroPython by excluding unneeded libraries and modules. Special functionality can be added to the firmware using C modules or frozen Python modules.

MicroPython for ESP32 SoC compiled SoC functionality into the firmwares using utilities provided by *ESP-IDF* (IoT Development Framework). Custom firmwares created for this project are based on MicroPython-V1.20.0-39 and ESP-IDF-V4.4.4 and are configured to exclude, BLE, _thread, and uasyncio, among others. These custom firmwares [14], on the other hand, include the **esp-now** C module and the **workers** frozen Python module, which respectively support the *ESP-NOW* connectionless communication protocol and tasks-based cooperative multitasking [13].

Four distinct custom firmwares are developed for the various ESP32 SoCs. Development boards are flashed with the appropriate firmware. This depends on which ESP32 SoC is installed on the board.

## 4.2   Communication

The *ESP-NOW* protocol operates at the link level, which is level 2 of the 7-layer OSI (Open Systems Interconnection) reference model [1]. Unique 6 bytes MAC (Media Access Control) addresses are used to identify nodes. Nodes communicate with each other using a connectionless communication protocol, i.e. each message packet sent by an application requires the source and destination MAC addresses.

The *ESP-NOW* supports: 1) one-to-one, 2) one-to-many, and 3) one-to-all communication modes. Consider four nodes with these MAC addresses: (1) `a2b388991111`, (2) `a2b388122222`, (3) `17ef23de3434`, and (4) `a2b389ba4545` (Table 2).

**Table 2.** ESP-NOW communication modes

| Protocol | | MAC | | Accessible nodes | Message Type |
|---|---|---|---|---|---|
| Mode | Transmission | Source | Destination | | |
| one-to-one | unicast | `a2b388991111` | `17ef23de3434` | (3) | `AUQ, AUR, MSG` |
| one-to-many | multicast | `a2b388991111` | `a2b388ffffff` | (2) | - |
| one-to-many | multicast | `a2b388991111` | `a2b3ffffffff` | (2, 4) | - |
| one-to-all | broadcast | `a2b388991111` | `ffffffffffff` | (2, 3, 4) | `HEY, BYE` |
| one-to-all | broadcast | `17ef23de3434` | `ffffffffffff` | (1, 2, 4) | `HEY, BYE` |

To do unicast and multicast, some part of the MAC address must be known in advance. In multicast (one-to-many), some lower bytes of a MAC address are changed to all ones, for example, `a2b388ffffff`. When all bytes are changed to all ones (`ffffffffffff`), the source node will send a broadcast (one-to-all) message.

An *ESP-NOW* object `ew` is created by calling `ew=espnow.ESPNow()`. All MAC addresses, for unicast, multicast and broadcast, must be added to the *ESP-NOW* object using `ew.add_peer(MAC)`. Otherwise, the message send command `ew.send(MAC, message)` will fail. For example, use `ew.add_peer(b'\xff'*6)` to add the MAC address for broadcast.

Sending a message to multicast and broadcast MAC addresses will always succeed. A `false` value is returned if a message is sent to a specific MAC address and the node is down or unreachable. In this project, only one-to-one and broadcast modes are used in the *ESP-NOW* communication between nodes, allowing dynamic meshes to be obtained without having to know the MAC addresses of the nodes in advance.

A node sends a broadcast message of type HEY or BYE to join or leave a mesh network. Any node within radio range of the sending node S will receive a broadcast message.

Upon receiving HEY, a node R sends a unicast message AUQ to S. When the S node reads the AUQ, it responds with a unicast message AUR. If the sender node S is able to decrypt the AUQ message, then the MAC of the receiver is appended to the its MESH array and added to the new peers by ew.add_peer(R). The receiver node R will do the same action on receipt AUR with respect to the sender's MAC address S. The AUQ and AUR are authentication handshake messages between sender and receiver.

When a node R receives BYE from a sending node S, it deletes S from its MESH array and removes S from known peers using ew.del_peer(S).

## 4.3  Security

The MESH array on a node serves two functions: 1) it contains a list of authenticated peers, and 2) it contains a list of peers in the mesh to which a message will be forwarded from the node.

The following functions are used to encrypt and decrypt the unicast AUQ and AUR message payloads:

```
from CryptoXo import Crypt
# encryption functions
crypt = Crypt() # only one object - not thread save!

def encrypt(mac):
    crypt.key(mac, 'erDt 17ysg#fsDDa= 2tY!!')
    return crypt.encrypt

def decrypt(mac):
    crypt.key(mac, 'erDt 17ysg#fsDDa= 2tY!!')
    return crypt.decrypt
```

By simply using a different second key for the two functions encrypt and decrypt, different secure mesh networks can be created between nodes in close proximity.

The AUQ message is assembled by pd=encrypt(S)(R); msg=b'AUQ'+pd, assuming the sender MAC address is S and the recipient MAC address is R. Reading a message gives, peer,msg=ew.recv(), where peer==S. After reading the AUQ message, node R decrypts the message with R=decrypt(S)(msg[3:]). S is authenticated at the receiver node if R is equal to the receiver's MAC address.

The receiving node responds with an AUR message, pd=encrypt(R)(S); msg=b'AUR'+pd. Node S decrypts the message with S=decrypt(R)(msg[3:]). If S is equal to its MAC address, then R is authenticated at node S.

The unicast message type MSG is the data carrier packet of the system. Each node will forward the received MSG messages to the next nodes. An MSG packet traverses the entire mesh network. Each MSG packet contains a header and a payload part and is formatted as shown below:

```
msg='MSGyyyyyyxxxxxxiiiiiiddddd....'  # less then 250 in size
target=msg[3:3+6]        # yyyyyy      - destination node
source=msg[3+6:3+6+6]  # xxxxxx      - source node
mid=msg[3+6:3+6+6+5]   # xxxxxxiiiii - message id
data=msg[3+6+6+5:]       # ddddd..     - data
```

The destination MAC address can be multicast or broadcast. The source MAC address and a timestamp form the message identifier. The source MAC address is used as part of the key to encrypt the data. The MSG is sent from the source to all authenticated peers in the MESH array.

```
target=b'\xffffffffffff'  # sent to all
    mid=b'%s%05d'%(MAC, hash('%d'%time.ticks_us())) # 11 bytes
    msg=b'MSG'+target+mid+encrypt(MAC)(payload)
    for peer in MESH: # send to all authenticated peers
        try:
            w=ew.get_peer(peer)
            ok = ew.send(peer, msg) # forward the message
            if not ok:
                print('Fail to send MSG to', peer.hex())
                MESH.remove(peer) # peer may be down or out of reach
            yield # one at a time
        except:
            print('Peer', peer.hex(), 'not found (send_msg)')
```

Upon receipt of an MSG, the receiving node will process the packet and forward the message to all peers in its MESH array, provided that the packet is new, the receiving node is not the destination, and the next node is not the source of the packet.

```
elif msg_typ == b'MSG':
    print('Get MSG from', peer.hex(), 'message', msg[:20], '...')
    if peer in MESH:    # authenticated peer?
        if len(msg)<20: continue
        msg_id = msg[9:20] # message id: 11 bytes
        if msg_id not in MID: # new packet
            MID[midp]=msg_id; midp=(midp+1)%100
            target=msg[3:9]
            source=msg[9:15]
            payload = msg[20:] # rest of bytes at pos 20 onward
            if len(payload)==0: continue
            # process payload - task
            mt.worker(process, (source, payload))
            if MAC==target:  # distination reach
                print('Distination', target.hex(), 'reached')
```

```
         else:
              # forward msg to known peers but not to peer
  # it came from or the source node
              mt.worker(forward, (peer, source, msg))
```

The MID is an array of message identifiers. MID has a fixed size of 100. A pointer variable midp is the index to the next location where a new message identifier will be inserted. MID and midp implement a circular buffer of message identifiers. The purpose of MID is to prevent circular forwarding of messages in the mesh network.

## 4.4  Application

The payload of the MSG packet is structured similarly to MQTT (Message Queuing Telemetry Transport). There is, however, no central broker. In the MSG packet, any node can send any type of data. MSG packets with broadcast destination MAC address will be read by each node. The message's topic indicates what the sender has published. Because all packets pass through all nodes, the receiver can subscribe to any topic of interest. Topics are hierarchical strings that are used to classify messages. They are made up of one or more levels that are separated by slashes (/). For instance, "sensors/light" could be a topic for light sensor data, whereas "switch/light" could be a topic for light switches.

The application designers decide which topics each node publishes and which topics it subscribes to. Because the maximum packet size is 250 bytes, data must be sent in chunks. These chunks must be assembled in the correct transmission order at the application level.

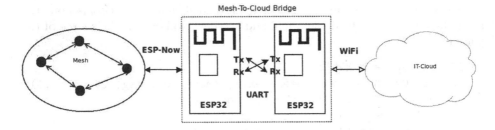

**Fig. 3.** Two ESP32 with UART perform a Mesh-To-WiFi Bridge

## 4.5  Cloud/Server

No IoT system is complete without the ability to send data to and receive instructions from the IT cloud.

The *ESP-NOW* protocol takes control of the physical layer of a device. The radio chip is tied to the *ESP-NOW* protocol stack and normal WiFi is no longer possible. A simple solution, shown in Fig. 3, is to use two ESP3 boards with UART (Universal Asynchronous Receiver/Transmitter) serial connection to interface them. Data from the mesh *ESP-NOW* side can be sent to the WiFi cloud side. This setup serves as a mesh-to-cloud gateway.

## 5   Conclusion

*ESP-NOW* is a connectionless communication protocol, which means that a node acts as a sender and receiver at the same time. A node can send and read data packets from another node without first establishing a connection or binding.

There are other technologies such as 5G, Zigbee, LoRaWAN (Long Range Wide Area Network) that provide similar functionality. However, ESP-NOW is available on all ESP32 MCUs without any additional wireless components.

Dynamic secure mesh networking is an important concept for IoT connectivity and utility. We have shown here that *ESP-NOW* can be used to build a practical implementation. The use of MicroPython with supporting modules such as espnow, workers, and CryptoXo for both development and deployment is proving to be feasible.

*ESP-NOW* is a non-standard protocol designed and supported only for the ESP32 MCU. However, this is not a reason not to consider it in a commercial product. The same can be said for MicroPython. Modern MCUs have enough resources and capabilities to run a high-level language interpreter, making development, deployment, and maintenance of an IoT application much easier than using C or assembly language, for example.

MicroPython is written in C and has a flexible configuration mechanism that makes it easy to create custom MicroPython firmware. MicroPython can be included in a commercial product. Perhaps it is time to reconsider developing an embedded product where dynamic scripting replaces the compiled application. There is a lot of productivity gain to consider.

IoT applications such as smart home automation, smart cities, smart grid, smart healthcare, IIoT (Industrial IoT), environmental monitoring, disaster response and recovery, smart agriculture and farming, smart transportation, wildlife tracking and conservation are among the many possible applications.

With a dynamic secure mesh network, supported by a dynamic programming environment with distributed concurrent collaborative tasks, an AI (artificial intelligence) driven system may be achievable in the near future.

## References

1. Day, J.D., Zimmermann, H.: The OSI reference model. Proc. IEEE **71**(12), 1334–1340 (1983). https://doi.org/10.1109/PROC.1983.12775
2. Winsemann, T., Köppen, V., Saake, G.: A layered architecture for enterprise data warehouse systems. In: Bajec, M., Eder, J. (eds.) CAiSE 2012. LNBIP, vol. 112, pp. 192–199. Springer, Heidelberg (2012). https://doi.org/10.1007/978-3-642-31069-0_17

3. Cilfone, A.; Davoli, L.; Belli, L.; Ferrari, G. Wireless mesh networking: an IoT-oriented perspective survey on relevant technologies. Future Internet **11**, 99 (2019). International Research Journal of Engineering and Technology (IRJET) Volume: 07 Issue: 06 June 2020. e-ISSN: 2395–005. https://doi.org/10.3390/fi11040099

4. Rosenberg, C., Luo, J., Girard, A.: Engineering wireless mesh networks. In: IEEE 19th International Symposium on Personal. Indoor and Mobile Radio Communications, Cannes, France 2008, pp. 1–6 (2008). https://doi.org/10.1109/PIMRC.2008.4699918

5. Sanni, M.L., Hashim, A.A., Anwar, F., Ahmed, G.S.M., Ali, S.: How to model wireless mesh networks topology. In: IOP Conference Series: Materials Science and Engineering, vol. 53 (2013). https://doi.org/10.1109/PIMRC.2008.4699918

6. Pasic, R., Kuzmanov, I., Atanasovski, K.: ESP-NOW communication protocol with ESP32. Izzivi prihodnost (2021). https://doi.org/10.37886/ip.2021.019

7. Eridani, D., Rochim, A.F., Cesara, F.N.: Comparative performance study of ESP-NOW, Wi-Fi, Bluetooth protocols based on range, transmission speed, latency, energy usage and barrier resistance. In: International Seminar on Application for Technology of Information and Communication (iSemantic). Semarangin, Indonesia 2021, pp. 322–328 (2021). https://doi.org/10.1109/iSemantic52711.2021.9573246

8. Kviesis, A., Komasilovs, V., Ozols, N., Zacepins, A.: Bee colony remote monitoring based on IoT using ESP-NOW protocol. PeerJ Comput. Sci. **9**, e1363 (2023). https://doi.org/10.7717/peerj-cs.1363

9. Hoang, T.N., Van, S.-T., Nguyen, B.D.: ESP-NOW based decentralized low cost voice communication systems for buildings. In: International Symposium on Electrical and Electronics Engineering (ISEE). Ho Chi Minh City, Vietnam 2019, pp. 108–112 (2019). https://doi.org/10.1109/ISEE2.2019.8921062

10. Schwarzwald, H.V., Würl, S., Langer, M., Trinitis, C.: MicroPython as a satellite control language. In: CF '22: Proceedings of the 19th ACM International Conference on Computing Frontiers May 2022, pp. 227–229 https://doi.org/10.1145/3528416.3531531

11. Gaspar, G., Fabo, P., Kuba, M., Flochova, J., Dudak , J., Florkova, Z.: Development of IoT applications based on the MicroPython platform for Industry 4.0 implementation. In: 2020 19th International Conference on Mechatronics - Mechatronika (ME), Prague, Czech Republic, 2020, pp. 1–7. https://doi.org/10.1109/ME49197.2020.9286455

12. Horst, U.T., Hasberg, H., Schulz, S.: MicroPython-based sensor node with asymmetric encryption for ubiquitous sensor networks. In: IEEE International IOT, Electronics and Mechatronics Conference (IEMTRONICS), Toronto, ON, Canada 2021, pp. 1–6 (2021). https://doi.org/10.1109/IEMTRONICS52119.2021.9422596

13. Workers Framework Micropython https://github.com/shariltumin/workers-framework-micropython. Accessed 16 May 2023

14. Dynamic Esp-Now Mesh Micropython https://github.com/shariltumin/mesh-espnow-micropython. Accessed 16 May 2023

# Art in the Machine: Value Misalignment and AI "Art"

Alyse Marie Allred[✉] and Cecilia Aragon

University of Washington, Seattle, WA 98195, USA
allreda@uw.edu

**Abstract.** Why have online artist communities largely rejected AI image generators when they have embraced other technologies? We focus on cooperative design and community values to first frame these communities as digital counterculture akin to transformative fandom. Then, we use this framework to explore the online art community's core principles in order to surface four key values (accessibility, distributed mentoring, gift economy, and authenticity), and illustrate their fundamental disconnect with the values espoused by advocates of current AI image generators. Finally, we conclude with suggestions for human and value-centered design of these technologies in collaborative creative visual communities to prevent similar unintended consequences.

**Keywords:** AI · creative collaboration · online communities · creativity · distributed creativity · distributed mentorship · informal learning · accessibility · art

## 1 Introduction

October 2022 saw the public launch of the stable diffusion based AI image generator DALL-E 2, followed shortly by competing programs like Midjourney [1]. However, as the programs rapidly gained popularity, a number of critical design flaws surfaced concerning safeguards against deepfake pornography [2], data privacy, and the opaqueness surrounding the algorithm and training datasets. After investigation, it was found that the image dataset contained non-consensually shared pornography and ISIS beheadings [3]; as well as private medical records [4].

In the unfolding discourse surrounding AI image generators, the online artist community has in large part outright rejected the technology [5, 6]. This community is a strongly collaborative group that has produced visual imagery in a supportive and highly interconnected fashion for many decades. Although collaboration and creative work are regular topics in cooperative design and the broader HCI community, there is limited insight into online artist communities and their reaction to AI image generators. Even prior to DALL-E 2's public launch, industry artists such as RJ Palmer warned against the risks the technology posed to working artists [5]. In the following months, these fears have been realized. Fantasy artist Greg Rutkowski was one of the early victims.

His works have been scraped non-consensually thousands of times, so much that search-ing his name yields more AI generated images than his original work [6]. Many other online artists from around the world have come forward after experiencing similar issues, claiming theft, copyright infringement, and financial harm [7–10].

Advocates of the new technology have argued that AI image generators "democ-ratize" art, framing concerned artists as luddites gatekeeping the concept of "art" out of fear of replacement [11]. However, this is an inaccurate portrayal that situates the discourse on the unanswerable question of "What is art?" rather than a deeper under-standing of how the online artist community functions to create, develop, share, and value art through a collaborative process. In this paper, we seek to address this gap.

Our hypothesis is that this tension occurs because the online artist community oper-ates on a fundamentally different value system from those advocating for AI image generators. This piece seeks to explore the dissonance between advocates of AI "art" and the collaborative beliefs and values of the online artist community. To accomplish this, we first frame this community as a digital counterculture akin to transformative fandom. Then, we use this framework to explore the online art community's core values in order to surface four key values. Finally, we use those values to better understand the community's rejection of AI art generators, their methods of resistance, and the implications this has for the technology moving forward.

## 1.1 Positionality

**Fig. 1.** Illustrative work by the primary author

In qualitative research on human values, it is often helpful to start with the authors' positionality—their social context and background that has influenced their research [12]. This can illustrate a depth of understanding of the values studied, as well as reveal unconscious biases. The discussion and analysis is built strongly on the first author's personal experiences and situated knowledge in the online artist community. She has interacted with this community as an artist since 2012, by way of transformative fandom.

With no formal art education, she honed her skill with the help of the community's informal mentorship. In 2016 she began freelancing professionally, and has since contributed over fifty professional-quality illustrations to various collaborative projects (see Fig. 1). The second author has studied cooperative visualization, the design and values of online communities, and transformative fandom for over a decade, publishing multiple papers and a book on these subjects [13–15].

## 2 Background

The online artist community is largely decentralized, distributed across the internet. Individual artists frequently experiment in mediums and techniques while posting their work across several social media sites or chatrooms. Given the diversity of age, location, and artistic skill or qualification, two unifying aspects of the online artist community are: a) communal participation in the creation of art and b) the internet as the primary method of sharing, networking, or supporting said art.

What makes the collaboration process of the online artist community unique is that it is built not on a medium or platform, but rather on an underlying system of values. Previously, these values were, for the most part, implicitly understood; they have only been forcibly surfaced in response to the emergence of AI image generators.

### 2.1 Online Artist Communities and Digital Counterculture

Collaboration and creative work are regular topics in cooperative design and HCI, but less research has been conducted into online artist communities. Existing work focuses on innovative tools or applications often occurring in the boundary space between the digital and the physical. These often take the form of presentations, music exhibits, or public displays that showcase the artistic potential of new technology [16–18]. While groundbreaking, these demonstrations tend to highlight the work of singular artists or teams, and are often isolated from the daily reality and communal workings of the online artist community.

The most comprehensive record comes from Perkel's ethnographic dissertation work on the online portfolio platform DeviantArt, which focuses on the interactions between teenaged users [19]. However, in addition to the limited scope to a single demographic on a specific platform, the study approaches the community as an outsider to the study site, eventually contributing comments and feedback rather than engaging as an artist situated in the space. As a result, insights specifically into online artist culture are relatively surface level, failing to capture most of the implicit values that run throughout the larger community.

To begin surfacing these values, we start by framing the online artist community as a digital counterculture. Lingel describes digital countercultures as communities of *alterity*, defined by their sense of otherness [20]. Art and artists are often created in reaction to the personal and cultural contexts in which it is situated as a form of identity work or activism. Subject matter frequently leans towards the grotesque or socially taboo in order to bring awareness to a cause or move it forward. This precedent has been maintained as art communities have shifted online, such as Wolfson's description of the new media focused group he dubs the "cyber left" [21].

Another important concept Lingel introduces is transferability, which she defines as "moving between—tracing connections between field sites rather than generalizing or making universal claims" [20]. The application of this concept brings us to the final framework in analyzing the online artist community: transformative fandom.

### 2.2 Online Artist Communities and Transformative Fandom

Transformative fandom refers to the collective communities of media fans that engage with source material through creative remix, producing artifacts such as fanfiction, fanvids, and fanart. Over the past few decades, academic scholarship has identified transformative fandom as both a digital counterculture and the original participatory culture [22], wherein participants explore mainstream media through alternative lenses, such as feminism or queerness. The resulting creative content often covers subversive topics surrounding sex, gender, and sexuality, leading to a long history of legal persecution by the corporations that own the intellectual property (IP).

Transformative fandom and online artist communities share significant overlaps. Online artists often begin honing their craft in internet-based fandom communities, providing the foundation for long-term artistic development [23]. Industry artists frequently engage with fandom on public sites, both for personal enjoyment and professional benefit. For example, the realistically rendered Pokémon fanart of the aforementioned concept artist, RJ Palmer, landed him a role on *Detective Pikachu* [24].

Many artists, including the first author, were introduced to the online artist community through transformative fandom. It is rare to find an online artist that has not previously engaged in transformative fandom in some capacity. In the next section, we argue that there is sufficient evidence from existing literature [23, 25] that the values and frameworks of transformative fandom can be transferred and applied to the larger online artist community.

## 3 Community Values

### 3.1 Diversity, Inclusion, and Accessibility

The online artist community is a participatory culture, defined by low barriers to artistic involvement, access to informal mentorship, and the sharing and support of creative endeavors [22]. Some of this can be observed through its similarities to transformative fandom; however, where fandom necessitates some familiarity with media, being an online artist requires creating and posting art online. To this end, social media sites such as Instagram, Tumblr, or DeviantArt are freely accessible.

However, this accessibility extends beyond the platforms of interaction. Digital art, the most common artistic medium present in the online artist community, is also one of the most accessible forms of art in history.

This accessibility is the result of two affordances, the first of which involves the tools by which the art is created. Although top-model devices, such as Wacom Cintiqs

**Fig. 2.** The diversity of digital art, featuring Kreftropod (MS Paint) [26], Catallenakat (Microsoft PowerPoint) [27], and L. C. Honora (Microsoft Word) [28]

(650+ USD) [29], are framed as an industry standard, affordable alternatives, such as the Huion HS64 (40+ USD) [30] are readily available. Similarly, Adobe's increasing prices and service based model [31] have alienated much of the online art community, leading artists to favor cheaper alternatives (Clip Studio Paint, Procreate) or freeware (FireAlpaca, Krita). Failing this, piracy is the go-to method of obtaining specialized art software—something of a necessity for the artists from the global south, where subscriptions may not even be offered, let alone financially viable.

However, specialized software and devices do not present a hard limit for online artists. Some favor outdated software like MS Paint as their tool of choice. Others turn to programs not designed for art, such as the Microsoft Office suite, to create complex and stylistic illustrations (see Fig. 2).

The second affordance is related to the nature of digital artifacts. Traditional art, such as sculpture and painting, is deeply connected to its physical embodiment; there is no way to digitally translate the size and scale of Michelangelo's David. These traits do not translate well across other mediums—a print reproduction will fail to capture the entire intended experience of an art piece. However, most people must settle for the reproductions, as access and opportunity to visit the works in person are tied to physical ability and financial means.

By contrast, digital artwork is ephemeral in its original form. It is disconnected from physical reality in a way that allows infinite reproducibility, so that anybody connected to the internet might access the intended experience regardless.

The importance of physicality (or lack thereof) around digital art and the online artist community is well illustrated by Anthony Collins. An online artist, Anthony is a queer, disabled transgendered person who experienced periods of homelessness in his young life. During this period, his laptop and tablet provided a lifeline, as when supplemented with internet and electricity from the local library, he was able to maintain some form of income while living out of his car [32].

Today, Anthony is housed and stable, but his declining health has further impacted his mobility. His continued connection and participation in the online artist community is reliant on the affordances outlined above, allowing him to adapt his space to address his physical and mental disabilities.

Anthony's case is not uncommon in the online art community, as evidenced by the way that community members actively work towards accommodation for a spectrum of disabilities. A recent example is an ongoing push on Tumblr to make the site more accessible to the visually impaired by adding alt text to otherwise undescribed images. This movement originated in fandoms around narrative podcasts, to maintain the accessibility afforded by the source material's original format. It has since spread to other fandoms and the online artist community as a whole, and is applied to both past and present works.

This sort of community-wide attempt at providing disability accommodations is by no means unique. Over the past decade, there have been debates around how to help other members of the community curate their space, such best practices for content warnings or establishing guidelines for tagging flashing imagery that might trigger seizures. Not every attempt at accommodation is successful, such as how content warnings for scopophobia (the intense fear of being stared at) were attached to any images where eyes were present. However, even these fumbles highlight how accessibility is something the online artist community actively strives for.

## 3.2 Informal Learning and Mentorship

Another trait shared between transformative fandom and the online artist community is how their decentralized, participation-based interactions facilitate informal learning and mentorship. Models of informal learning such as distributed mentoring—which were initially developed from the non-hierarchical, communal method of mentorship seen in fanfiction communities [13]—have proven broadly applicable to distributed creativity on the internet [33].

This community-wide dedication to accessible education tools is no accident, as can be seen in the history of cosplay (a performance art where participants design and wear costumes). In a 2017 reflection, cosplayer Penwiper recalled how, prior to the early 2000s, the costuming scene of media fandom was dominated by an older generation of master craftsmen who were extremely proprietary around trade knowledge. In this knowledge vacuum, young cosplayers began developing completely novel methods for costume creation. Unlike the previous generation of costumers, these techniques were created with accessibility in mind, utilizing broadly available crafting tools and materials that could be purchased on a budget. Critically, there was an active push against gatekeeping this new knowledge. Penwiper and other cosplayers created tutorials and guides, posting them publicly to early social media sites and personal hand-coded webpages. In the years since, this non-proprietary approach to trade knowledge in the cosplay community has become standardized, encouraging experimentation with the intention of passing on that knowledge for the benefit of future costumers [34].

Informal mentorship of this type is not limited to the cosplay community. The broader online art community shares a similar ethos, and boasts a wealth of educational resources, which range from beginner tutorials for watercolor to technical instructions for 3D rigging to detailed explorations of the human musculature. Some materials are designed to fill gaps in opportunity, an acknowledgment that not many are offered the chance of a proper art education. Other materials are created to fill the gaps in education, such as providing resources that are overlooked or lacking in a formal education, such as how to respectfully depict non-white, non-normative bodies. Most, however, are created on the implicit understanding that gatekeeping has no place in the community.

### 3.3  Gift Economy

Like many contemporary countercultures, the online artist community has strong anti-capitalist underpinnings, reflected in their attitudes around the accessibility of art. Instead, they lean heavily into a system of social capital, specifically a gift economy.

Approaching from the lens of transformative fandom offers additional insight. Like fandom's gift economy, the unit of currency, the gift, is any object that requires skill to create. However, in radical rejection of commercial exchange, the value of this gift is not determined by the quality of craftsmanship, but on what it symbolizes—the time, effort, and intention put towards the act of creation.

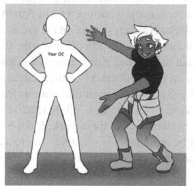

**Fig. 3.** (left) Promotional material from Sunny's art challenge [35]; (middle, right): The vibrant and transformative work of Vietnamese artist Baku Nguyễn [36, 37]

Take, for example, Sunny, a webcomic artist and product designer. In 2023, Sunny ran a small art competition, challenging participants to creatively respond to a couple of prompts related to her ongoing webcomic (see Fig. 3). At the conclusion of the challenge, the six winners that Sunny selected were given an option of two prizes: a bundle of her merchandise *or* a custom art piece. Ultimately, all but one of the winners opted for the custom art piece, valuing that over the merchandise bundles that were worth up to 60 USD each [35].

Given the value placed upon an art piece's context, art theft is a serious offense in the online artist community. Art theft is not limited to plagiarism, which is difficult to catch and prove in a large, decentralized community inclined to remix. A far more common form comes as a result of reposting, wherein a person who is not the original creator of a work posts that work to another social media account or platform altogether. Within a gift economy, the act of removing the original context of a work effectively strips the markers of value from it, depriving its creator of social capital. At best, this practice is frustrating, watching another person receive thousands of likes or comments while the original work receives a fraction of that attention. At worst, the lack of credit is actively harmful, making invisible already marginalized artists and potentially depriving them of opportunities for work.

At first glance, the inclusion of transformative work almost seems to contradict these attitudes surrounding art theft, especially in the parts of the community where fanworks are converted to goods and merchandise. However, the contradiction merely reveals an understanding of fair use that does not align with US copyright law.

Rather than a judgment over who "owns" intellectual property, online artists consider a calculation of harm. In the case of indie media spearheaded by single artists or small teams, it is widely understood that the sale of bootleg materials poses active harm to the original creators by competing for the limited financial support of a small fanbase. By contrast, the sale of remix work by individual artists poses virtually no financial harm to large companies. Transformative work is rooted in reclaiming control over mainstream stories in conjunction with the greater online artist community's dedication to removing barriers to art and creativity.

In addition to a general attitude of resistance, the evolving understanding of fair use reflects the way that the online artist community is increasingly removed from American, or even western, ideals. Vietnamese illustrator Baku Nguyễn stated that the greatest harm comes not from a theft of credit, but a theft of autonomy [38]. In other words, the harm of not only stripping an art piece's context, but some third party actively assigning a *new* meaning. Much of Baku's work centers on the exploration of their cultural identity, particularly through clothing design (see Fig. 3). Many of their illustrations feature colorful, complex explorations of traditional Vietnamese clothes. While relatively laissez-faire about the ways that others may adapt or iterate upon their work, Baku has explicitly requested that their clothing designs not be replicated, explaining: "there's a burden of knowledge there. These garments are the result of colonialism, and I do Not trust the broad range of strangers online to handle that delicately" [38].

The importance that Baku places on agency over their work—especially the aspects that are deeply entwined with cultural history—calls attention to the way that capitalism and colonialism continue to shape the art that we make. It also illustrates how the increasing diversity and inclusion of global perspectives in the online artist community influence their shared values.

### 3.4  Authenticity

Authenticity is, by far, the most nebulous of the values discussed here, as it deals with the relationship between an artist and their art. The act of creation necessitates that the creator give a piece of themselves. As a result, putting that art into the world is an act of extreme vulnerability.

One artifact of authenticity in the community is a practice known as Art vs the Artist. The most common incarnation involves selecting eight pieces of art that you feel best represent yourself. These eight works are then arranged in a 3 × 3 square, with the center of the matrix occupied by a picture of the artist. The exercise provokes self-reflection surrounding how they wish to be perceived by the greater community, and which of pieces of work they believe best communicate that.

The connection between authenticity and artistic identity also describes why the "online artist community" cannot be scoped down to a specific *type* of art. The space naturally resists categorization, as the artists jump organically between mediums and subject material. Ultimately, authenticity describes an inherent need to create.

A comic by David Shrigley captures the bone-deep itch that drives many artistic endeavors. The comic is a single panel, featuring a dog sitting at a piano. The text reads in heavy block letters: "He plays very badly but it stops him from destroying things" [39].

## 4   Art in the Machine

Viewed from within this system of values (accessibility, distributed mentoring, gift economy, and authenticity), AI image generators represent one of the most toxic incarnations of corporate art theft. As algorithms scrape an art piece, they disconnect it from its context and intention, disrespecting and denying the value of the gift. More than that, by removing the artist from the art, the algorithm simultaneously denies them credit *and* autonomy over their own work.

AI image generators were developed without considering online artists as stakeholders, despite how the technology hinges entirely on access to their creative work. A good faith reading of the situation posits ignorance; however, it is an ignorance that has bloomed into malice. As the months have passed and corporations have doubled down on the adoption and use of AI image generators, not even surface-level attempts have been made to address the escalating harm.

To add insult to injury, this effort has co-opted the values and language of the online art community in order to reframe their justified anger as hysteria. Talking points around how AI image generators "democratize" art by making it "accessible" are used to portray artists as gatekeepers of art, despite the community's long-running dedication to both education and accessibility. We see this further illustrated if we return to the story of Greg Rutkowski, the digital artist whose work was non-consensually fed to the algorithms. In addition to losing agency over what is presented as his work, it is important to note that the key reason his work was so easily and accurately scraped was because he went out of his way to make his work accessible to the visually impaired by adding extensive alt text [6].

To members of the online art community, AI image generators seek to profit from their work without consequence, to push marginalized people further to the margins by making them invisible, with the ultimate goal of removing the artist from art altogether. The apathy with which their complaints have been met has only solidified these beliefs.

## 5   Resistance

The online art community has mobilized in active resistance to the attempted normalization of AI image generators. On the legal front, a trio of online artists—Kelly McKernan, Karla Ortiz, and Sarah Anderson—have launched a class-action lawsuit against OpenAI, aiming to restrict the use of algorithms and expand artists' rights over their own work [40, 41]. Meanwhile, in a related community, the issue of AI has become a critical point in the ongoing WGA (Writers Guild of America) strike, as writers push back against arguments akin to those leveled earlier at online artists [42].

The online artist community has employed a mix of guerilla tactics and organized boycotts to combat encroaching technology. One example is an adaptation of a method for dealing with art-stealing Twitter bots [43]. These bots search the internet for images that received a user comment "I want this on a t-shirt," then non-consensually download the image in question and offer it as a t-shirt design on a third party website. In response, online artists en masse began tagging official Disney imagery with the same phrase, which has consistently led to the take-down of exploitative sites. The current adaptation involves community members "feeding" official Disney artwork to various AI image generators with similar intentions.

Over the past year, new methods for protection have become available. Researchers at the University of Chicago have launched Glaze, a program that creates a version of images with an invisible "cloak" that makes it more difficult to be scraped by AIs [44].

The most notable example of community-wide protests occurred after the online portfolio site, ArtStation, saw a flood of AI generated images—many of which had been scraped directly from the site itself. In response, artists began posting anti-AI images to clog up the site's feed display and to prevent further scraping. The protests saw some success, leaving the site's landing page barren for days. Although eventually ArtStation responded by actively hiding the anti-AI protest images, it was a clear illustration of the depth of outrage in the online artist community [45, 46].

## 6 Conclusion

In this paper, we have focused on how the values of a highly collaborative and technologically savvy community shape their design processes and ultimately their visual products. Rather than focusing on the technology exclusively, understanding community values and how they influence the community's technology choices can enable designers to build successful and thriving online communities. We surfaced four key values of the online artist community (accessibility, distributed mentoring, gift economy, and authenticity), and illustrated their fundamental disconnect with the values espoused by advocates of current AI image generators.

The surprising productivity, free knowledge sharing, and outright joy expressed by participants of online artist communities has been tempered by a strong degree of rage against mechanistic systems that AI tools have only exacerbated.

Or, as the artist Anthony passionately articulated: "These systems left me homeless, destitute, and actively suicidal. Leaving those systems to set up my own business was far from ideal, I would have been more than content to spend my life adding value to a corporation in exchange for a modest comfortable income. I wanted to work with/for/in these systems, even! I find collective work incredibly gratifying! But these systems, for whatever reason, have nigh universally determined I am an undesirable presence, and insufficient for their purposes, so they left me to starve and die" [32].

As the technology of AI image generators improves, it will be critical to apply features that take into account the underlying values of the humans who created and collaboratively shared the source images that have made the AI tools so successful. A human-centered and value-centered design process has always strengthened cooperative visualization and any type of creative work. It is absolutely essential that human and community values be centered in any future design of AI image generators, which are a formidable example of the unintended consequences of overly hasty attempts to launch generative algorithms in the visual design world.

# References

1. Foley, J.: DALL-E 2 Access is Now Open to Everyone, and that's Kind of Terrifying. https://www.creativebloq.com/news/dalle2-access-open-to-all
2. Vincent, J.: Stable Diffusion made Copying Artists and Generating Porn Harder and Users are Mad. https://www.theverge.com/2022/11/24/23476622/ai-image-generator-stable-diffusion-version-2-nsfw-artists-data-changes
3. Xiang, C., Maiberg, E.: ISIS Executions and Non-Consensual Porn Are Powering AI Art. https://www.vice.com/en/article/93ad75/isis-executions-and-non-consensual-porn-are-powering-ai-art
4. Edwards, B.: Artist Finds Private Medical Record Photos in Popular AI Training Data Set. https://arstechnica.com/information-technology/2022/09/artist-finds-private-medical-record-photos-in-popular-ai-training-data-set/
5. Plunkett, L.: AI Creating "Art" Is An Ethical and Copyright Nightmare. https://kotaku.com/ai-art-dall-e-midjourney-stable-diffusion-copyright-1849388060
6. Heikkilä, M.: This Artist is Dominating AI-Generated Art. And he's not Happy about it. https://www.technologyreview.com/2022/09/16/1059598/this-artist-is-dominating-ai-generated-art-and-hes-not-happy-about-it/
7. van Baarle, L.: Untitled Post. https://blog.loish.net/post/703723938473181184/theres-a-protest-going-on-against-ai-art-over-on (2022)
8. Lum, M.: Say no to AI Generated Art in the Exhibitors and... (2022) https://twitter.com/PuccaNoodles/status/1591896706509336576
9. Ki: Say no to AI art (2022). https://gawki.tumblr.com/post/703770072741707776/i-felt-the-need-to-share-here-as-well-say-no-to
10. Lee, D.J.: Untitled Post (2022). https://jdebbiel.tumblr.com/post/703480889851756544/my-works-got-stolen-last-week-and-were-used-to
11. Barnett, M.: Slightly Against Aligning with Neo-Luddites (2022). https://www.lesswrong.com/posts/9MZdwQ7u53oaRiBYX/slightly-against-aligning-with-neo-luddites
12. Bourke, B.: Positionality: Reflecting on the Research Process. TQR (2014). https://doi.org/10.46743/2160-3715/2014.1026
13. Campbell, J., Aragon, C., Davis, K., Evans, S., Evans, A., Randall, D.: Thousands of positive reviews: distributed mentoring in online fan communities. In: Proc of the 19th ACM Conf. on Computer-Supported Cooperative Work & Social Computing, pp. 691–704. ACM, San Francisco California USA (2016)
14. Aragon, C., Davis, K.: Writers in the Secret Garden: Fanfiction, Youth, and New Forms of Mentoring. The MIT Press, Cambridge, Massachusetts (2019)
15. Evans, S., et al.: More Than peer production: fanfiction communities as sites of distributed mentoring. In: Proceedings of the 2017 ACM Conference on Computer Supported Cooperative Work & Social Computing, pp. 259–272. ACM, Portland Oregon (2017)
16. Huang, M.X., Tang, W.W.W., Lo, K.W.K., Lau, C.K., Ngai, G., Chan, S.: MelodicBrush: a novel system for cross-modal digital art creation linking calligraphy and music. In: Proceedings of the Designing Interactive Systems Conference, pp. 418–427. ACM, Newcastle Upon Tyne United Kingdom (2012)
17. Jacobs, J., Mellis, D., Zoran, A., Torres, C., Brandt, J., Tanenbaum, T.J.: Digital craftsmanship: HCI Takes on technology as an expressive medium. In: Proceedings of the 2016 ACM Conference Companion Publication on Designing Interactive Systems, pp. 57–60. ACM, Brisbane QLD Australia (2016)
18. Clarke, R., Briggs, J., Light, A., Wright, P.: Situated encounters with socially engaged art in community-based design. In: Proc of the 2016 ACM Conf on Designing Interactive Systems, pp. 521–532. ACM, Brisbane QLD Australia (2016)

19. Perkel, D.: Making art, Creating Infrastructure: DeviantART and the Production of the Web (2011)
20. Lingel, J.: Digital Countercultures and the Struggle for Community. The MIT Press, Cambridge, MA (2017)
21. Wolfson, T.: Digital Rebellion: The Birth of the Cyber Left. University of Illinois Press (2014)
22. Jenkins, H.: Textual Poachers: Television Fans and Participatory Culture. Routledge, New York (2013)
23. Manifold, M.C.: Enchanting tales and imagic stories: the educational benefits of fanart making. Art Educ. **66**, 12–19 (2013). https://doi.org/10.1080/00043125.201
24. Palmer, R.: Art of RJ Palmer. https://www.rj-palmer.com
25. Allred, A.M., Gray, C.M.: "Be gay, do crimes": the co-production and activist potential of contemporary fanzines. Proceedings ACM Hum.-Computational Interaction **5**, 1–35 (2021). https://doi.org/10.1145/3479520
26. kreftropod: [insufficient] (2017)
27. catallenakat: Giselle (2020)
28. Honora, L.C.: Kim Kitsuragi 2 (2022)
29. Wacom: Wacom Cintiq: creative pen display. https://www.wacom.com/en-us/products/pen-displays/wacom-cintiq
30. Huion: Huion HS64 Android Drawing Tablet for Beginners. https://store.huion.com/products/huion-hs64
31. Adobe: Compare plans for individuals, students & teams, https://www.adobe.com/creativecloud/compare-plans.html
32. Collins, A.: Personal Communication (2023)
33. Literat, I.: Distributed Creativity on the Internet: A Theoretical Foundation for Online Creative Participation (2018)
34. penwiper: Untitled Post (2019). https://penwiper.tumblr.com/post/189251630312/so-a-couple-days-ago-some-folks-braved-my
35. Sunny: Untitled Post (2022). https://www.instagram.com/p/CkFDL2nLfn0/
36. Nguyễn, B.: palace wizard (2022)
37. Nguyễn, B.: cờ ngũ sắc (2021)
38. Nguyễn, B.: Personal Communication
39. Shrigley, D.: He Plays Very Badly but it Stops Him from Destroying Things (2022)
40. Chayka, K.: Is A.I. Art Stealing from Artists?. https://www.newyorker.com/culture/infinite-scroll/is-ai-art-stealing-from-artists (2023)
41. Dixit, P.: "It's Gross To Me": The Trio Of Artists Suing AI Art Generators Speaks Out. https://www.buzzfeednews.com/article/pranavdixit/ai-art-generators-lawsuit-stable-diffusion-midjourney
42. Hsu, J.: Why Use of AI is a Major Sticking Point in the Ongoing Writers' Strike. https://www.newscientist.com/article/2373382-why-use-of-ai-is-a-major-sticking-point-in-the-ongoing-writers-strike/
43. McKay, T.: I Want That on a T-Shirt, gizmodo.com/i-want-that-on-a-t-shirt-1840273177
44. Shan, S., Cryan, J., Wenger, E., Zheng, H., Hanocka, R.: Glaze: Protecting Artists from Style Mimicry (2023). https://glaze.cs.uchicago.edu/
45. Weatherbed, J.: ArtStation is Hiding Images that Protest Against AI art. https://www.theverge.com/2022/12/23/23523864/artstation-removing-anti-ai-protest-artwork-censorship
46. Edwards, B.: Artists Stage Mass Protest Against AI-Generated Artwork on ArtStation – Ars Technica. https://arstechnica.com/information-technology/2022/12/artstation-artists-stage-mass-protest-against-ai-generated-artwork/

# Exploring the Usability of the LCH Color Model for Web Designers

Frode Eika Sandnes(✉) ⓘ

Department of Computer Science, Oslo Metropolitan University, 0130 Oslo, Norway
frodes@oslomet.no

**Abstract.** Although the LCH color models have been around for many years, it has just recently been included in web specifications and is currently being implemented by browser vendors. Several voices argue that the LCH color model for web will drastically change how web designers work with colors and lead to improved results. This study explores the usability of the LCH model in context of web design and how the LCH model could affect accessibility. Two specific use cases are addressed, the selection of color harmonies and adherence to color contrast requirements. The results indicate that the LCH model is a worse choice than HSL when the model is used incorrectly to select color harmonies using textbook RYB color theory. Although LCH in some situations simplifies work with color contrasts compared to HSL it seems unlikely to drastically change how designers work with contrast. Several potential challenges with LCH from a pragmatic design usability perspective are discussed.

**Keywords:** Web design · Color harmony · Contrast · Low vision · LCH · RYB

## 1 Introduction

Color models help designers and developers represent and discuss colors. A vast array of color models has been proposed. One of the most widely used models is the hardware centric RGB model where a color is specified in amounts of red, green, and blue. However, as it is hard to perceive the relationship between RGB values and actual colors, the HSL and HSV models are instead used by individuals with more demanding color needs. HSL and HSV both define colors according to their hue, lightness (or value), and saturation. The main difference between HSL and HSV is that HSV can be viewed as a cone where white is in the center of the top disk, while HSL can be viewed as two cones with a touching disk where white is defined as the top tip. The mathematical mapping between HSV/HSL and RGB is relatively simple. Although HSV and HSL constitute an improvement over RGB they can also be challenging to use as the perceivable colors are unevenly distributed across the color space. For example, the colors yellow and blue may have identical lightness values yet be perceived as light and dark. Hence, there are discrepancies between the lightness parameter and the perceived lightness. To overcome such problems perceptually uniform color spaces have been proposed. One of the most cited perceptual color spaces is the CIElab color space and its cylindrical counterpart

© The Author(s), under exclusive license to Springer Nature Switzerland AG 2023
Y. Luo (Ed.): CDVE 2023, LNCS 14166, pp. 43–55, 2023.
https://doi.org/10.1007/978-3-031-43815-8_5

LCH (lightness, chroma, and hue). Hue is the perceived color, lightness can be considered the brightness of a color in relation to the brightness of white under similar lighting conditions, while chroma is the purity of a color or "colorfulness" (similar to saturation).

HSL and LCH hues are typically denoted using polar coordinates. The HSL color wheel is a projection of the RGB color space onto a plane defined by the black point with a normal towards white. The resulting color wheel therefore has a recognizable pattern with the red, green, and blue components equidistant 120 degrees apart with yellow, cyan, and magenta in-between. The greens consume a disproportionately large sector of the color wheel compared to other hues where it can be hard to visually perceive hues. It is pointed out by W3CSchools, a widely used source for information about web-design, that the "RGB Green is different from the HTML color named Green" [1]. The LCH model is designed such that the resulting color wheel leads to perceptual changes in hues that are related to angle distance. Another key difference is that the 12 o' clock hue is red in HSL while it is magenta-red in LCH.

The lack of support for improved color spaces in design tools and web standards is probably the main reason for its limited use in practice. For example, HSL is a more recent addition to RGB in web technology (first introduced in CSS3 some 20 years ago). Recently, LCH has also been added to the web standard [2] although listed as experimental technology at the time of writing. Most research on color models has exclusively focused on visual properties, and few studies have addressed their practical usability. It is therefore relevant to assess potential consequences of these changes. This study focuses on two common and important use cases faced by web designers, namely working with color harmonies and working with accessible color contrasts.

Designers may rely on color harmonies taught in design education. This is often referred to as "color theory". The RYB-color wheel as it is probably the most cited model in art and design. RYB (red, yellow, and blue) stems from painting where color palettes are generated by mixing red, yellow, and blue. To generate a color wheel the red, yellow, and blue (primary colors) are placed at 120 degrees apart on the wheel with red at 12 o'clock. The mixed primary colors (secondary colors) are placed between the primary colors (namely orange, green, and magenta). Although there are no rules for which colors go well together, there are rule-of-thumb suggestions that can help novice and beginner designers make sensible choices that have esthetical qualities. Common color harmonies include monochrome, analogous, complementary, triads and split complementary. Harmonies are typically illustrated on the RYB color wheel in textbooks. Colors close on the wheel appear more harmonious while colors further apart on the wheel become more noticeable and create tension. The RYB color wheel equally divides the colors into "warm" and "cold" colors. W3CSchools argues that "RYB is the best color wheel to identify the colors that go well together." and "The RYB wheel can be used to create pleasing color schemes for the web." [1].

Still, many electronic tools with color wheels before LCH were based on HSL. At first glance the HSL and RYB models may appear similar. Some designers may not be aware of differences and may therefore make color RYB harmony decisions in HSL space. RYB color harmonies applied to HSL can also be observed in academic texts [3, 4]. It is also argued that traditional color theory is not optimal as it is not based on empirical evidence [5]. Yet, design literature has a different emphasis than color science literature with a designer-oriented view on colors. For instance, Jalal et al. [6] argues that key color operations include sampling (eyedropper), understanding and adjusting colors, manipulating color relationships, combining colors with other elements, and revisiting existing color choices. Kim and Suk [7] argue that the sharing of design resources is an important part of design. While color science literature has a global view of the color space, some voices in the design literature argue for tools that facilitate exploration and tweaking of local colors in the color space [8].

This work rests on a perceived gap between the color scientists' emphasis on empirical evidence, and the pragmatic needs of web designers and their mental models of color. This paper attempts to contribute new perspectives on possible implications of introducing designers to LCH color tools. Irrespective of what is the "correct" definition of color harmony, this work assumes that RYB color theory constitutes an established well-understood universal reference that allows designers to describe and discuss colors. One objective of this work was thus to assess how RYB color harmony decisions made in LCH space affect the intended visual effect. One key question is how different the (reference) RYB-color wheel is to the LCH color wheel. For instance, complementary colors in RYB are on opposite sides of the wheel (180 degrees), while LCH has other hue pairs on the opposite sides of the color wheel.

Next, it has been argued that the LCH model will lead to improved accessibility as it becomes easier to work with contrast in a perceptually uniform space. For instance, Vidra and Pešička [9] claim that "LCH ensures that different colors with the same lightness have almost identical contrast ratios". There are currently few examples of how designers are encouraged to use LCH to ensure accessibility in practice. By itself, the model does not reveal what is sufficient color contrast and it is still necessary to rely on additional contrast calculations. One question is whether LCH simplifies the process? Imagine a team that modifies a contrast compliant palette. To what degree will the modified palette need to be rechecked using contrast calculations?

## 2 Related Work

Color is studied from many perspectives such as color theory, psychology, visualization, human computer interaction, and art. The topic of this study is the LCH color model [10]. This study focuses primarily on how designers relate to colors as they are represented in digital tools such as color pickers [11–13]. Two key issues are the selection of color harmonies [14], and tool support for accessible color contrasts [15]. Several approaches for incorporating color contrasts in color pickers have been selected [15–18], and some of these accessibility ideas have eventually made their way into commercial tools such as Google Chrome. Tool support that suggests accessible colors have been demonstrated [19, 20], as well as tools that automatically correct insufficient color contrasts on live web sites [21]. There has also been a recent growing interest in the effects of dark-mode interfaces [22, 23].

# 3  Method

To explore the usability of the LCH model this study employed several simulations based around two common use cases faced by web designers, namely the selection of color harmonies and working with contrasts.

## 3.1  Use Case 1: Color Harmony

This use case relates to how designers may select a set of colors for a design that are aesthetically pleasing. For this they may use one of common color harmony patterns defined by the respective angles between pairs of colors on the color wheel. For example, complementary colors are defined as being 180 degrees apart, triadic colors are 120 degrees apart, analogous colors are approximately 30 degrees apart and monochrome colors have identical hue angles. To explore this the hues of the LCH, HSL and RYB color wheels are first compared. Next, the angles between pairs of color pairs are compared across the three color-spaces.

## 3.2  Use Case 2: Color Contrast

This use case involves selecting color pairs for text and text background that have sufficient contrast. The Web Content Accessibility Guidelines (WCAG) provides widely used limits. Typically, a web designer starts by selecting a pair of colors and then checks that this color pair provides sufficient contrast using some sort of contrast calculator. Other developers may test their web design using automatic accessibility checking tools and correct detected accessibility violations.

In practical situations, designers want to adjust or make totally different color decisions throughout a project. With RGB and HSL such changes need to be rechecked to ensure that the revised color palette adheres to minimum contrast limits. However, the question is whether this task is simplified with the LCH model as the space is perceptually uniform. Can lightness, chroma, and hues be altered independently of each other without affecting the resulting color contrast of a palette. A consequence of such properties would reduce the need to validate the contrast level with any color change.

A set of simple calculations were conducted by systematically and independently varying the hues, chroma and lightness of a color and recording the corresponding changes in contrast in relation to a fixed second color.

## 3.3  Procedure

The color calculations conducted herein was done in JavaScript using Dave Eddy RYB routines (https://github.com/bahamas10/RYB/blob/gh-pages/js/RXB.js# L252-L330), and Jonathan Neal's color (LCH, HSL, and RGB) conversion and contrast routines (https://github.com/jonathantneal/convert-colors). Hue angle differences were computed using dot products of color wheel unit vectors.

# 4   Results

## 4.1   Hue Discrepancies

Figure 1 illustrates the color wheels of hues for the RYB, HSL and LCH color models. Note that the LCH color wheel is rotated clockwise such that the red hue is aligned with the red of HSL and RYB. Visual inspections of these color wheels reveal large discrepancies. Red and magenta are the only hues that are relatively aligned as most other hues are positioned quite differently around the circle. RYB and LCH appear the most dissimilar with HSL appearing somewhere in between the two. The detailed hue discrepancies will be explored in the following. Figure 1 shows that the 50/50 division of the RYB wheel into warm and cold colors does not apply to HSL and LCH.

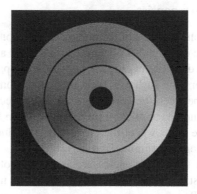

**Fig. 1.** Hue angles in RYB (outer ring), HSL (middle ring), LCH (inner ring). Note that the LCH hues are rotated 40 degrees anticlockwise. Saturation = 70% and lightness = 60%).

Figure 2 shows the absolute differences in angles between identical hues between each pair of the three color models as it can be hard to distinguish small hue differences visually. Clearly, the color wheel of LCH has no communalities with the RYB color wheel whatsoever as the differences range between 20 and 120 degrees. The plot shows that HSL and LCH share two hue angles with close to identical hues, and that HSL and RYB share four such hue angles.

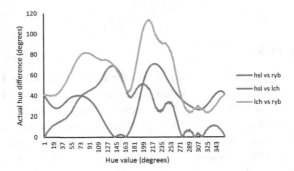

**Fig. 2.** Uncorrected hue discrepancies between polar RYB, HSL and LCH color models.

## 4.2 Color Harmony Discrepancies

To explore the potential consequences of the hue differences on color harmony choices, the discrepancies between LCH and RYB angles, and HSL and RYB for references, were computed. This was done by investigating every angle pair around the hue circle in steps of one degree. For each such pair their angle was computed and compared to the corresponding angle between the corresponding hue directions on the RYB color wheel. Clearly, color harmonies are determined relatively on the color wheel and the absolute orientation of the color wheel therefore has no influence. The results of the angle difference comparisons are summarized in Table 1.

The results show that the discrepancies are large for both HSL and LCH when compared to RYB. Interestingly, the LCH discrepancies are notably larger than those for HSL in relation to RYB.

For LCH the median discrepancy is more than 7%, while for HSL it is just above 6%. For 75% of LCH angles the discrepancies constitute 12.5% (HSL is just above 10%). It must be noted that the worst-case scenario is a discrepancy of more than 25% for LCH and 20% for HSL.

**Table 1.** Distribution of discrepancies of hue angle (degrees) for HSL, HSL, and RYB.

| Quartile | LCH-RYB | HSL-RYB | HSL-LCH |
|---|---|---|---|
| Min | 0 | 0 | 0.0 |
| Q1 | 12.4 | 9.6 | 6.0 |
| Median | 26.4 | 21.7 | 14.8 |
| Q3 | 45.6 | 37.0 | 30.5 |
| Max | 95.9 | 79.8 | 73.0 |

Table 2 lists the hue pairs that have both very different and very similar distances on the RYB vs LCH color wheels for sets of neighbor, triadic, and complementary color harmonies. For example, according to RYB green and blue are neighboring colors, but their angle in LCH is 122 suggesting that these are triads. Moreover green-yellow and red are triads according to RYB while this is not the case in LCH as the corresponding angle is less than 60 degrees. Similarly, green and red are complementary colors in

RYB, while their angle is just 96 in LCH which is half the complementary angle of 180 degrees.

Color pairs with very similar relative distances on the RYB and LCH color wheels are the neighbor orange vs green-yellow, the triad turquoise vs green-yellow and the complementary blue and orange.

It is quite interesting to note the large discrepancies between the perceptually uniform LCH color wheel and the RYB wheel that traditionally has been the reference representation of aesthetic perception of unique colors.

**Table 2.** Minimum and maximum hue value differences (based on the same visual hues) between RYB and LCH for neighbors, triadic, and complementary color pairs.

| | Minimum angle discrepancy | | | Maximum angle discrepancy | | |
|---|---|---|---|---|---|---|
| | neighbor | triad | compl. | neighbor | triad | compl. |
| LCH hue 1 | 64 | 210 | 233 | 269 | 88 | 135 |
| | Orange | Turquoise | Blue | Blue | Green-yellow | Green |
| LCH hue 2 | 94 | 89 | 51 | 146 | 32 | 39 |
| | Green-yellow | Green-yellow | Orange | Green | Red | Red |
| RYB diff. | 30 | 120 | 180 | 29 | 120 | 179 |
| LCH diff. | 30 | 120 | 179 | 122 | 56 | 96 |

## 4.3 Accessibility Through Color Contrast

Table 3 shows the results of varying the hues in a resolution of 1 degree around the hue color wheel, with fixed chroma and lightness. According to these results it seems that the claim that the contrast will remain constant by varying the hue does not hold in a strict sense as the resulting contrasts indeed varies. The spread of the variations seems to be related to the magnitude of the difference in lightness between the two colors. For small lightness changes (10) the difference was just noted at the third decimal point, with differences of 20 in lightness the variations are noticeable for the second decimal point, for difference of 40 there are variations in the third decimal point and for a large lightness difference (80) the variation is noticed as the contrasts varied from below and above 8.

**Table 3.** Distribution of contrasts as a function of varying hue (for different lightness changes).

| | Lightness change | | | | | | | |
|---|---|---|---|---|---|---|---|---|
| Quartile | 10 | 20 | 30 | 40 | 50 | 60 | 70 | 80 |
| Min | 1.391 | 1.891 | 2.511 | 3.265 | 4.166 | 5.228 | 6.463 | 7.885 |
| Q1 | 1.394 | 1.898 | 2.523 | 3.285 | 4.195 | 5.269 | 6.518 | 7.956 |
| Median | 1.396 | 1.905 | 2.537 | 3.308 | 4.230 | 5.317 | 6.584 | 8.043 |
| Q3 | 1.398 | 1.908 | 2.543 | 3.318 | 4.245 | 5.342 | 6.618 | 8.090 |
| Max | 1.399 | 1.912 | 2.551 | 3.331 | 4.265 | 5.368 | 6.654 | 8.135 |

Table 4 shows the results of varying the chroma from 0 to 230 in a resolution of 1, with fixed hue and lightness fixed. Again, the results show that there is a variation in the resulting contrast level as a function of chroma changes. However, the variations are very small.

**Table 4.** Distribution of contrasts as a function of varying chroma (for different lightness changes).

| | Lightness change | | | | | | | |
|---|---|---|---|---|---|---|---|---|
| Quartile | 10 | 20 | 30 | 40 | 50 | 60 | 70 | 80 |
| Min | 1.348 | 1.777 | 2.295 | 2.911 | 3.632 | 4.497 | 5.426 | 6.515 |
| Q1 | 1.350 | 1.782 | 2.304 | 2.925 | 3.653 | 4.497 | 5.466 | 6.567 |
| Median | 1.352 | 1.787 | 2.313 | 2.949 | 3.673 | 4.526 | 5.504 | 6.618 |
| Q3 | 1.354 | 1.792 | 2.323 | 2.955 | 3.697 | 4.559 | 5.549 | 6.676 |
| Max | 1.358 | 1.801 | 2.337 | 2.977 | 3.729 | 4.602 | 5.606 | 6.749 |

Figure 3 shows the results of varying lightness while keeping hue and chroma constant. The second color is obtained by adding the brightness change to the (base) brightness of the first color in the pair. The results show that the resulting contrasts vary as a function of lightness level (base lightness of the first color), and that the degree of variation is also a function of change in lightness (affecting lightness of the second color in the pair). For example, with a lightness change of 60 the contrast level varies from a maximum of 8 to a 4 (for the limited range studied herein). Moreover, this change is obviously non-linear. The effect of lightness changes is smaller for very dark colors and the effect becomes higher with medium dark colors. The effect of contrast changes is yet smaller with bright colors.

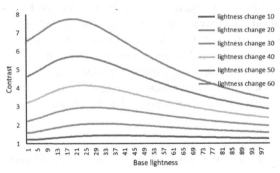

**Fig. 3.** Contrasts between two colors as a function of base lightness with fixed lightness changes in lightness (10 to 60 in steps of 10).

# 5  Discussion

## 5.1  Color Model Discrepancies

Both the LCH and HSL models refer to lightness and hue. The comparative analysis of hues of RYB, HSL and LCH revealed large differences. Hence, the same words are used to refer to quite different scales. Consequently, if a designer has intuitively learned the hue angles in one model it can be challenging to move to another model. Moreover, this assumes that the designer is aware of the differences, an assumption that may not necessarily hold in practice. One key intention of LCH is to provide an improvement over HSL by offering perceptual uniformity. A fixed change in one of the LCH parameters should result in perceptually fixed change in color, while for HSL the change depends on where one is on the scale. On one hand the reuse of the words lightness and hue help designers reuse their mental model of HSL and thereby be able to use the model immediately. One may ponder whether it would result in less confusion to give these parameters unique names, for example LCH-hue and HSL-hue to clearly signal that although they share similarities, they have different definitions. This will draw designers' attention towards differences in the respective scales. However, the chroma versus saturation parameters may cause less confusion due to the different names suggesting that they represent different parameters.

Another potential challenge is the parameter order. The LCH model is also known as HCL model (the reverse abbreviation). Yet, it has been decided that the LCH abbreviation will be used in the context of web design. However, many web designers are used to working with the HSL model. With HSL vectors the hue comes first and lightness last (or second last if there is also an alpha value). However, with LCH vectors the lightness value comes first and hue value comes last, which is the opposite of HSL. It is highly plausible that someone used to working with HSL vectors occasionally will erroneously swap the hue and lightness values out of habit. While reading rapidly, we tend to decode entire words, not individual letters, and the string LCH is likely to be recognized as a word and not be decoded as an instruction for which order to place the parameters. If the HCL variation was chosen such situations would be less likely to occur. Clearly, parameter order confusions are limited to situations where designers and developers are editing code and stylesheets. This problem will not likely be an issue with visual color picker tools.

It is unlikely that web designers will be interested in familiarizing themselves with the computational details of the LCH model. Moreover, Wikipedia describes LCH models in plural form and denotes that there are several LCH models with similar goals, i.e., to achieve a perceptually uniform cylindrical color space where colors are defined according to lightness, chroma, and hue. Fortunately, the W3C CSS Color Module Level 4 specification gives a precise definition of LCH in context of the web.

## 5.2  Color Harmonies

The hue definition has no effects on monochrome harmonies, i.e., when a color pair shares identical, or close to identical, hues (with variations in lightness and chroma). This is because the difference between two identical angles will be zero regardless of which hue definition is used. Moreover, the discrepancies are in most cases limited for analogous harmonies (neighbor colors), as the hue angles are similar. When taking into consideration that monochrome and analogous color harmonies probably are among the most used as these are harmonious and non-provocative, one may get an explanation as to why designers to this date may have deduced color harmonies incorrectly from the HSL color wheel without noticing the discrepancies.

The results show that discrepancies occur with larger hue angles such as found with complementary and triadic color harmonies. Moreover, the results indicate that the LCH model results in even larger discrepancies than the HSL model in situations where designers are applying RYB color harmonies on the LCH color wheel. As such, the LCH model is not an improvement compared to HSB. Still these observations are based on RYB as a frame of reference in terms of textbook color theory. Yet, RYB color harmonies are recommendations and not hard rules that must be followed. One could argue that the chroma and hue values are less important if designers actively employ lightness to establish contrast between visual distinct elements.

### 5.3 Color Contrast

The contrast simulations show that the variations in contrast resulting from hue alterations are too small to have practical significance. Hence, it seems that the claim the LCH model simplifies working with accessibility holds for hue changes, in that the hue can be altered independently in LCH space without affecting the contrast. A similar pattern was observed for chroma, also chroma variations appear sufficiently small to have practical significance. Consequently, it seems that LCH allows chroma changes to be made to color palettes without affecting the contrast levels. Whether these contrast variations are caused by chroma or hue changes, caused by lack of precision in the calculations, or whether they can be shown theoretically is beyond the scope of this study.

With regards to lightness changes to color palettes, contrast levels were not preserved when shifted. Moreover, the non-linear relationship probably means that few designers can perform such shifts without consulting some contrast tools. Therefore, the LCH model does not seem to help designers with lightness adjustments. In situations where there is insufficient contrast one can adjust the lightness of one of the colors.

Although the variations in contrast due to hue and chroma changes may be practically insignificant, they could be judicially significant. In terms of the current WCAG2.1 guidelines one may end up with a situation where a color pair just meets the minimum contrast requirements before an alteration but drop just below the limit after changes to either chroma or hue. Formally, the guideline would not be met thereby could trigger a formal accessibility violation during an accessibility audit.

### 5.4 Color Tools

Discrepancies in hue can easily be compensated for in software tools. It is relatively trivial to implement LCH color wheels that point to matching color harmonies using RYB definitions. For example, a complementary color may be illustrated by an angle that is less than 180 and triads with angles that are different to 120 degrees. Similarly, it is relatively straightforward to incorporate contrast checks and contrast visualizations within LCH color pickers in a similar manner to which they are realized in some HSL color pickers.

It will be interesting to see how tools for working with LCH will develop once the web technology becomes widely available. There are already many examples of LCH color picking tools. Some of these do not reveal the underlying LCH space while others do. Figure 4 shows the example of one LCH color picker that visualizes the range of valid parameter values. Clearly, these relationships are complex as the space is irregularly shaped compared to the simple HSL and RGB models (cubes and cones). For example, the valid maximum chroma values follows a complex curve that changes drastically with the lightness adjustments. It seems thus hard to manually predict what are valid chroma values for a given lightness value will be, and one may speculate whether tool support is an absolute necessity when working with LCH. Further user studies are needed to gain insight into how designers perceive the LCH space as it is communicated via software tools.

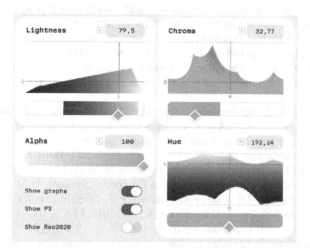

**Fig. 4.** LCH parameter ranges are dependent on the parameters. LCH color picker (https://github.com/evilmartians/okLCH-picker).

## 6  Conclusions

The LCH color model was assessed from web designers' usability perspective. The results show that the LCH model is resulting in larger discrepancies than HSL if using it to select RYB-type color harmonies, and from this perspective the LCH model does not offer improvements. In terms of working with accessibility the LCH model is likely to simplify the task of providing accessible colors with sufficient contrast as in large chroma and hue changes can be made without significantly affecting the resulting contrast. However, lightness changes in color palettes do affect the contrast in non-linear relationships. Most web designers will therefore still need contrast specific tool support. Further work is needed to understand how web designers with varying levels of training will start to use the LCH model once it becomes widely deployed. Such insights are needed to improve the usability of color tools.

# References

1. W3C Schools: Color wheels (2022). https://www.w3schools.com/colors/colors_wheels.asp
2. Vidra, V., Pešička, O.: LCH is the Best Color Space! (2022). https://atmos.style/blog/LCH-color-space
3. Meier, B.J., Spalter, A.M., Karelitz, D.B.: Interactive color palette tools. IEEE Comput. Graphics Appl. **24**(3), 64–72 (2004)
4. Hu, G., Pan, Z., Zhang, M., Chen, D., Yang, W., Chen, J.: An interactive method for generating harmonious color schemes. Color. Res. Appl. **39**(1), 70–78 (2014)
5. Ou, L.C., Luo, M.R., Cui, G.: A colour design tool based on empirical studies. In: Design Research Society Conference 2008, Sheffield Hallam University, Sheffield, UK (2009)
6. Jalal, G., Maudet, N., Mackay, W.E.: Color portraits: From color picking to interacting with color. In: Proceedings CHI 2015, pp. 4207–4216. ACM (2015)
7. Kim, E., Suk, H.J.: Thoughts and tools for crafting colors: Implications from designers' behavior. In: Proceedings DIS 2017, pp. 321–331, ACM (2017)
8. Shugrina, M., Zhang, W., Chevalier, F., Fidler, S., Singh, K.: Color builder: A direct manipulation interface for versatile color theme authoring. In: Proceedings CHI 2019. ACM (2019)
9. MDN (2023): https://developer.mozilla.org/en-US/docs/Web/CSS/color_value/LCH
10. Sarifuddin, M., Missaoui, R.: A new perceptually uniform color space with associated color similarity measure for content-based image and video retrieval. In: Proceedings of ACM SIGIR 2005 Workshop on Multimedia Information Retrieval (MMIR 2005), ACM (2005)
11. Douglas, S., Kirkpatrick, T.: Do color models really make a difference?. In: Proceedings of the SIGCHI Conference on Human Factors in Computing Systems. ACM (1996)
12. Brathovde, K., Farner, M.B., Brun, F.K., Sandnes, F.E.: Effectiveness of color-picking interfaces among non-designers. In: Luo, Y. (ed.) CDVE 2019. LNCS, vol. 11792, pp. 181–189. Springer, Cham (2019). https://doi.org/10.1007/978-3-030-30949-7_21
13. Henry, P., Westland, S.: The role of gamut, intuition and engagement in colour management in a design context. Color. Technol. **136**(3), 255–262 (2020)
14. Tokumaru, M., Muranaka, N., Imanishi, S.: Color design support system considering color harmony. In: Proceedings FUZZ-IEEE'02, pp. 378–383. IEEE, (2002)
15. Sandnes, F.E., Zhao, A.: An interactive color picker that ensures WCAG2. 0 compliant color contrast levels. Procedia Computer Sci. **67**, 87–94 (2015)
16. Sandnes, F.E., Zhao, A.: A contrast colour selection scheme for WCAG2. 0-compliant web designs based on HSV-half-planes. In: Proceedings SMC2015, pp. 1233–1237. IEEE (2015)
17. Sandnes, F.E.: Understanding WCAG2. 0 color contrast requirements through 3D color space visualization. Stud. Health Technol. Inform, **229**, 366–375 (2016)
18. Tigwell, G.W., Flatla, D.R., Archibald, N.D.: ACE: a colour palette design tool for balancing aesthetics and accessibility. ACM TACCESS **9**(2), 1–32 (2017)
19. Sandnes, F.E.: An image-based visual strategy for working with color contrasts during design. In: Miesenberger, K., Kouroupetroglou, G. (eds.) ICCHP 2018. LNCS, vol. 10896, pp. 35–42. Springer, Cham (2018). https://doi.org/10.1007/978-3-319-94277-3_7
20. Hansen, F., Krivan, J.J., Sandnes, F.E.: Still not readable? an interactive tool for recommending color pairs with sufficient contrast based on existing visual designs. In: Proceedings of the ASSETS 2019, pp. 636–638. ACM (2019)

21. Sandnes, F.E.: Inverse color contrast checker: automatically suggesting color adjustments that meet contrast requirements on the web. In: Proceedings ASSETS 2021. ACM (2021)
22. Pedersen, L.A., Einarsson, S.S., Rikheim, F.A., Sandnes, F.E.: User interfaces in dark mode during daytime–improved productivity or just cool-looking?. In: Proceedings UAHCI 2020, LNCS, pp. 178–187. Springer, (2020)
23. Xie, X., Song, F., Liu, Y., Wang, S., Yu, D.: Study on the effects of display color mode and luminance contrast on visual fatigue. IEEE Access **9**, 35915–35923 (2021)

# Modeling and Visualization of Complex Systems with the Use of GraphTool

Iwona Świderska, Ewa Grabska[✉], and Wojciech Palacz

Faculty of Physics, Astronomy and Applied Computer Science, Jagiellonian University, ul. prof. Stanisława Łojasiewicza 11, 30-348 Kraków, Poland
{ewa.grabska,wojciech.palacz}@uj.edu.pl

**Abstract.** This paper proposes a model of a complex design system in the form of a system of graphs with attributed and labeled not only nodes and edges but also entire graphs. The primary task of the graph system is to collect data from information provided by the context and organize this data according to the relationships between them, including adding metadata represented by layers with graph labels that designate the appropriate graphs for layers. At the layer level, we can define relationships between layers as relationships between nodes of graphs belonging to different layers. The proposed model has been implemented in GraphTool which is designed to support modeling and visualization of this graph system type using computer tools for graph transformation. The approach presented in this paper will be illustrated by an example that, concerns human resources management in a large software company and is an example of a description of human cooperation.

**Keywords:** graph · modeling · visualization

## 1 Introduction

System modeling and generation are two important phases of the whole design process aided by computers. Both the ever-growing amount of knowledge and the necessity to use techniques adhering meaning to data have led researchers to search for new methodologies for semantics-driven modeling and generation [5]. This paper aims to propose a new model of a complex design system in the form of a system of graphs with attributed and labeled not only nodes and edges but also entire graphs. In the graph system, data is collected from information provided by the context and organized according to the relations between them, including adding metadata represented by layers with graph labels that designate the appropriate graphs for layers. At the layer level, we can define relationships between layers as relationships between nodes of graphs belonging to different layers. The proposed model has been implemented in GraphTool which is designed to support both the modeling and modifying of the variability of design structures by graph rewriting rules, i.e., the technique of creating a new graph out of an original graph algorithmically.

© The Author(s), under exclusive license to Springer Nature Switzerland AG 2023
Y. Luo (Ed.): CDVE 2023, LNCS 14166, pp. 56–67, 2023.
https://doi.org/10.1007/978-3-031-43815-8_6

The paper is organized as follows: In Sect. 2 some most popular world widely used systems for graph rewriting are presented. With such a context Sect. 3 the GraphTool application is introduced as a new tool offering a graphical editor for defining different types of graphs and rules describing their transformation. The next Sect. 4 is focused on providing formal model of design structure using graphs and generative procedure that in Sect. 5 is used to present a model supporting problem-oriented design solution based on a semantically enriched system of graphs. In the last Sect. 6 we present an example illustrating the system of graphs related to human resources management in a large software company created in GraphTool.

## 2   State of the Art

There are many approaches to graph rewriting. Several of them were both theoretical approach and implementations in the form of graph transformation toolkits. They can be used to develop graph models and transformation rules corresponding to a specific problem; this is in essence identical to using a traditional programming language to develop data structures and procedures for this problem.

PROGRES (PROgrammed Graph REwriting Systems) works with models which are a kind of object-oriented directed graphs. For transformation rules PROGRES uses a hybrid programming language, with both visual and textual elements [9]. Simple rules are represented visually, with optional textual fragments representing rule application condition and attribute assignments. Complex transformation procedures which use local variables, invocation of simple rules, conditionals, loops, etc. are specified textually. Graph models on which PROGRES operates are kept in an external database management system known as GRAS. This allows for some advanced functionality, like nondeterministic execution of transformation procedures with backtracking out of dead ends, but at the same time complicates deploying POSTGRESusing applications.

Fujaba (From UML to Java and Back Again) is another system which utilizes graph transformations. It was designed as a tool for model-driven software engineering [2]. It uses UML class diagrams to represent the structure of a computer application, and UML activity diagrams together with so-called "story pattern" diagrams to specify the behavior of the application [3]. These diagrams are then converted into Java code. Operations on node attributes are implemented as operation on Java object properties; the diagrams can contain textual fragments with Java code, which can access objects being processed by transformation rules.

GROOVE (Graphs for ObjectOriented Verification) is a tool for exploring results produced by a given set of transformation rules, and for checking if generated graphs satisfy specific properties [7]. Transformation rules are represented diagrammatically. Control program which schedules them is textual, written in a special nondeterministic programming language. Information about allowed node types, node attributes and connecting edges must be provided in advance by means of a type graph.

The GraphTool system, that is used to model an example in this paper, is less strict than PROGRES, Fujaba, etc. - it requires only a global list of attributes and their domains to be defined in advance. Attributes from this list can then be assigned to arbitrary nodes. GraphTool is envisioned as a tool for creating graphs and graph transformation rules, and for applying rules to a graph chosen as a starting point. The order in which rules are applied to this graph is determined by a control diagram. A control diagram, in its simplest form, is just another graph. Choosing it as a way of directing the derivation process differentiates GraphTool from other graph rewriting systems which use specialized programming languages, and makes it accessible to a broader audience of potential users.

The distinctive feature of GraphTool among the other applications are layers. They increase readability of graph and rule diagrams displayed in the GraphTool UI, which also makes it more accessible to users.

## 3   Notes About the GraphTool

The motivation for work on GraphTool - a tool for graphs was to propose an unified environment that offers the possibility not only to create a structure of graphs with semantic levels, but to generate new graphs in an automatic manner as well [8]. GraphTool uses Java SDK 11.0 environment. It is based on Eclipse Rich Client Application graphical editor for modeling and generating graphs [1]. The base perspective GraphTool application is shown on Fig. 1. It is divided into several working areas. GraphTool supports different types of graphs as it was shown in [6] and [10].

The navigator view (marked as area 1 on Fig. 1) is used to present the current content of the workspace. Within the workspace the user can define own projects. In each project a set of graph transformation rules, a control diagram for these rules and a collection of initial graphs for transformations are specified.

In GraphTool the user can model a graph by creating its graphical representation (area 3 on Fig. 1) and specify its additional properties (area 2 on Fig. 1.)

A graph rule called a production is defined by two graphs, left-hand side and right-hand side graphs. Application of a production to a graph results in its transformation to a new graph by replacing a subgraph being a copy of left side to the graph with the copy of right side of the production. The production can have associated predicate that is a logical statement describing a condition when the rule can be applied. Within the tool transformation rules can be built from scratch or on the top of existing ones. The same rules as in case of graph definition apply to productions. The example production modeled in GraphTool is shown in area 5 in Fig. 1. Any inconsistencies regarding created graph or transformation rules are detected and presented (area 4 in Fig. 1).

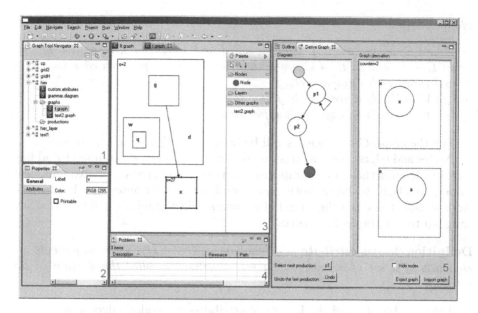

**Fig. 1.** A screenshot of GraphTool

Transformation rules can be grouped and then the order of their application is determined by the control diagram. It is a directed graph with highlighted start and stop nodes. The other nodes represent the productions. The diagram is valid when at least one path exists from the start to the end node. The concept of the graph can be extended by adding the semantic level represented by attributes. The attribute is a function defined on a domain assigning the value from this domain to a graph element. The declaration of a new attribute is understood as specification of an unique name and its domain (the available types are integer numbers, floating-point numbers, strings, enums and arrays). Additionally, the user can specify the default value.

## 4    Modeling of the Design Structure and Generative Procedure Using Graphs

Before modeling the structure and simulating a flow for human resource management the formal definitions of graph preliminaries will be presented in order to leverage the introduction of the selected graph structure and graph transformations. Let $\Sigma_V$ and $\Sigma_E$ be *alphabets* containing elements named *labels*. Let us assume that these sets are disjunctive $\Sigma_V \cap \Sigma_E = \emptyset$. Let us denote a union of sets $\Sigma_V$ and $\Sigma_E$ as $\Sigma$, it means $\Sigma = \Sigma_V \cup \Sigma_E$.

**Definition 1.** *A directed graph labelled over the alphabet $\Sigma$ is a tuple*

$$G = (V, E, s, t, l_V, l_E)$$

*where:*

- *V and E are finite set of elements called nodes and edges, respectively,*
- $s : E \rightarrow V$ *and* $t : E \rightarrow V$ *are functions that assign for each edge its source and target nodes, respectively,*
- $l_V : V \rightarrow \Sigma_V$ *is a node labeling function,*
- $l_E : E \rightarrow \Sigma_E$ *is an edge labeling function.*

For the graph $G$ its elements will be denoted as $V_G, E_G, s_G, t_G, l_{V_G}, l_{E_G}$.

Nodes and edges create a structure of a graph. It can be extended by adding a semantic level that in the graph theory is defined using attributes and their values. Similarly to labels both nodes' and edges' attributes can be defined. Additionally, there is a third kind of elements called graph's attributes that are assigned to the graphs themselves.

**Definition 2.** *An **attribute** is a function* $a : O_a \rightarrow D_a$, *where arguments are elements of a set of objects, and a set of values is called the domain of the attribute.*

Let sets $A_V$, $A_E$ and $A_G$ be sets of attributes for nodes, edges and a graph, respectively, such that $A_V \cap A_E = \emptyset$, $A_V \cap A_G = \emptyset$, $A_E \cap A_G = \emptyset$. Denote by A the sum of all aforementioned sets of attributes, i.e. $A = A_V \cup A_E \cup A_G$.

**Definition 3.** *An **attributed graph over A** is a tuple:*

$$G_A = (G, \; att_{\Sigma_V}, \; att_{\Sigma_E}, \; att_G),$$

*where:*

- *G is a directed, labelled graph*
- $att_{\Sigma_V} : \Sigma_V \rightarrow 2^{A_V}$ *is an attribute function for labels of nodes,*
- $att_{\Sigma_E} : \Sigma_E \rightarrow 2^{A_E}$ *is an attribute function for labels of edges,*
- $att_G : \{G\} \rightarrow 2^{A_G}$ *is an attribute function for the graph.*

**Definition 4.** *A **valued graph** $G_I$ is a pair $G_I = (G_A, val)$ where:*

- $G_A$ *is an attributed graph built on top of the directed, labelled graph G,*
- $val = \{ f_a : a \in A \}$ *is a set of partial functions that assign values for the attributes of nodes, edges and the graph itself.*

*Functions assigning values for the attributes fulfill following requirements:*

- *if* $a \in A_V$, *then* $f_a$ *is a partial function from V into* $D_A$ *(it means that* $f_a : V \nrightarrow D_a$*) and it is defined over the set* $\{ v \in V : a \in att_{\Sigma_V}(l_V(v)) \}$;
- *if* $a \in A_E$, *then* $f_a : E \nrightarrow D_a$ *and it is defined over the set* $\{ e \in E : a \in att_{\Sigma_E}(l_E(e)) \}$;
- *if* $a \in A_G$, *then* $f_a : \{G\} \nrightarrow D_a$ *and it is defined only for its single defined only if* $a \in att_G(G)$.

To simplify the notation instead of $f_a(x)$ the format $a(x)$ will be used. In case of considering multiple graphs simultaneously and the need of using the indexes pointing to the graphs to highlight the chosen one the following notation can be used $salary_G(o_4)$ instead of $f_{salary_G}(o_4)$, $salary_H(o_4)$ instead of $f_{salary_H}(o_4)$, etc.

The graphs can be transformed by means of a transformation rule that is defined by two graphs known as the left-, the right-hand side and embedding transformation. A rule can be applied to a graph $G$ only if a part of $G$ is the same as a left side of the rule. Formally, there exists an homomorphism between the left graph and a subgraph of $G$.

Let $\mathcal{G}_A(\Sigma_V, \Sigma_E)$ be a set of all directed, labeled graphs $\Sigma = \Sigma_V \cup \Sigma_E$ and attributed over the set $A$.

**Definition 5.** *Let $G$ and $H$ belong to $\mathcal{G}_A(\Sigma_V, \Sigma_E)$. The mapping $f = (f_V, f_E)$: $V_G \times E_G \to V_H \times E_H$, we call **a graph homomorphism** and we write $f : G \to H$ when:*

- *$f_V : V_G \to V_H$ and $f_E : E_G \to E_H$,*
- *$\forall e \in E_G : f_V(s_G(e)) = s_H(f_E(e))$ and $\forall e \in E_G : f_V(t_G(e)) = t_H(f_E(e))$,*
- *$\forall v \in V_G : l_G(v) = l_H(f_V(v))$, $att_{\Sigma_{V_G}}(l_G(v)) = att_{\Sigma_{V_H}}(l_H(f_V(v)))$,*
- *$\forall e \in E_G : l_G(e) = l_H(f_E(e))$, $att_{\Sigma_{E_G}}(l_G(e)) = all_{\Sigma_{E_H}}(l_H(f_E(e)))$,*
- *$att_G(G) = att_H(H)$.*

Graph homomorphism $f : G \to H$ is said to be an isomorphism if $f$ is a bijection.

## 5    System of Graphs

In [4] a new approach to graphs was proposed - a system of graphs. The basic definition of system of graphs can be extended by adding labels and attributes to internal graphs. Taking into consideration its advantages related to the leverage of describing context this type has been chosen to simulate a flow for human resource management.

Let $\mathcal{S}$ be an alphabet where $\mathcal{S} \cap \Sigma = \emptyset$. The elements of this alphabet are used to denote the layers of graphs.

**Definition 6.** *An **n-layer system of graphs over** $\mathcal{S} \cup \Sigma$ for $n \geq 2$ is a tuple:*

$$H = (X, ch, E, s, t, lab)$$

*where:*

- *$X$ is a n-element set of nodes, called layers such that: $\forall g \in \mathcal{G}_A(\Sigma_V, \Sigma_E)$ $V_g \cap X = \emptyset$*
- *$ch : X \ni x \to g_{ch(x)} \in \mathcal{G}_A(\Sigma_V, \Sigma_E)$ is a function assigning for each layer $x$ a nested graph $g_{ch(x)}$ so that for each $x \in X$ their matching graphs $g_{ch(x)}$ have disjunctive sets of both nodes $V_{ch(x)}$ and $E_{ch(x)}$,*

- $E$ is a set of external edges so that $\forall x \in E_{ch(x)} \cap E = \emptyset$,
- $s,\ t:\ E \to \bigcup_{x \in X} V_{ch(x)}$ are functions assigning for each edge from the set of external edges a source and target nodes, respectively. These nodes cannot belong to the same layer: $\forall x \in X,\ e \in E : s(e) \in V_{ch(x)} \Rightarrow t(e) \notin V_{ch(x)}$,
- $lab : X \to S$ is an injective function labeling layers of set $X$

The introduction of a new type of graph in the form of an n-layer graph system requires new definitions of its homomorphism and graph rules along with their application.

**Definition 7.** *Let $M$ and $N$ be n-layer graphs of systems over $S \cup \Sigma$. A system of graphs homomorphism $m = (m_{X1}, ..., m_{Xn}, m_E, m_{lab})$ is a $n + 2$-tuple, where:*

- $\forall i \in \{1, .., n\}\ \exists x \in X_M \exists\ y \in X_N :$ *there is a graph homomorphism $m_{Xi}$ :* $ch_M(x) = ch_N(m_{Xi}(y))$,
- $m_E : E_M \to E_N,\ \forall e \in E_M : l_M(e) = l_N(m_E(e))$,
- $\forall e \in E_M : m_V(s_M(e)) = s_N(m_E(e))$ *and* $m_V(t_M(e)) = t_N(m_E(e))$,
- $m_{lab} : S \to S,\ \forall x \in X_M : lab_M(x) = m_{lab}(lab_N(x))$.

Let $L$ and $R$ be the left- and the right-hand side of a rule, respectively. Let $G$ be a system of graphs to be transformed. Let $m : L \to G$ be a homomorphism that has been found and fixed. The system of graphs $G$ can then be split into two subgraphs, the first one induced by $m(V_L)$, the second one induced by $V_G - m(V_L)$. In other words, $G$ is split into an image of $L$ (which will be removed and replaced by $R$) and the remainder.

An embedding transformation can be used to define the procedure for dealing with dangling edges between both parts of the system of graph $L$. It can be also used to add new edges.

**Definition 8.** *Let $L$, $R$ be two sides of a transformation rule for a system of graphs. An embedding transformation $ET = (S, T)$ is a pair of functions* $S, T : \Sigma_E \times \bigcup_{x \in X_L} V_{ch_L(x)} \to 2^{\Sigma_E \times \bigcup_{x \in X_R} V_{ch_R(x)}}$.

The $S$ and $T$ are functions assigning for labels of each edge (outgoing and incoming respectively) from the left side of the production the set of pairs representing the labels of edges that will connect the right graph side of the production after its embedding into remainder of the systems of graphs.

**Definition 9.** *A transformation rule over $S \cup \Sigma$ is a triple:*
$$p = (L, R, ET),$$
*where:*

- $L$ *and* $R$ *are graphs of systems over $S \cup \Sigma$ and they are called the left-, the right-hand side, respectively,*
- $ET$ *is an embedding transformation for $L$ and $R$*

Let $AE$ be a set of all edges for given system of graphs, $AE = E \cup \bigcup_{x \in X} E_{chx}$. Let $as : AE \to \bigcup_{x \in X} V_{ch(x)}$, $at : AE \to \bigcup_{x \in X} V_{ch(x)}$ be functions assigning both (internal and external) edges its source and target nodes.

**Definition 10.** *Let $G$ and $H$ be graphs of systems over $S \cup \Sigma$. Let $p$ be a transformation rule. The system of graphs $H$ is a **direct derivation** from $G$ by $p$ (denoted as $G \overset{p}{\Rightarrow} H$) if and only if:*

- *there exists a homomorphism $m : L \to G'$ where $G'$ is a subgraph of $G$,*
- *there exists a homomorphism $n : R \to H'$ where $H'$ is a subgraph of $H$,*
- *$G - G' = H - H'$,*
- *let $IN_G = \{e \in AE_G : as_G(e) \notin G' \wedge t_G(e) \in G'\}$,*
- *let $IN_H = \{e \in AE_H : as_H(e) \notin H' \wedge t_H(e) \in H'\}$,*
- *let $OUT_G = \{e \in E_G : s_G(e) \in G' \wedge t_G(e) \notin G'\}$,*
- *let $OUT_H = \{e \in E_H : s_H(e) \in H' \wedge t_H(e) \notin H'\}$,*
- *$\forall e_1 \in IN(H', H) \; \exists \; e_2 \in IN(G', G) : \quad (l_E(e_1), \; n(t(e_1))) \in T(l_E(e_2), \; m(t(e_2)))$, so for each incoming edge $e_1$ belonging to embedding of $H'$ in $H$ there exists an incoming edge $e_2$ belonging to embedding of $G'$ in $G$ such that the edge $e_1$ belongs to embedding transformation for edge $e_2$,*
- *$\forall e_1 \in OUT(H', H) \; \exists \; e_2 \in OUT(G', G) : \quad (l_E(e_1), \; n(s(e_1))) \in S(l_E(e_2), \; m(s(e_2)))$ (similarly for outgoing edge as above).*

## 6 Example of an N-Layer System of Graphs

As an example of an n-layer system of graphs the structure of the IT team including tasks between its members will be modelled. The layer will be used to group members into subteams. Let the following sets be the sets of labels of vertices and edges accordingly:

- $\Sigma_V = \{manager, architect, dev, intern, testLeader, tester, admin\}$
- $\Sigma_E = \{supervises, assigns, verifies, describes, shares\}$

Let us define following attributes:

- *salary, lang, os* $\in A_V$ where $D_{salary} = \mathbb{N}$, $D_{lang} = \{Java, C, Ruby\}$ and $D_{os} = \{Linux, Windows\}$,
- *time* belonging to $A_E$ from $D_{time} = \mathbb{R}_{\geq 0}$,
- *location* belonging $A_G$ z $D_{city} = \{Cracow, Warsaw\}$.

Let the following functions be defined for each $G \in \mathcal{G}_A(\Sigma_V, \Sigma_E)$:

- $att_{\Sigma_V} : \Sigma_V \to 2^{A_V}$

$$att_{\Sigma_V}(l) = \begin{cases} \{salary\} & \text{for } l \in \{manager, architect, tester, testLeader\} \\ \{salary, lang\} & \text{for } l = dev \\ \{os\} & \text{for } l = admin \end{cases}$$

- $att_{\Sigma_E} : \Sigma_E \to 2^{A_E} : att_{\Sigma_E}(assigns) = att_{\Sigma_E}(shares) = \{time\}$
- $att_G : \{G\} \to 2^{A_G} : att_G(G) = \{location\}$

Let us define the following graphs over the set $\Sigma = \Sigma_V \cup \Sigma_E$:

- a graph $C = (V_C, E_C, s_C, t_C, l_{V_C}, l_{E_C})$, where:

- $V_C = \{o1\}$,
- $E_C = \emptyset$, $s_C, t_C : \emptyset \to V_C$,
- $l_{V_C}(o1) = manager$, $l_{E_C} : \emptyset \to \Sigma_E$,
- $salary(o1) = 1000$
- a graph $P = (V_P, E_P, s_P, t_P, l_{V_P}, l_{E_P})$, where:
  - $V_P = \{o2, o3, o4, o5\}$,
  - $E_P = \{e2, e3, e4, o5\}$,
  - $s_P(e2) = s_P(e3) = o2$, $s_P(e4) = s_P(e5) = o4$, $t_P(e2) = o4$, $s_P(e3) = s_P(e5) = o3$, $t_P(e4) = o5$,
  - $l_{V_P}(o2) = architect$, $l_{V_P}(o3) = l_{V_P}(o4) = dev$, $l_{V_P}(o5) = intern$,
  - $l_{E_P}(e2) = l_{E_P}(e3) = assigns$, $l_{E_P}(e4) = supervises$, $l_{E_P}(e5) = reviews$,
- a graph $Q = (V_Q, E_Q, s_Q, t_Q, l_{V_Q}, l_{E_Q})$, where:
  - $V_Q = \{o6, o7, o8\}$,
  - $E_Q = \{e10, e11\}$,
  - $s_Q(e10) = s_Q(e11) = o6$, $t_Q(e10) = o8$, $t_Q(e11) = o7$,
  - $l_{V_Q}(o6) = testLeader$, $l_{V_Q}(o7) = l_{V_Q}(o8) = tester$,
  - $l_{E_Q}(e10) = l_{E_Q}(e11) = assigns$,
  - $salary(o6) = 500$, $salary(o7) = 400$, $salary(o8) = 450$, $time(e10) = 2.5$, $time(e11) = 4$
- a graph $D = (V_D, E_D, s_D, t_D, l_{V_D}, l_{E_D})$, where:
  - $V_D = \{o9, o10\}$,
  - $E_C = \emptyset$, $s_D, t_D : \emptyset \to V_D$,
  - $l_{V_D}(o9) = l_{V_D}(o10) = admin$, $l_{E_D} : \emptyset \to \Sigma_E$
  - $os(o9) = Linux$, $os(o10) = Windows$

Let $H_{it}$ be a 4-layers system of graphs with $S_{it} = \{CEO, DEV, QA, DevOps\}$. According to the Definition 6 the graph $H_{it}$ can be defined as follows:

- $X_{it} = \{x_C, x_P, x_Q, x_D\}$, and for each of them the functions $ch$ are defined as follows: $ch(x_C) = C$, $ch(x_P) = P$, $ch(x_Q) = Q$, $ch(x_D) = D$,
- $E_{it} = \{e1, e6, e7, e8, e9, e12, e13, e14, e15\}$, $l_E(e1) = l_E(e9) = l_E(e12) = l_E(e13) = supervises$, $l_E(e6) = l_E(e7) = verifies$, $lE(e8) = describes$, $lE(e14) = lE(e15) = shares$,
- $s_{it}(e1) = s_{it}(e9) = s_{it}(e12) = s_{it}(e13) = o1$, $s_{it}(e6) = o8$, $s_{it}(e7) = o7$, $s_{it}(e8) = o2$, $s_{it}(e14) = o9$, $s_{it}(e15) = o10$, $t_{it}(e1) = o2$, $t_{it}(e6) = o4$, $t_{it}(e7) = o3$, $t_{it}(e8) = t_{it}(e9) = o6$, $t_{it}(e12) = o9$, $t_{it}(e13) = o10$, $t_{it}(e14) = t_{it}(e15) = o8$,
- $lab_{it}(x_C) = CEO$, $lab_{it}(x_P) = DEV$, $lab_{it}(x_Q) = QA$, $lab_{it}(x_D) = DevOps$

In Fig. 2 graphical representation of $H_{it}$ is shown.

For the given n-layer system of graphs the transformation rules can be introduced. They can be used to represent possible changes in the IT team structure.

The first of them models a scenario when a new intern is hired. As an inexperienced employee he has to be supervised by a developer who has worked so far. What's more, a new tester has to be assigned so that this person will be responsible for verifying the functionality coded by the intern. This tester has to be also supervised by another tester who has been already in the team. The embedding transformation has to cover existing edges for $dev$ and $tester$ nodes:

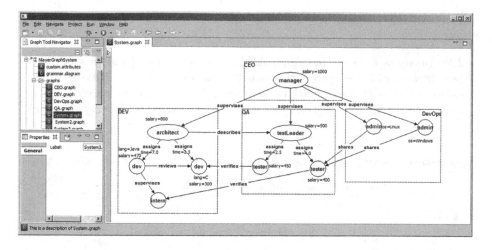

**Fig. 2.** Graphical representation of $H_{it}$

- $IN$ : $(reviews, o4) \rightarrow \{(reviews, o4)\}, (assigns, o4) \rightarrow \{(assigns, o4)\},$ $(assigns, o7) \rightarrow \{(assigns, o7), (assigns, o11)\}$

The embedding transformation defines that the all incoming edges to nodes from left side are not changed. A new edge will be added to mark new tester will be have assigned tasks by the same node (*testLeader*) who assigns now tasks to existing tester. The transformation rule is shown in Fig. 3.

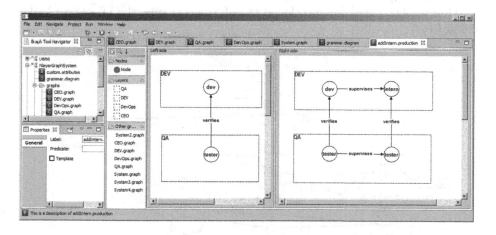

**Fig. 3.** Graph transformation rule adding new intern

The second transformation rule that can be applied after the aforementioned one is related to assigning resources that can be used by the new intern and tester. Due to the limited amount of available resources, the admin needs to remove existing assignments and share them with these new employees (see Fig. 4).

- $IN$ : $(assigns, o11) \rightarrow \{(assigns, o11)\}, (assigns, o7) \rightarrow \{(assigns, o7)\},$
  $(supervises, o12) \rightarrow \{(supervises, o12)\}, (assigns, o8) \rightarrow \{(assigns, o8)\},$
  $(shares, o8) \rightarrow \{(shares, o8)\}, (supervises, o9) \rightarrow \{(supervises, o9)\}$
- $OUT$ : $(verifies, o7) \rightarrow \{(verifies, o7)\}, (verifies, o8) \rightarrow \{(verifies, o8)\},$

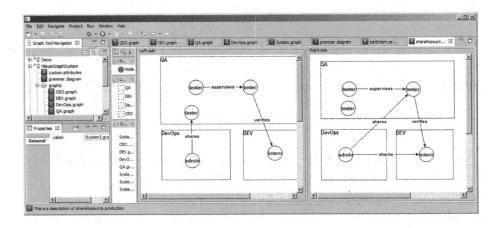

**Fig. 4.** Graph transformation rule sharing resources

After applying the aforementioned transformation rule, the IT system looks like in Fig. 5.

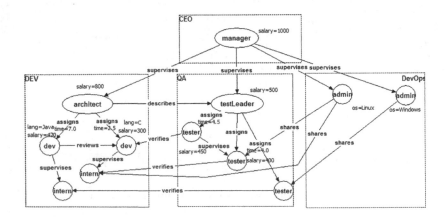

**Fig. 5.** Graphical representation of $H_{it}$ after transformations

# 7    Conclusion

GraphTool has been successfully used to model an issue from human resources management. The proposed system of graphs by means of this application can be used as a support tool for designers for the process of modeling related to the visualisation of structure of complex systems and their resources. On the other hand using the modularization this type of graphs can be regarded as a model of collaboration that is based on the knowledge exchange between subsystems considering their context.

# References

1. https://wiki.eclipse.org/Rich_Client_Platform
2. Burmester, S., et al.: Tool integration at the meta-model level: The fujaba approach. STTT, 203–218, August 2004. https://doi.org/10.1007/s10009-004-0155-8
3. Geiger, L., Zündorf, A.: Statechart modeling with fujaba. Electr. Notes Theor. Comput. Sci. **37–49**, 03 (2005). https://doi.org/10.1016/j.entcs.2004.12.029
4. Grabska-Gradzińnska, I.: Creating a computer role-playing game narrative using graph transformations. Ph.D. thesis. (in Polish). Uniwersytet Jagielloński, Kraków (2023)
5. Nunzio Arena, D.: Towards semantics-driven modelling and simulation of context-aware manufacturing systems (2019)
6. Palacz, W., Ryszka, I., Grabska, E.: Graphs with layers - a visual tool for conceptual design and graph generation. In: 21st International Workshop: Intelligent Computing in Engineering (EG-ICE 2014) (2014)
7. Rensink, A.: The GROOVE simulator: A tool for state space generation, vol. 3062, September 2003. ISBN 978-3-540-22120-3. https://doi.org/10.1007/978-3-540-25959-6_40
8. Ryszka, I., Grabska, E.: Graphtool - a new system of graph generation (2013)
9. Schürr, A., Winter, A.J., Zündorf, A.: The PROGRES approach: language and environment (1999)
10. Strug, B., Ryszka, I., Grabska, E., Ślusarczyk, G.: Generating a virtual computational grid by graph transformations. Remote Instrumentation for eScience and Related Aspects, pp. 209–226 (2012)

# Pruning CapsNet for Hand Gesture Recognition with sEMG Signal Based on Two-Dimensional Transformation

Zheng Wang[1]([✉])(iD), Sheng Wei[2](iD), Hangyao Tu[1](iD), and Yanwei Zhao[3]

[1] School of Computer and Computational Sciences, Zhejiang University City College, Hangzhou, China
wang-cc23@caai.cn

[2] College of Computer Science and Technology, Zhejiang University of Technology, Hangzhou, China

[3] School of Engineering, Zhejiang University City College, Hangzhou, China

**Abstract.** The sEMG signal-based recognition is broadly used in the field of human-computer interaction. To improve the signal classification accuracy, this paper proposes a two-dimensional transformation pruning capsule network (TDPCAPS) to recognize different hand gestures. To apply deep learning methods to signal classification, a two-dimensional transformation method is proposed, which converts feature vectors into two-dimensional feature data. Moreover, using the capsule network to explore the characteristics of the sEMG signal, as this model overcomes the defect that the convolution neural network fails to capture the correlation among features. However, the capsule network requires a lot of computing resources, so this paper adopts a pruning mechanism to reduce the number of coupling coefficients and speed up the calculating process. In the experiments of electrode displacement and several subjects, the recognition accuracy of TDPCAPS reaches 84.92% and 80.31%, respectively. Meanwhile, the classification time for a window is reduced by 11.39%. The experimental results show that the proposed method can ensure recognition accuracy and improve computational efficiency at the same time.

**Keywords:** CapsNet · sEMG · pruning · two-dimensional transformation · gesture recognition

## 1 Introduction

The bioelectric signals of human contain rich information about human body, especially the information related to motion intention. Among them, the surface electromyography (sEMG) signal, which is produced on the skin surface, is generated along with the process of muscle contraction [26]. It has the advantages of low acquisition cost and ease of use. At present, it is widely used in muscle fatigue, human-computer interaction and other fields [22]. To apply sEMG into use, faster methods with higher accuracy to recognize sEMG are expected to

Y. Luo (Ed.): CDVE 2023, LNCS 14166, pp. 68–84, 2023.
https://doi.org/10.1007/978-3-031-43815-8_7

obtain human motion intention. The amplitude of sEMG signal is rather small, which is easily influenced by the noise of the signal acquisition device or the wearing position, and the signal characteristics of different people are quite different [21]. Therefore, the accuracy of sEMG signal in practical application needs to be improved. In order to meet the practical application requirements, there is an urgent need for methods that can mine more potential information and improve the classification performance.

In earlier years, the recognition of sEMG signal mainly depends on feature extraction and machine learning methods, such as support vector machine (SVM) [2], random forest (RF) [12], etc., Good results have been achieved then. However, these methods are extremely dependent on features selected and the effect is not good when faced with large datasets or more gestures [23]. Besides, as machine learning methods have developed for many years, the changes of models often turn out to be less effective than the original ones. Therefore, researchers turn to deep learning for help, as deep learning models are usually end-to-end and have achieved good results on diverse fields [15].

However, the commonly used deep learning models still have limitations. On the one hand, deep learning usually uses pooling operation to sample features and reduce parameters, but pooling operation discards a large amount of data in the receptive field. The lost information may play a crucial role in specific gesture recognition. On the other hand, convolution is often used as a means of feature extraction in deep learning, but commonly used models like convolutional neural networks can only reflect the existence of a certain feature, ignoring the potential links among features [6]. With the increasing number of gesture recognition, the relationship between features is also an important source of information. That's why capsule network is applied in this paper. Capsule network combines several neurons as the basic component to ensure that the links among neurons are kept along with the calculating process [3], which also causes the increase of computing resources.

Besides, because the sEMG signal is a time series, which belongs to one-dimensional signal, and there are few processing models for one-dimensional data in deep learning. Therefore, it is often used to transform the EMG signal into two-dimensional data for training. Different data transformation methods have great influence on the recognition results.

Based on the above discussion, a two-dimensional transformation pruning capsule network is proposed to solve the problem of recognizing sEMG signal and accelerate the calculating process. The main contributions are listed below.

(1) This paper proposes a method to transform the feature vectors to two-dimensional data, allowing more convenience to apply deep learning methods. The generated two-dimensional data has less redundant information than the existed transformation methods and are proven to be effective in representing the characteristics of sEMG signal. It is based on the combination of features and allows the exploration of potential inner links.

(2) To reduce unnecessary calculation and accelerate calculating process, a pruning mechanism is added to the dynamic routing process of capsule network. This

mechanism sets a threshold for coupling coefficients. If the threshold is large, this model doesn't pay attention to details of input, otherwise does. The value of threshold is also analysed in this paper to enable better result of sEMG signal recognition.

(3) This paper has done several experiments and achieves good results. For sEMG signal recognition, the situation of electrode displacement and several subjects are done, having the accuracy of 84.92% and 80.31%, respectively. The effectiveness of pruning mechanism is proved, with computing time decrease of 11.39% for a single time window. All these prove that the proposed model has the ability to ensure the accuracy and reduce computing time.

## 2   Related Works

### 2.1   Existing Two-Dimensional Transformation Methods to Transform sEMG

It is a common practice to transform sEMG signal into two-dimensional data, as there are lots of effective models to deal with two-dimensional data and the results of 1-d convolution are not that satisfying.

Geng et al. [8] first proposed the concept of high-density sEMG image, which converted the sEMG signals collected by high-density electrode equipment into two-dimensional matrix according to the electrode positions. Combined with CNN, 52 gestures of Ninapro DB1 dataset were recognized, and the accuracy rate was 65.1%, which was the highest at that time.

Inspired by high-density sEMG image, Cheng et al. [5] put forward the concept of sEMG feature image. By subdividing the time window of sEMG and extracting the features, the feature matrix was obtained. Combined with CNN's experiment on Ninapro DB1 dataset, the accuracy rate was 82.54%. It can be seen that the features have stronger representation than the signals themselves.

Ha et al. [9] proposed to transform EEG signal into two-dimensional data by short-time Fourior transformation and sent the input into capsule network. This work has achieved better results than previous CNN-based approaches.

Chen et al. [4] proposed two-dimensional method to convert the feature vectors used in machine learning into 2D in the form of Cartesian product, and combined with spatial attention capsule network to recognize gestures. The accuracy rates on his own data set were 84.77% and 81.90%.

All these methods transform the input into two-dimensional data for end-to-end training. As high-density electrode equipment are usually expensive, which will add to the pressure for application cost, it is not a universal solution. sEMG feature image is a more suitable method for wide application, but it fails to consider the correlations between features. As for Chen's two-dimensional method, it contains much redundant information in a feature map, which will be a waste of computing resources.

## 2.2   Capsule Network

Capsule network was proposed by Hinton et al. [10], which overcomes the short-coming of CNN that the correlations among features cannot be reflected. As a single capsule is a vector composed of several neurons, the relative relation among features will be kept during iterations. Therefore, this model has more potential when faced with complex datasets.

Hinton et al. [10] proposed that the input and output of the capsule should be represented by matrix, and the expectation maximization algorithm should be used instead of dynamic routing. By designing capsules into binary groups of attitude matrix and activation probability, the matrix network overcomes the shortcoming that vector capsules can't extract complex features, but it also increases the complexity of dynamic routing calculation.

McIntosh et al. [17] put forward a method of detecting actors and actions in videos through natural language problems by using capsule network. Video and text input are encoded in the form of capsules, and actors and action videos are segmented from sentences. Specifically, there are common entities in video and sentence input, and the similarity between these entities can be found by using dynamic routing, which proves the potential of capsule network in semantic segmentation.

Zhao et al. [25] proposed using capsule network for text classification, and proposed three strategies to stabilize the dynamic routing process, so as to reduce the interference of noise capsules that may contain irrelevant information or unsuccessful training. Experiments on six different text classification benchmark data sets show that the capsule network is effective in text classification, and it is found that the capsule network has great promotion potential in converting single-label text classification into multi-label text classification.

Zhang et al. [24] put forward an enhanced capsule network for medical image classification. Based on the original capsule network, feature decomposition module and multi-scale feature extraction module are introduced, which can extract richer features, ensure that important information in low-level capsules is not missed, reduce the amount of calculation and speed up the convergence of the network. The experimental results show that capsule network can achieve good results in the task of medical image recognition and classification.

The capsule network can retain the spatial and temporal characteristics of the original signal. Considering the advantages of the capsule network, it has great potential for the recognition and classification of sEMG signals with strong time series characteristics.

## 3   The Proposed Method

The framework is mainly composed of two parts, as is shown in Fig. 1. sEMG signal is converted into feature matrix by two-dimensional transformation method, and then sent to the pruning capsule network for classification to obtain the final result.

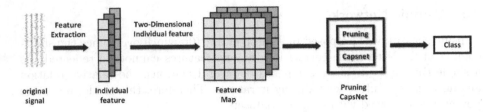

**Fig. 1.** The structure of TDPCAPS framework.

## 3.1   Two-Dimensional Transformation Method

In machine learning, the attributes of a sample are usually represented in the form of feature vector, which is used to deal with linear classification problems. As for sEMG signal classification, feature extraction can extract features that are less linearly related and have strong ability to help distinguish different gestures. Compared with extracting features of sEMG with convolutions or other two-dimensional methods, the correlation degree of internal information is smaller and the redundancy is lower when the feature vector is used as input. However, the feature vectors cannot be directly sent into the deep learning model. Inspired by the idea of two-dimensional transformation [4], the feature vectors is converted based on the method of Cartesian product. Define the feature vector $F$ in Eq. 1, which consists of m features plus the number 1:

$$f = [1, x_1, x_2, \ldots, x_i, \ldots, x_n] \tag{1}$$

where xi represents the i-th feature extracted from sEMG signal.

If the Cartesian product operation is directly applied to the vector f, features in vector f are combined in pairs. Since the calculation order between two features has no influence on the result, only half of the information in a feature map is valid, which will waste a lot of calculation resources. Therefore, consider squaring the discrete feature information in the feature vector $f_2$:

$$f^2 = \left[1, x_1^2, x_2^2, \ldots, x_i^2, \ldots, x_m^2\right] \tag{2}$$

After the feature vector $f^2$ is obtained, the Cartesian product operation is performed with the feature vector $f$ and $f^2$. The specific conversion formula is as follows:

$$F = D\left(f, f^2, \alpha, \beta\right) = G\left(\partial \cdot \left(f \times f^2\right)^\beta\right) = \text{sigmoid}\left(\partial \cdot \left(f \times f^2\right)^\beta\right) \tag{3}$$

where $\alpha$ and $\beta$ are conversion parameters, is the symbol of Cartesian product operation; F is the feature map obtained by two-dimensional operation between $f$ and $f^2$. Formula 4 combines two discrete features into a new composite feature by product form. The detailed process is shown in Fig. 2.

$$f \times f^2 = \left\{\left(f_j \cdot f_i^2\right) \mid f_j \in f \wedge f_i^2 \in f^2\right\} \tag{4}$$

In order to solve the problem of amplitude difference among different features, the obtained feature map F needs to undergo the maximum-minimum normalization process, and the data is converted to a limited range, as shown in Formula 5.

$$X_{\text{narn}} = \frac{X_i - X_{\min}}{X_{\max} - X_{\min}} \tag{5}$$

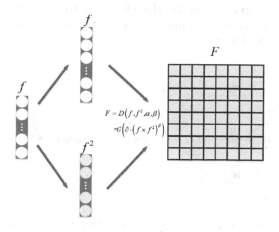

**Fig. 2.** The process of two-dimensional transformation.

## 3.2    The Structure of Capsule Network

Capsule network is the special form of CNN, whose basic component is a capsule [16]. To be specific, a capsule, similar to a vector, is made up of several neurons. In this way, the relative relations among neurons will be kept in the calculating process [11].

The network contains 3 layers without regard to input or output layer, which are a convolution layer, a primary capsule layer, and a senior capsule layer. The output of the first convolution layer is reshaped into capsules of shape 8D. As for the calculating method between primary capsule layer and senior capsule layer, it is a special mechanism called dynamic routing [10].

This model adopts the capsule length to represent the possibility of whether a certain attribute exists. The loss function is shown in Eq. 6.

$$\text{Loss} = \sum_{j=1}^{N} \left( T_j \max \left( 0, m^+ - \|v_j\| \right)^2 + \lambda \left( 1 - T_j \right) \max \left( 0, \|v_j\| - m^- \right)^2 \right) \tag{6}$$

where $N$ means the number of categories, $\|v_j\|$ is the length of the vector output of capsule $j$, $T_j = 1$ indicates class $j$ exists, otherwise it is 0, $m^+$ is the penalty for false positive set as 0.9 and $m^+$ is the penalty for false negative set as 0.1, $\lambda$ is a weight parameter, which is used to reduce the influence of wrong predictions set as 0.5.

### 3.3   Dynamic Routing with Pruning Mechanism

The capsule network is not perfect, because the dynamic routing mechanism in the capsule network is relatively cumbersome and generates a large number of parameters.

To solve this problem, a pruning mechanism is introduced to reduce the number of coupling coefficients. That is, to reduce unnecessary parameter calculation time to speed up the iteration efficiency, and to ensure the accurate while simplifying the dynamic routing mechanism appropriately. The specific pruning operation is shown in Fig. 3.

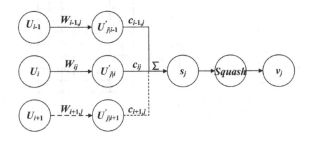

**Fig. 3.** The dynamic routing process with pruning mechanism.

If the contribution of low-level capsule $U_{i+1}$ to high-level capsule $s_j$ is not high, that is, low-level capsules and high-level capsules are separated from each other. Once the value of the coupling coefficient $c_{i+1,j}$ of the link is less than the set threshold, the value of the coupling coefficient $c_{i+1,j}$ of the link is set to 0 to prune the dynamic route (the pruning operation in the figure is indicated by a dotted line). Also, the backward propagation and update of the link are prohibited, so as to reduce unnecessary parameter calculation time and speed up the training and prediction of the model. Define $\lambda_c$ as the coupling coefficient threshold and $\zeta$ as the elastic parameter, and the dynamic routing process can be written as follows:

$$U'_{j|i} = W_{ij}U_i \tag{7}$$

where $U_i$ is the output of the $i$-th primary capsule and $W_{ij}$ is the weight matrix that connects capsule $i$ and $j$, $U'_{j|i}$ is the prediction vector of the $i$-th primary capsule for the $j$-th senior capsule.

$$s_j = \sum_i c_{ij}U'_{ji} \tag{8}$$

where $s_j$ is the output of the capsule $j$ and $c_{ij}$ is the coupling coefficients that sum to 1. $c_{ij}$ is calculated as Eq. 8:

$$c_{ij} = \begin{cases} \dfrac{\exp(b_{ij})}{\sum_\eta \exp(b_{i\eta})}, & \dfrac{\exp(b_{ij})}{\sum_\eta \exp(b_{i\eta})} \geq \lambda_c \\ 0, & \dfrac{\exp(b_{ij})}{\sum_\eta \exp(b_{i\eta})} < \lambda_c \end{cases} \tag{9}$$

$$\lambda_c = \frac{1}{\zeta N} \tag{10}$$

where $\lambda_c$ is the threshold for coupling coefficients and $b_{ij}$ is the log prior probabilities that capsule $i$ should be coupled to capsule $j$. Prior probability $b_{ij}$ is 0 initially and will be updated in the subsequent iterations to update the coupling coefficient $c_{ij}$.

$$v_j = \frac{\|s_j\|^2}{1 + \|s_j\|^2} \frac{s_j}{\|s_j\|} \tag{11}$$

where $v_j$ is the output of action capsule $j$. In order to represent whether an entity present by the capsule exists in the input, a squash function is applied to restrict the vector length, whose range is slightly above zero for short capsules and slightly below 1 for long capsules.

$$b_{ij} = b_{ij} + U'_{j|i} \bullet v_j \tag{12}$$

The coupling coefficients $c_{ij}$ for next iteration is determined by the updated value of the prior probability $b_{ij}$. The prior probability $b_{ij}$ updates by adding the product of predicted vector $\hat{U}_{j|i}$ and output vector $v_j$. In this way, capsules that share similar directions will be have bigger coupling coefficients during iterations.

## 4    Experiments

### 4.1    Dataset

In this experiment, eight healthy people's upper limb sEMG signals were collected as the experiment data, and five gestures were selected in order to truly reflect the actions needed in human daily life. The five gestures are Hand Closed (HC), Hand Open (HO), Radial Flexion (RF), Wrist Extension (WE) and Wrist Flexion (WF), as shown in Fig. 4.

In each period, each subject performed five gestures, and the signals of each gesture were recorded. During the collection of gesture actions, each action last for at least 12 s. To avoid muscle fatigue, the subjects should rest for 10 s after completing a gesture. After one group of movements, keep the device at the same position. There is a rest for about 30 min and then the subject began to repeat the previous gestures. The device can be took off only when 3 groups of dada are collected. After an interval of 6 h, the subjects collected the other three groups of data according to the same steps. In order to exclude the transition state between two gestures, only the middle 10 s of the sEMG signal of each gesture is marked as valid.

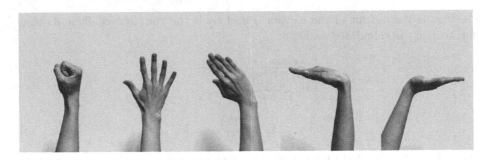

**Fig. 4.** Five hand gestures selected.

## 4.2 Implementation Details

Since the sampling frequency of the acquiring device is set to 1 kHz and 16 channels are deployed, the size of sEMG dataset for each gesture is $10,000 \times 16$. The original surface EMG signal of the data set is $8 \times 6 \times 5 \times 10,000 \times 16$, that is, $240 \times 10,000 \times 16$.

The signal was processed with window analysis method. Set the number features $m = 14$, the window length $w = 300$, the increment interval $t_w = 50$, the conversion parameters $\alpha$ and $\beta$ of the two-dimensional method are 0.5 respectively, and the iteration number of dynamic routing of capsule network is 3. The features used in the experiment are RMS [19], MAV [19], WL [19], ZC [19], DASDV [19], LOG [19], SSI [19], TM3 [19], TM4 [19], TM5 [19], FR [13], IEMG [13], MFMN [13] and MFMD [13], respectively.

The experimental environment is Windows 10, GPU 1660Ti, and the platform is Tensorflow 1.14. Adam algorithm is used to optimize the target in the experiment. The batch-size is 32 in the case of electrode displacement and 16 in the case of several subjects.

## 4.3 The Experiments

**Under the Case of Electrode Displacement.** In practice, it is inevitable that the equipment will be put on and off, which have an impact on the recognition accuracy. Therefore, the signal collected by one subject in different time periods was used to simulate this situation, in which the signal collected in the morning was used as the training set and the signal in the afternoon was used as the test set. The specific experimental results are shown in Table 1.

As the muscles contracted in different gestures may not have much differences, it is easy to misjudge. When identifying sEMG signal affected by electrode displacement, machine learning methods have advantages over WE and WF, but fail to perform well on other gestures, which suggests that these methods have some defects.

The classification accuracy of CNN model, which directly uses the signal as input is obviously lower than that of other models, although it has a slight

**Table 1.** The accuracy of different methods under the case of electrode displacement.

| Model | Different Gestures | | | | | Whole Accuracy |
|---|---|---|---|---|---|---|
| | HC | HO | RF | WE | WF | |
| SVM+FE [18] | 61.54 ± 0.00% | **13.85 ± 0.00%** | 93.33 ± 0.00% | **100.00 ± 0.00%** | **100.00 ± 0.00%** | 73.33 ± 0.00% |
| BP+FE [14] | 76.26 ± 6.60% | 0.26 ± 0.26% | **94.26 ± 4.85%** | 99.13 ± 2.62% | 99.94 ± 0.17% | 73.56 ± 1.15% |
| CNN [1] | **95.08 ± 5.24%** | 9.18 ± 6.71% | 28.46 ± 11.22% | 96.05 ± 5.30% | 96.50 ± 6.98% | 64.56 ± 1.79% |
| CNN+F [1] | 81.64 ± 3.54% | 1.74 ± 1.40% | 90.41 ± 5.36% | 99.95 ± 0.15% | **100.00 ± 0.00%** | 74.35 ± 0.73% |
| CNN+FE+TD [1] | 89.64 ± 3.77% | 7.13 ± 4.87% | 92.00 ± 2.81% | **100.00 ± 0.00%** | 99.89 ± 0.33% | 77.39 ± 1.45% |
| Caps+FE+TD [10] | 97.54 ± 2.09% | 37.49 ± 21.42% | 83.38 ± 10.44% | 96.87 ± 3.42% | 82.89 ± 11.38% | 79.58 ± 3.04% |
| SpectroCNN [7] | 95.18 ± 1.66% | 47.18 ± 5.03% | 85.49 ± 4.80% | 51.95 ± 5.72% | **100.00 ± 0.00%** | 75.58 ± 0.86% |
| TCN [20] | 69.33 ± 8.99% | 23.38 ± 8.47% | 1.74 ± 1.66% | 99.54 ± 1.38% | 99.72 ± 0.83% | 58.10 ± 2.29% |
| TDPCAPS* | 92.41 ± 2.62% | **86.82 ± 8.71%** | 92.56 ± 4.42% | 84.27 ± 5.82% | 62.11 ± 16.87% | **84.92 ± 0.82%** |

advantage in the recognition of action HC. However, if the features of sEMG signal are extracted in advance, the recognition performance of most gestures can be improved. Therefore, feature extraction of sEMG signals is a good method for data reduction and purification. Compared with CNN+FE model, CNN+FE+TD model with two-dimensional method improves the classification accuracy of HC and RF gestures by 8.00% and 1.59% respectively, but it has a poor accuracy for HO.

Caps+FE+TD model is inferior to CNN+FE+TD model in the case of RF, WE and WF, but it greatly improves the classification accuracy of HO on the premise of ensuring good recognition result for other gestures.

From the results, TDPCAPS model has achieved excellent recognition effect on HC, HO and RF gestures, and the average accuracy rate of recognizing all gestures has reached 84.92%. The combination of CapsNet and two-dimensional transformation method further improves the overall classification accuracy by 5.34%. It is worth noting that the accuracy of TDPCAPS on HO is 86.82%, which shows that the method proposed in this paper can well characterize the characteristics of HO, while the accuracy of other methods on HO is less than 50%.

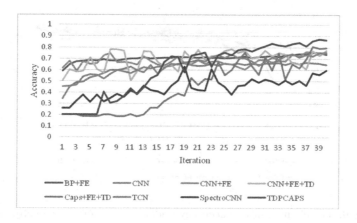

**Fig. 5.** The changes of test accuracy under the case of electrode displacement.

The test accuracy changes with the process of iteration are shown in Fig. 5. As can be seen from the figure, the classification accuracy of each model is constantly rising. Compared with CNN and BP network, CapsNet's classification accuracy is relatively low at the initial stage, but after a certain number of iterations, CapsNet can better recognize different gestures and achieve a better recognition effect.

**Under the Case of Several Subjects.** sEMG signal vary from person to person, it's important to mine universal characteristics of the signal. In the experiment, the sEMG data of 7 subjects were used as the training set, and the rest data were used as the test set. The results are listed below, as shown in Table 2.

The classification accuracy of CNN model is obviously the lowest of all methods, although it has the best performance on WF. When two-dimensional transformation methods are applied, the accuracy reach a relatively high level. TDP-CAPS has the highest average accuracy of recognizing all gestures that reaches 80.31%. Although the model has not achieved the best accuracy in a single action, the accuracy of all actions has been improved. It shows that the method proposed in this paper can make the model pay more attention to the information contained in the input. Compared with Caps+FE+TD model, the overall classification accuracy of TDPCAPS model is improved by 3.18%, and the recognition effects of four gestures are improved in different degrees, by 0.07%, 2.12%, 1.56%, 2.56% and 6.94% respectively.

Figure 6 shows the changes of test accuracy with the increase of training iterations. The proposed method falls behind at the very beginning but succeeds in getting the highest accuracy.

To sum up, the experiments verify that the TDPCAPS model can effectively recognize the sEMG signals in different situations, and the recognition result of most gestures is not bad, with strong generalization ability.

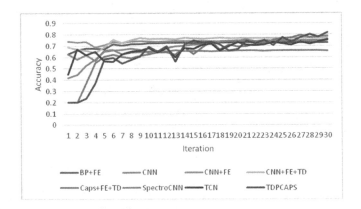

**Fig. 6.** The changes of test accuracy under the case of several subjects.

**Table 2.** The accuracy of different methods under the case of several subjects.

| Model | Different Gestures | | | | | Whole Accuracy |
|---|---|---|---|---|---|---|
| | HC | HO | RF | WE | WF | |
| SVM+FE [18] | 78.38 ± 0.00% | 74.10 ± 0.00% | 51.88 ± 0.00% | **98.21 ± 0.00%** | 64.86 ± 0.00% | 73.52 ± 0.00% |
| BP+FE [14] | 86.38 ± 4.66% | 63.30 ± 4.36% | 62.68 ± 3.99% | 97.76 ± 0.13% | 49.17 ± 1.00% | 71.96 ± 0.68% |
| CNN [1] | 73.85 ± 3.02% | 45.74 ± 2.99% | 45.41 ± 2.79% | 96.33 ± 0.78% | **67.21 ± 1.84%** | 65.70 ± 0.68% |
| CNN+FE [1] | 97.95 ± 2.39% | 64.05 ± 12.46% | 75.92 ± 10.42% | 96.90 ± 1.26% | 39.59 ± 8.52% | 75.04 ± 1.10% |
| CNN+FE+TD [1] | **99.73 ± 0.36%** | 76.20 ± 3.41% | 63.90 ± 3.57% | 95.60 ± 1.38% | 49.64 ± 2.07% | 77.13 ± 0.79% |
| Caps+FE+TD [10] | 99.18 ± 1.57% | 76.07 ± 10.16% | 79.19 ± 8.94% | 95.68 ± 2.20% | 43.20 ± 4.50% | 78.82 ± 0.98% |
| SpectroCNN [7] | 99.01 ± 1.27% | **87.26 ± 0.55%** | 76.46 ± 4.66% | 96.54 ± 2.23% | 14.62 ± 3.08% | 75.05 ± 0.48% |
| TCN [20] | 86.76 ± 6.42% | 69.84 ± 7.22% | **80.09 ± 5.52%** | 97.25 ± 1.34% | 43.91 ± 6.82% | 75.71 ± 0.78% |
| TDPCAPS* | 99.25 ± 3.89% | 78.19 ± 5.12% | 74.97 ± 5.96% | 97.24 ± 0.62% | 50.14 ± 5.50% | **80.31 ± 1.09%** |

## 4.4 Validation for Pruning Mechanism

In order to verify the effectiveness of pruning mechanism, this section calculates the training time of various models mentioned in previous experiments. The specific training time is and recognition time are shown in Table 3.

**Table 3.** Training time and recognition time for different models.

| Model | Electrode Displacement Training Time (s) | Different people Training Time (s) | Recognition Time (ms) |
|---|---|---|---|
| BP [14] | 40.89 ± **5.86** | 319.15 ± **51.99** | 0.295 ± 0.036 |
| CNN [1] | 184.01 ± 4.54 | 940.98 ± 47.60 | 0.297 ± 0.032 |
| CNN+FE [1] | 54.96 ± 3.90 | 344.40 ⊥ 47.78 | **0.129 ± 0.031** |
| SpectroCNN [7] | 329.35 ± 6.41 | 3556.99 ± 63.63 | 1.623 ± 0.036 |
| TCN [20] | 156.37 ± 4.86 | 806.45 ± 45.66 | 0.439 ± 0.028 |
| TDCAPS | 292.11 ± 7.85 | 2784.19 ± 75.05 | 1.721 ± 0.044 |
| TDPCAPS* | 287.40 ± 4.76 | 2712.68 ± 80.24 | 1.545 ± 0.036 |

Compared with TDCAPS, TDPCAPS can slightly reduce the time required for model training under the same experimental conditions. Compared with BP, CNN, TCN and other networks, TDPCAPS still takes a long time, but this network can reduce the training time of the model with a certain recognition accuracy. This shows that the dynamic routing pruning mechanism can effectively cut off unnecessary links, speed up the model training and simplify the model, so as to meet the time delay requirement of sEMG gesture recognition in reality.

## 4.5 Threshold Analysis for Pruning Mechanism

The threshold of coupling coefficients of dynamic routing pruning mechanism is an uncertain item, which is easily influenced by the elastic parameter $\zeta$ and thus greatly affect the pruning of dynamic routing links. When the coupling coefficients adopt different thresholds, the model will change slightly because of different combinations of input links. Therefore the changes of the coupling coefficient threshold will greatly affect the recognition accuracy of the models. Therefore, in this section, the influence of the change of coupling coefficient threshold on the accuracy of model identification is considered with other parameters unchanged, and the specific results are shown in Fig. 7.

Among them, the solid line is the specific recognition accuracy rate that changes with the coupling coefficient threshold, and the surrounding area that gradually becomes lighter is the range where the recognition accuracy rate can fluctuate when a certain coupling coefficient threshold is taken. The lighter the colour, the smaller the probability. It can be seen from the figure that, when recognizing the surface EMG signals in different situations, the recognition accuracy of the model increases with the decrease of the coupling coefficient threshold, and finally slowly tends to be stable. When the threshold value of coupling coefficient is large, it means that the spatial attention capsule network will ignore more detailed features, and the lack of information will make the final abstract features fail to represent the essence of surface EMG signals, so the recognition effect of the model is not ideal. When the threshold value of coupling coefficient is small, the dynamic routing links with less contribution can be connected, and some tiny information can no longer be ignored. The spatial attention capsule network can summarize highly abstract features, so the recognition accuracy of the model will be continuously improved.

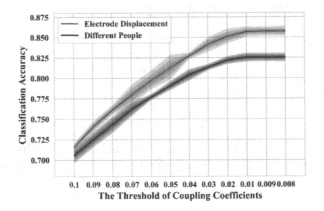

**Fig. 7.** Classification accuracy varies with the threshold of the coupling coefficient.

Of course, the change of the coupling coefficient threshold will also affect the training time of the model. Because when the coupling coefficient takes different thresholds, the number of calculation parameters of the model will change, and sometimes the links with less contribution need not be pruned, which will greatly affect the generation of the model. Therefore, this chapter discusses the variation range of training time when the coupling coefficient threshold changes, and the specific results are shown in Fig. 8.

Among all lines, the solid line is the average training time that varies with the threshold of coupling coefficient, and the surrounding area that gradually

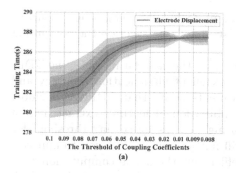
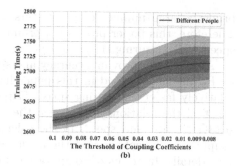

**Fig. 8.** Training time varies with the threshold of the coupling coefficient.

becomes lighter is the range where the training time can fluctuate when a certain threshold of coupling coefficient is taken. The lighter the colour is, the smaller the probability that it can be achieved. It can be seen from the figure that the curve of training time increases continuously with the decrease of the threshold of coupling coefficient, and finally tends to be stable, no matter under what conditions. This shows that when the threshold value of coupling coefficient is large, it means that the capsule network doesn't need to pay attention to too many details. So it ignores more links to speed up the training of the model. When the threshold value of coupling coefficient is small, it means that the space capsule network needs to pay attention to the tiny correlations between features, so most links need to be calculated and thus the training time also increases. As a whole, the training time increases at first and then decreases, which shows that the coupling coefficients of most links with less contribution are clustered around 0.04 to 0.07, as expected. Because softmax function is a generalization of logistic function, dynamic routing applies softmax function to generate coupling coefficient, which makes the coupling coefficient of links with less contribution tend to zero, so the speed of decline is also from fast to slow.

Generally speaking, it is ideal to set the coupling coefficient threshold $\lambda_c$ = 0.01. Under the limit of the current coupling coefficient threshold, although the model sacrificed some training time, it keeps the ideal recognition accuracy, which is very important for gesture recognition of sEMG signal.

## 5 Conclusion

This paper proposes a two-dimensional transformation pruning capsule network, which includes a two-dimensional transformation method to transform feature data and the capsule network with pruning mechanism to classify gestures. Two-dimensional feature method can construct the combination of one-dimensional vector features into two-dimensional data, reducing redundant information of existing methods and explore the potential links between features. In addition, although the capsule network can reduce the information loss and mine the correlation between features, the dynamic routing mechanism in the network brings a large number of parameters and more loss of computing resources. Therefore, this paper proposes a pruning strategy to accelerate the computing speed while ensuring the accuracy.

Aiming at improving accuracy and speed up the calculating time, the TDP-CAPS model proposed in this paper has excellent classification accuracy and relatively faster calculating speed. Experiments verify that TDPCAPS model can find the relationship between the combination of features extracted from sEMG signals, and speed up the calculating process by setting threshold for coupling coefficients so that the model will not pay much attention to unnecessary details. In terms of computational efficiency, the single computation time is about 1 millisecond, which is 10.2% less than that without pruning, which verifies the effectiveness of pruning mechanism and can meet the time delay requirement of real-time identification. However, the feature data obtained by two-dimensional method may have the problem of sparse effective information, which is the future improvement direction.

**Acknowledgement.** This work is supported by National Natural Science Foundation of China under Grant (No. 51875524), the Foundation of Zhejiang University City College (No. J202316) and the Open Project Program of the State Key Lab of CAD&CG (Grant No. A2210), Zhejiang University.

# References

1. D Atzori, M., Cognolato, M., Muller, H.: Deep learning with convolutional neural networks applied to electromyography data: a resource for the classification of movements for prosthetic hands. Front. Neurorobotics **10** (2016). https://doi.org/10.3389/fnbot.2016.00009
2. Bian, F., Li, R., Liang, P.: Svm based simultaneous hand movements classification using semg signals. In: 14th IEEE International Conference on Mechatronics and Automation, ICMA 2017, August 6, 2017 - August 9, 2017, pp. 427–432. 2017 IEEE International Conference on Mechatronics and Automation, ICMA 2017, Institute of Electrical and Electronics Engineers Inc. (2017). https://doi.org/10.1109/ICMA.2017.8015855
3. Chao, H., Dong, L., Liu, Y.L., Lu, B.Y.: Emotion recognition from multiband EEG signals using capsnet. Sensors **19**(9) (2019). https://doi.org/10.3390/s19092212
4. Chen, G.Q., Wang, W.L., Wang, Z., Liu, H.H., Zang, Z.L., Li, W.K.: Two-dimensional discrete feature based spatial attention capsnet for semg signal recognition. Appl. Intell. **50**(10), 3503–3520 (2020). https://doi.org/10.1007/s10489-020-01725-0
5. Cheng, Y.W., et al.: Gesture recognition based on surface electromyography-featureimage. Concurrency Computation-Practice Exp. **33**(6) (2021). https://doi.org/10.1002/cpe.6051
6. Cruz, M.V., Namburu, A., Chakkaravarthy, S., Pittendreigh, M., Satapathy, S.C.: Skin cancer classification using convolutional capsule network (capsnet). J. Sci. Ind. Res. **79**(11), 994–1001 (2020)
7. Duan, N., Liu, L.Z., Yu, X.J., Li, Q.Q., Yeh, S.C.: Classification of multichannel surface-electromyography signals based on convolutional neural networks. J. Ind. Inf. Integr. **15**, 201–206 (2019). https://doi.org/10.1016/j.jii.2018.09.001

8. Geng, W.D., Du, Y., Jin, W.G., Wei, W.T., Hu, Y., Li, J.J.: Gesture recognition by instantaneous surface EMG images. Sci. Rep. **6** (2016). https://doi.org/10.1038/srep36571

9. Ha, K.W., Jeong, J.W.: Decoding two-class motor imagery EEG with capsule networks. In: 2019 IEEE International Conference on Big Data and Smart Computing, BigComp 2019, February 27, 2019 - March 2, 2019, p. IEEE; Korean Institute of Information Scientists and Engineers (KIISE). 2019 IEEE International Conference on Big Data and Smart Computing, BigComp 2019 - Proceedings, Institute of Electrical and Electronics Engineers Inc. (2019). https://doi.org/10.1109/BIGCOMP.2019.8678917

10. Hinton, G., Sabour, S., Frosst, N.: Matrix capsules with EM routing. In: 6th International Conference on Learning Representations, ICLR 2018, April 30, 2018 - May 3, 2018. 6th International Conference on Learning Representations, ICLR 2018 - Conference Track Proceedings, International Conference on Learning Representations, ICLR (2018)

11. Jia, L., Miao, H., Qi, B., Wang, J.: Vehicle type recognition based on improved capsule network. In: 6th IEEE International Conference on Consumer Electronics - Taiwan, ICCE-TW 2019, May 20, 2019 - May 22, 2019. 2019 IEEE International Conference on Consumer Electronics - Taiwan, ICCE-TW 2019. Institute of Electrical and Electronics Engineers Inc. (2019). https://doi.org/10.1109/ICCE-TW46550.2019.8991734

12. Jia, R., Yang, L., Li, Y., Xin, Z.: Gestures recognition of semg signal based on random forest. In: 16th IEEE Conference on Industrial Electronics and Applications, ICIEA 2021, August 1, 2021 - August 4, 2021, pp. 1673–1678. Proceedings of the 16th IEEE Conference on Industrial Electronics and Applications, ICIEA 2021, Institute of Electrical and Electronics Engineers Inc. (2021). https://doi.org/10.1109/ICIEA51954.2021.9516350

13. Kubo, T., Yoshida, M., Hattori, T., Ikeda, K.: Feature selection for vowel recognition based on surface electromyography derived with multichannel electrode grid. In: Zhang, Y., Zhou, Z.-H., Zhang, C., Li, Y. (eds.) IScIDE 2011. LNCS, vol. 7202, pp. 242–249. Springer, Heidelberg (2012). https://doi.org/10.1007/978-3-642-31919-8_31

14. Li, Y., Tian, Y., Chen, W.: Multi-pattern recognition of semg based on improved BP neural network algorithm. In: Proceedings of the 29th Chinese Control Conference, CCC'10, pp. 2867–2872. Proceedings of the 29th Chinese Control Conference, CCC'10. IEEE Computer Society (2010)

15. Liu, Y., et al.: Multi-channel EEG-based emotion recognition via a multi-level features guided capsule network. Comput. Biol. Med. **123** (2020). https://doi.org/10.1016/j.compbiomed.2020.103927

16. Mazzia, V., Salvetti, F., Chiaberge, M.: Efficient-capsnet: capsule network with self-attention routing. Sci. Rep. **11**(1) (2021). https://doi.org/10.1038/s41598-021-93977-0

17. McIntosh, B., Duarte, K., Rawat, Y.S., Shah, M.: Visual-textual capsule routing for text-based video segmentation. In: 2020 IEEE/CVF Conference on Computer Vision and Pattern Recognition. Institute of Electrical and Electronics Engineers Inc. (2020). https://doi.org/10.1109/cvpr42600.2020.00996

18. Oskoei, M.A., Hu, H.S.: Support vector machine-based classification scheme for myoelectric control applied to upper limb. IEEE Trans. Biomed. Eng. **55**(8), 1956–1965 (2008). https://doi.org/10.1109/TBME.2008.919734

19. Sabour, S., Frosst, N., Hinton, G.E.: Dynamic routing between capsules. In: 31st Annual Conference on Neural Information Processing Systems (NIPS). Advances in Neural Information Processing Systems, vol. 30. Neural Information Processing Systems (Nips), LA JOLLA (2017)

20. Tsinganos, P., Cornelis, B., Cornelis, J., Jansen, B., Skodras, A.: Improved gesture recognition based on SEMG signals and TCN. In: 44th IEEE International Conference on Acoustics, Speech, and Signal Processing, ICASSP 2019, May 12, 2019 - May 17, 2019. ICASSP, IEEE International Conference on Acoustics, Speech and Signal Processing - Proceedings, vol. 2019-May, pp. 1169–1173. Institute of Electrical and Electronics Engineers Inc. (2019). https://doi.org/10.1109/ICASSP.2019.8683239

21. Wang, H., Zhang, Y., Liu, C., Liu, H.H.: SEMG based hand gesture recognition with deformable convolutional network. Int. J. Mach. Learn. Cybern. 13(6), 1729–1738 (2022). https://doi.org/10.1007/s13042-021-01482-7

22. Wei, W.T., Hong, H., Wu, X.L.: A hierarchical view pooling network for multichannel surface electromyography-based gesture recognition. Comput. Intell. Neurosci. 2021 (2021). https://doi.org/10.1155/2021/6591035

23. Zhang, X.F., Hu, Y.P., Luo, R.M., Li, C., Tang, Z.C.: The impact of load style variation on gait recognition based on SEMG images using a convolutional neural network. Sensors 21(24) (2021). https://doi.org/10.3390/s21248365

24. Zhang, Z., Ye, S.W., Liao, P., Liu, Y., Su, G.P., Sun, Y.: Enhanced capsule network for medical image classification. In: 42nd Annual International Conferences of the IEEE Engineering in Medicine and Biology Society: Enabling Innovative Technologies for Global Healthcare EMBC'20, pp. 1544–1547 (2020)

25. Zhao, W., Ye, J., Yang, M., Lei, Z., Zhang, S., Zhao, Z.: Investigating capsule networks with dynamic routing for text classification. In: 2018 Conference on Empirical Methods in Natural Language Processing (EMNLP 2018), pp. 3110–3119 (2018)

26. Zhao, Y., Li, F., Xu, L.: A SEMG-based hand motions recognition system with dimension-reduced FFT. In: 31st Chinese Control and Decision Conference, CCDC 2019, June 3, 2019 - June 5, 2019, pp. 1415–1420. Proceedings of the 31st Chinese Control and Decision Conference, CCDC 2019, Institute of Electrical and Electronics Engineers Inc. (2019). https://doi.org/10.1109/CCDC.2019.8832516

# Tool for Game Plot Line Visualization for Designers, Testers and Players

Leszek Nowak[1]([✉]) [iD], Iwona Grabska-Gradzińska[2] [iD], Wojciech Palacz[3] [iD],
Ewa Grabska[3] [iD], and Maria Guzik[4]

[1] Department of Information Technologies, Faculty of Physics, Astronomy and Applied
Computer Science, Jagiellonian University, Krakow, Poland
`leszek.nowak@uj.edu.pl`
[2] Department of Games Technology, Faculty of Physics, Astronomy and Applied Computer
Science, Jagiellonian University, Krakow, Poland
`iwona.grabska@uj.edu.pl`
[3] Department of Design and Computer Graphics, Faculty of Physics, Astronomy and Applied
Computer Science, Jagiellonian University, Krakow, Poland
`{wojciech.palacz,ewa.grabska}@uj.edu.pl`
[4] Faculty of Physics, Astronomy and Applied Computer Science, Jagiellonian University,
Krakow, Poland

**Abstract.** This paper presents a tool for automatic and interactive visualization
of game plots, which can be used to check whether the designers' work meets
the constraints of the world, to help testers control played game story paths. The
referential designers' game plots can be imported from any flowchart diagrams as
an XML file and the actual gameplay variant is generated on the fly and applied
to the original design based on detected common diagram points.

**Keywords:** Collaborative Design · Plot Lines Testing · Design Diagrams

## 1 Introduction

The designers' work requires both imagination and specialized tools that enables the
formalization of ideas already in the conceptual design phase for further processing,
comparison, and documentation. The risk of using highly specialized tools is that they
often create project limitations that are not intended by design, and can negatively impact
the creative process or simply block certain solutions.

For this reason, some designers prefer to use a piece of paper and a pencil as it is
the most unrestrictive design tool; unfortunately, even if this solution works in the early
phases of the design, it does not allow the design to be automatically transferred to further
work stages in the production system [1]. The choice of design support tools depends on
the design domain; in the case of plot development, the most important thing is to depict
cause-and-effect relationships, the succession of events and references to objects of the
story and world, that is why design tools based on flowchart systems are very popular.

© The Author(s), under exclusive license to Springer Nature Switzerland AG 2023
Y. Luo (Ed.): CDVE 2023, LNCS 14166, pp. 85–93, 2023.
https://doi.org/10.1007/978-3-031-43815-8_8

Depending on the needs of the designer and the sophistication of the tool, it is possible to add extra information to graph nodes, e.g. concept art, links to assets, audio dialogs, etc. An example of such a diagram, based on the Arcweave application [2] is shown in Fig. 1. The general practice, is to place the relationships represented as edges of the graph and label the vertices according to the events / characters they represent. The common feature that offers flexibility in developing various stages of the plot is the ability to export/import the diagram to a file format such as JSON or XML. This allows for the interchangeable flow of data between tools.

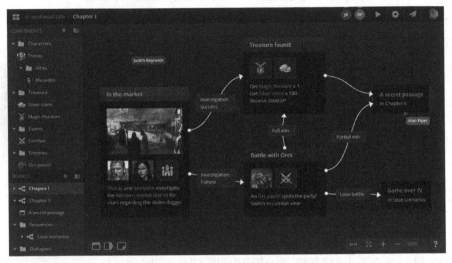

**Fig. 1.** Example use of the story flowchart containing extra narrative information paired with game art to visualize possible outcomes. (image from: https://arcweave.com/).

The players do not see the design flowchart, but they create sequences of the events which can be compared to the original design to show plot paths, resource efficiency and goals reached by the players. Their decisions and events appearing in the game can be logged for analysis, enabling comparison of differences between the order of the events as created in design diagram, and events triggered by the player.

For the automatization purposes the export and import process should be lossless and convertible. The description of the events in the design diagram should be comparable to the log entries from the gameplay. In such a case, it is possible to recreate an event diagram based on the gameplay and the player's decision. This allows one to identify or analyze the paths taken by the player that allowed him to reach story milestones.

## 2   Testing Plot Lines in Video Games

The nonlinearity is the greatest challenge of narrative storytelling in games. Creating the flowcharts for the plot and testing gameplays in terms of possible narrative paths is a daunting task [3, 4]. Even if the flowcharts include only the key events, the number of different game paths the player can take increases with every possible narrative event. The player in his playthrough generates only one path in the story, but testers have to check many possible event sequences. For this reason game designers often try to "tunnel" player choices by creating collapsing story branches creating an illusion of choice.

### 2.1 Problem of Testing Nonlinear Plot

In this paper, the workflow for plot lines comparison and testing is presented. The workflow uses the original graph-based framework for collaborative game plot design, paired with a plot line visualization module.

The graph model as a theoretical approach and its implementation in the Godot game engine [5] was presented in [6, 7]. For the design diagram visualization, the draw.io [8] platform was chosen as the popular free and open-source tool with the crucial functionality to export diagrams to XML files. The log files generated by the framework use the XML notation and allow for visualization of the plot event and actions taken by the players. The presented tool is used by testers to analyze all the designed plot paths, and enable designers to generate plot patches, which were not originally included in design diagram. To match the events from the log to the design diagram elements only the name of the event type, characters and relevant items are shown on generated diagram. This is done for the sake of visual simplicity. So far (as of 2022) the module was used by 13 groups of 3–4 students to design, present and test original stories.

### 2.2 Visualization of the Plot Lines in Testing Process

In the framework described in [9] there is an option to test the plot in two ways:

- without additional information of the narrative arc structure
- with the design diagram as a referential narrative arc structure

In the first option the player (or tester) decisions create the line of events. During the second and next tests, the variant parts of the story line are added as branches and the co-part of the plotlines is colored in red. The events sequence is visualized using the Graphviz dot engine. Graphviz is the library which enables automatic graph drawing [10, 11]. The Fig. 2 shows a simple linear sequence of events generated on a base of one playthrough.

In the second option, when the original design diagram is available, tester can follow one of the presented paths or create his own sequence on the base of the original diagram. Figure 3. Presents more complex nonlinear plot structure with few possible variants and one path distinguished as main plot (yellow rectangle). The need for such tool was mentioned in [9]. In the example below the white and green squares stand for two types of action, but after the action is taken during gameplay the node turns red. The nodes in a shape of circles stands for possible gameplay endings. Black circles mean the main character death.

The design diagram can be shown to the tester during the gameplay and actualized with the information of reached nodes or shown only after passing the gameplay. The four different playthroughs of the same story are shown in Figs. 4, 5, 6 and 7.

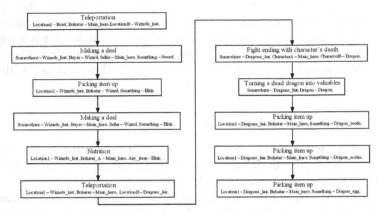

**Fig. 2.** The visualization of the plotline generated on a base of player decisions. The plotline represents short sequence of actions in which the player uses an magic elixir to defeat the dragon.

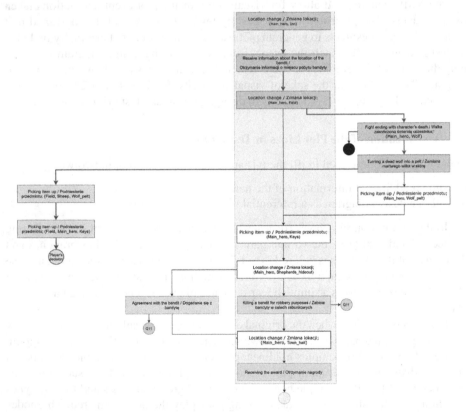

**Fig. 3.** Nonlinear plot with few possible variants and line plot generated during the gameplay. Red nodes stand for the events, which were both proposed by the designer and performed by the player. Blue nodes stand for the player's actions, which do not fit to any event invented by the designer.

In the playthrough the player makes autonomous decisions by choosing any of the available actions. The player makes decisions based on knowledge of the relationship between the elements of the game world, their attributes and the narrative layer associated with the elements. The player's knowledge is fueled by actions such as "Conversation," "Read an announcement," etc. The gathered knowledge is contained in the character diary, to which the player has access at any time.

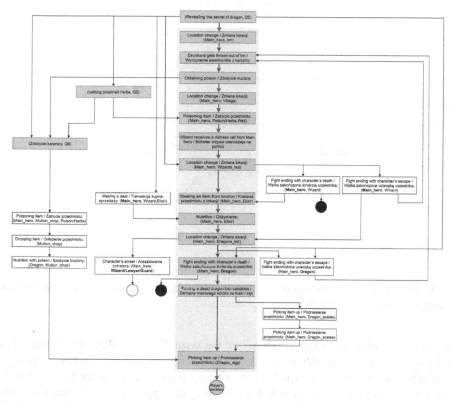

**Fig. 4.** The players decisions lead to exactly the same plot as the main plot arc proposed by designer.

Figure 4 represents a playthrough in which the player is following the plot exactly as planned by the designer. The intended plot is the one with a yellow background. It depicts a coherent story with no initial conditions and an ending resulting in the player receiving a reward.

Players may choose to "shortcut" the quest by trying to complete only the final objective. For the story designer sequence of such actions might not be desired and an alternative ending might be added that will punish the player. This situation is shown in Fig. 5 where omitting a large part of the designed storyline results in failing the game. Depending on the game this may or may not be the intended outcome.

Figure 6 is a variant of gameplay that depends on the player's temperament, for example, is a variant in which the player enters the mission with a certain amount of

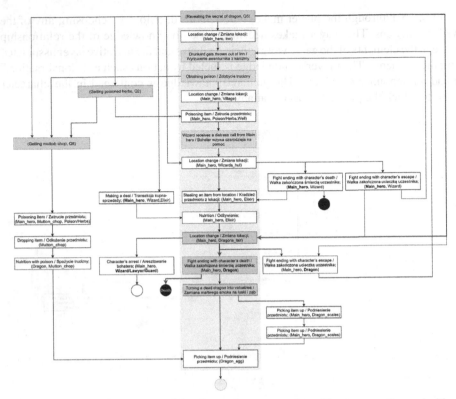

**Fig. 5.** The player makes some crucial and most dangerous action without preparation and without securing an advantage, so the main hero dies quickly.

cash, and instead of using the poison to lure the wizard to the village, he will sell it at the market, and adding the obtained money to his resources will legally buy the potion. He will be poorer, but will not run the risk of being arrested after the theft. Presumably, however, such a player will not only take the dragon's egg, but will also meticulously collect dragon's teeth and dragon's scales to sell them later at the market, thanks to which he will regain the invested funds. In turn, he will complete the entire mission without breaking the law or risking criminal penalties.

Figure 7 represents a playthrough variant proving that the player is well grounded in pop culture will be a sequence in which the player, having obtained poison, uses it to poison a sheep, which he substitutes for the dragon and thus avoids a fight with the dragon, embodying an idea from a Polish folk legend present also in fantasy genre narratives.

To create the new diagram the .DRAWIO file is exported to its XML representation. On the base of xml dependencies, the internal graph representation is done. The module uses the deep-first search to find events in the diagram that corresponds to decisions made by the tester on the fly. The recognized and fit nodes are marked in red. If there is no matching in any branch, it adds a new node to the left of all existing ones (to prevent collisions) and highlights it in blue.

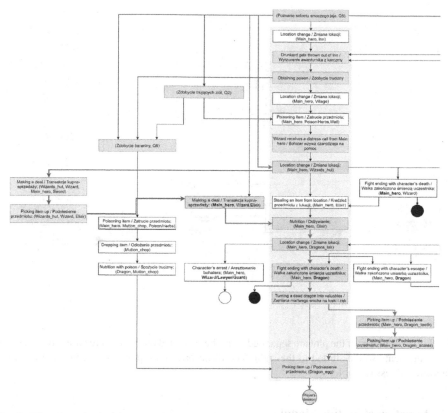

**Fig. 6.** The player's decisions partially correspond with the designer's proposition (red nodes). The additional nodes are placed next to the left margin. All the previous nodes are shifted to the right by the width of the rectangle to avoid node collision.

When the tester finishes, the graph structure is converted back into the.DRAWIO file and saved as a diagram for further transformations and analysis.

In Fig. 7 a node-edges overlapping can be observed, making the diagram less readable. Since the diagrams are auto generated via draw.io, the visualization can be improved by user input, or by creating a dedicated tool for visualization purposes.

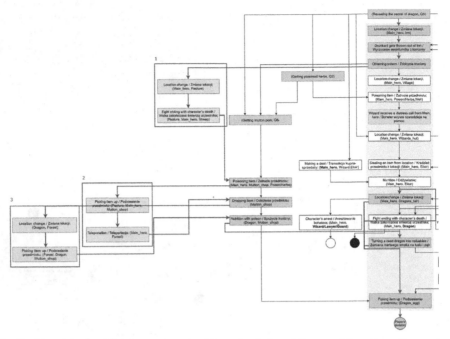

**Fig. 7.** Three pieces of the plot are separated from the designed diagram. Three times the previous drawn elements where shifted to the right. The three branching points result in more complex diagram and less readable.

## 2.3  Function of Testing Module

In the basic variant of the module behavior, the tester is supposed to run the gameplay freely and will only see the visualization of the gameplay after it is completed, so as not to suggest the available solutions. During the gameplay, a log of the player's decisions is generated, containing information about the state of the world after each move. Since each node of the visualization is associated with a specific entry in the log, it is possible when testing the next plotline – partially overlapping with the previous one – to indicate the event in the sequence from which we want to start the new plotline. This saves the tester time.

Another variant of script behavior is connected with the early-stage testing, when the tester wants to know if it is possible to do a playthrough exactly as proposed by the designer. The visualization of the diagram is shown during the testing and changes after each player's move.

The visualization can be prepared long after the test is finished based on the log file.

## 3  Conclusion and Future Works

Testers who used the visualization module admitted that it made their work faster and easier. It also improved the efficiency of finding untested plot variants and making additional transitions between gameplay variants. The tool also improved the subsequent analysis by enabling the comparison of gameplay variants in visual form rather than by comparing log records. Design process is complex, and the attempts to allow for plot nonlinearity and the wide range of possibilities of action combining lead to problems with consistency and considering all dependencies during the design process.

A powerful and complete set of plot variant tests enables you to make bolder design decisions and spend less time tediously checking them.

Ongoing work focuses on creating dedicated user interfaces to ease creating and visualizing the diagrams in more contained and flexible environments that limit the need for third-party software.

# References

1. Ewa Grabska Projektowanie wizualne wspomagane komputerem, Akademicka Oficyna Wydawnicza EXIT (2007)
2. Arcweave – Game design for teams. https://arcweave.com/. Accessed 05 2023
3. Kubiński, P.: Videogames in the light of transmedia narratology and the concept of storyworld. Tekstualia 4(43), 23–36 (2015). https://doi.org/10.5604/01.3001.0013.4243
4. Nobaew, B., Ryberg, T.: Interactive narrator in ludic space: a dynamic story plot underneath the framework of MMORPGs storytelling system. In: Felicia, P. (ed.) Proceedings of the 6th European Conference on Games Based Learning (ECGBL 2012), pp. 600–608. Academic Conferences and Publishing International (2012)
5. Godot Engine – cross-platform game engine. https://godotengine.org/. Accessed 05 2023
6. Grabska-Gradzińska, I., et al.: Towards automatic generation of storyline aided by collaborative creative design. In: Proceedings of the 17th International Conference on Cooperative Design, Visualization and Engineering (CDVE 2020) (2020)
7. Grabska-Gradzińska, I., Nowak, L., Palacz, W., Grabska, E.: Application of graphs for story generation in video games. In: Stanger N., Joachim, V. L. (eds.) Proceedings of the Australasian Computer Science Week Multiconference 2021 (ACSW 2021) : 1st–5th February 2021, University of Otago, Dunedin, New Zealand (Virtual). The Association for Computing Machinery (2021). https://doi.org/10.1145/3437378.3442693
8. DrawIo – diagramming for teams. https://www.drawio.com/
9. Grabska-Gradzińska, I., Grabska, E., Palacz, W., Nowak, L., Argasiński, J.: Data structure visualization as an aid in collaborative game design. In: Luo, Y. (ed.) Cooperative Design, Visualization, and Engineering. CDVE 2022. LNCS, vol. 13492. Springer, Cham (2022). https://doi.org/10.1007/978-3-031-16538-2_24
10. Ellson, J., et al.: Graphviz and dynagraph – static and dynamic graph drawing tools. In: Jünger, M., Mutzel, P. (eds.) Graph Drawing Software. Mathematics and Visualization. Springer, Berlin, Heidelberg (2004). https://doi.org/10.1007/978-3-642-18638-7_6
11. Gansner, E.R., Koutsofios, E., North, S.: Drawing graphs with dot (2015)

# A BIM-Based XR Solution for Cooperative Infrastructure Design

Nobuyoshi Yabuki$^{(\boxtimes)}$ ⓘ, Atsuhiro Yamamoto, and Tomohiro Fukuda ⓘ

Osaka University, 2-1 Yamadaoka, Suita, Osaka 565-0871, Japan
yabuki@see.eng.osaka-u.ac.jp

**Abstract.** In recent years, efforts have been made to improve productivity in Architecture, Engineering, and Construction (AEC) through Building Information Modeling (BIM), which involves sharing 3D models across the entire project. In civil engineering projects, which involve various stakeholders, remote meetings have been employed to reduce travel time and costs. However, conventional remote meetings using flat displays have faced challenges in terms of participant presence, understanding the three-dimensional shape of objects under discussion, tracking model changes, and grasping the evolution of the model during construction. Therefore, this research aimed to develop a remote meeting system for civil engineering design discussions using BIM and Extended Reality (XR) to support remote participants. The system consists of MR remote meetings, design change tracking, collaborative 3D model editing functionality, and 4D simulation for construction planning. A prototype system was developed, and a comparative evaluation was conducted between the proposed method and the conventional method.

**Keywords:** Teleconference · Construction Information Modeling · Extended Reality

## 1 Introduction

In civil engineering, the adoption of Building Information Modeling (BIM) has increased, along with the use of remote meetings to save costs and time. However, conventional remote meetings using flat displays face challenges in participant engagement, understanding 3D objects, comparing designs, and grasping construction plans. Fukuda et al. [2] developed a Mixed Reality (MR) remote meeting system using point cloud streaming, focusing on real-time point clouds of physical models under discussion, but not handling 3D virtual design models such as BIM.

The objective of this study is to develop an Extended Reality (XR) remote meeting system using BIM models and design change tracking to enhance three-dimensional perception and participant presence, improve design change understanding, and facilitate spatial change understanding during construction planning. The system integrates MR remote meetings, design change tracking, cloud-based 3D editing, and 4D simulation.

Y. Luo (Ed.): CDVE 2023, LNCS 14166, pp. 94–99, 2023.
https://doi.org/10.1007/978-3-031-43815-8_9

A comparative experiment is conducted to validate the proposed system against the conventional remote meeting approach using flat displays.

Previous studies have investigated remote meetings using Virtual Reality (VR) and flat displays. Sun et al. [3] developed a VR remote meeting system for architectural and urban design, but it lacks MR/VR integration for stereoscopic viewing. Studies on immersive VR remote meetings include Yamamoto et al. [7]'s integration of BIM and immersive VR and Pouliquen-Lardy et al. [8]'s stereoscopic flat display system. In terms of design change tracking, Yabuki et al. [13] proposed general tracking methods for asynchronous design processes. Cloud-based 3D model editing studies include Adamu et al. [15]'s remote meeting system for editing BIM models. For the 4D simulation of construction plans, Sampaio et al. [19] developed a VR system for visualizing construction plans. Integration of these subsystems for remote design discussions in a shared space is currently limited and requires further research and development.

## 2 Proposal

This study proposes an XR remote conference method for civil engineering structures. The method includes a shared space, a 3D model, and user avatars, with remote participants using an HMD. It consists of two subsystems: one for viewing and reviewing 3D models using MR, and the other for editing and conducting 4D simulations using VR. The MR subsystem includes remote conference and design change tracking, while the VR subsystem offers cloud-based 3D editing and construction plan simulation.

XD remote conference: The XR remote conference functionality includes participant avatar manipulation and object manipulation. Participant avatar manipulation displays and synchronizes avatars in the shared space, enabling collaborative interaction. Object manipulation involves displaying, modifying, and synchronizing the 3D model of the object under consideration among users.

Design change tracking: The design change tracking functionality includes three subsystems: design change history loading, visualization, and option switching. It involves reading the design change history file, establishing object-design change links, and identifying modified portions of the 3D model. By referencing the stored design change history, the system enables switching design options based on the changes. This supports collaborative design using Cooperative Information Modelling (BIM) and defines a general model for 3D models with design changes.

Characteristics of Collaborative Design Changes with 3D Models: 1. Iterative synchronous/asynchronous processes; 2. 3D model identification; 3. Shape and attribute inheritance; 4. Multiple participant involvement; 5. Editing completion time determination.

Based on these five characteristics, the general model for 3D models in the design change history can be defined, as shown in Eq. (1).

$$M\left(S_i, M_j, P(\text{List of } M_k), A_n, T_{i-j}\right) \tag{1}$$

where $M$ is the target 3D model, $S_i$ is the session number ($i = 1, 2, 3...$), $M_j$ is the model number ($j = 1, 2, 3...$), $M_k$ is the model number of the parent model from which $M$ inherits ($k = 1, 2, 3...$), $P(\text{List of } M_k)$ is the list of model numbers of the parent models of $M$, $A_n$ is the code of the engineer who edited $M$ ($n = 1, 2, 3...$), and $T_{i-j}$ is the editing completion time of $M$.

The design change history display functionality presents the stored design change history on the console panel, enabling participants to review the history of design changes. Design option switching displays alternative design options, highlights differences, and synchronizes the displayed options. This facilitates comparative evaluations and enhances understanding of design changes compared to traditional remote conferences.

3D editing and 4D simulation: The 3D model editing functionality enables users to edit the shape and attribute information of the model and synchronize these edits among participants. With the proposed system, remote participants can share a VR space, grasp the scale of the construction project, and understand the 4D simulation of the construction plan. The 4D simulation functionality includes data loading, integrating productivity data with the BIM model, and executing the simulation by changing dates and construction plan options, synchronized among users.

X-Reality Design Teleconference (XRDT) System: In this research, a prototype system named XRDT is developed. Unity 3D is used as the development platform, as for visual and voice communication, Photon Realtime and Photon Voice are applied, and the experience devices are HoloLens and Oculus Rift from MR and VR side. The flow chart of the system is shown in Fig. 1.

The image of the remote conference is shown in Fig. 2a. Meanwhile, in Fig. 2b, the function of design change tracking is described, in Fig. 2c, the cloud-based 3D editing capabilities are described, in Fig. 2d, the 4D simulation function for construction plans is performed.

## 3 Evaluation

### 3.1 Preparation

A survey was conducted to evaluate the proposed method and the conventional method after each experiment, with 2 male engineering student participants in their 20s for each experiment. The survey utilized a 7-point categorical scale and included open-ended responses. The system configurations of the proposed method and conventional method are presented in Table 1, with differences in video output, conversation functionality, system operation method, and 3D model sharing. Validation experiments were conducted for the design stage (Validation Experiment 1) and construction planning stage (Validation Experiment 2) using the XRDT system, which supports both design and construction planning processes.

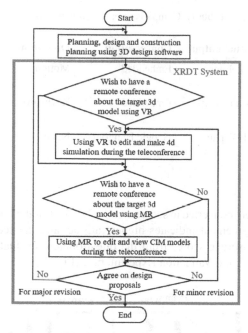

**Fig. 1.** System flow chart.

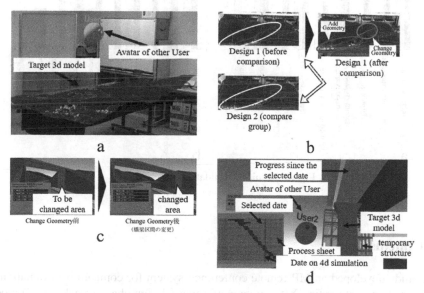

**Fig. 2.** Description of system functions.

**Table 1.** Comparison between methods.

|  | **Visual output** | **Conversation** | **Operation** | **3D model sharing** |
|---|---|---|---|---|
| Proposed method (MR) | HoloLens | Embedded | Motion | Yes |
| Proposed method (VR) | Oculus Rift | Embedded | Keyboard | Yes |
| Previous work | 2d Display | Google Hangouts | None | No |

### 3.2 Results

The survey ratings were converted to scores on a 1–7 scale. For the question about system fatigue, the higher agreement indicates higher fatigue, and the scores were reversed. Figure 3 shows the average scores from the questionnaire evaluations for Validation Experiment 1 (Fig. 3a) and Validation Experiment 2 (Fig. 3b).

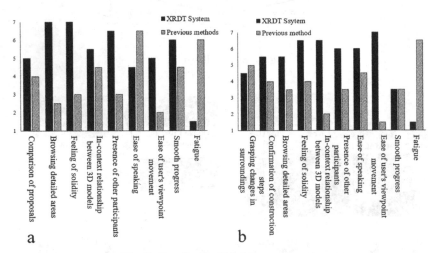

**Fig. 3.** Results of validation experiments.

## 4 Conclusion

This study developed an MR remote conference system for comparative evaluation of civil structures, integrating XR remote conference, design change tracking, 3D model editing, and 4D simulation. The XRDT system prototype was evaluated through a comparative experiment with a traditional remote conference using a flat display, using a simulated project. The evaluation was collected via a questionnaire to assess the proposed method. The contributions of this study are as follows:

- The study developed the XRDT system, an MR remote conference system integrating XR functionality, design change tracking, cloud-based 3D editing, and 4D simulation for construction planning.
- The proposed method showed advantages over traditional remote conferences using flat displays in visual comparison, usability, and confirming construction steps.
- The proposed method faced challenges in terms of user fatigue and perceiving changes in the surrounding environment during construction.

# References

1. Fukuda, T., Zhu, Y., Yabuki, N.: Point cloud stream on spatial mixed reality-toward telepresence in architectural field. In: Proceedings of the 36th eCAADe Conference, vol. 2, pp. 727–734. Poland (2018)
2. Sun, L., Fukuda, T., Resch, B.: A synchronous distributed cloud-based virtual reality meeting system for architectural and urban design. Front. Architect. Res. **3**, 348–357 (2014). Elsevier (2014)
3. Yamamoto, A., Yabuki, N., Fukuda, T.: Immersive virtual reality teleconference system with design change tracking and 3D editing. In: Proceedings of the 18th International Conference on Construction Application of Virtual Reality (CONVR2018), pp. 302–310. New Zealand (2018)
4. Pouliquen-Lardy, L., Milleville-Pennel, I., Guillaume, F.: Remote collaboration in virtual reality: symmetrical effects of task distribution on spatial processing and mental workload. Virtual Real. **20**, 213–220 (2016). https://doi.org/10.1007/s10055-016-0294-8
5. Yabuki, N., Soubra, S., Lebegue, E., Gual, J., Artaud, G.: A proposed bridge information model IFC-BRIDGE and semantic comparison of synchronized product model data. In: Proceedings of 1st International Conference on Computational Design in Engineering, pp. 21–24 (2009)
6. Adamu, Z.A., Emmitt, S., Soetanto, R.: Social BIM: co-creation with shared situational awareness. J. Inf. Technol. Constr. **20**, 230–252 (2015)
7. Sampaio, A.Z., Martins, O.P.: The application of virtual reality technology in the construction of bridge: the cantilever and incremental launching methods. Autom. Constr. **37**, 58–67 (2014)

# Novice Behavior Analysis in Business Training by Using Tobii Eye Tracking Technology

Sutipong Sutipitakwong⬚ and Pornsuree Jamsri(⬚)

School of Information Technology, King Mongkut's Institute of Technology Ladkrabang,
Bangkok, Thailand
{61070369,pornsuree}@it.kmitl.ac.th

**Abstract.** Advanced technology exists in various business sectors. It is important to identify fundamental skills that are required in each business. This research aims to understand the situation or obstacles confronted by a novice staff individual while they perform required business tasks. This can provide an initial understanding of newly employed staff's behavior and tailor meaningful training for them. Each employee performs required job tasks based on their previous background knowledge and experiences. To succeed in new job tasks, a proposed training guideline can assist novices get started and cooperate successfully with others throughout the new business environment. With the use of Tobii Eye Tracking Technology, the researcher can gather a novice's behavior through eye tracking hardware—Tobii Glasses 3. This method discloses hidden thinking and level of task performance. Tobii Pro Lab is a software for doing analysis with 4 features: 1) gaze plots; 2) heat maps; 3) times of interest; 4) areas of interest to achieve the goal of providing information in training new employees.

**Keywords:** Eye Tracking · Novice Behavior · Cooperative Training · Business Training · Digital Marketing

## 1 Introduction

This project implements the use of eye tracking technology to understand the focus points, attention span, and obstacles a novice confronts when on the job. Providing a clear understanding of the challenges and obstacles in the thinking process of a novice staff individual can greatly benefit them in overcoming job challenges [1]. The novice chosen for this study works in the field of digital marketing. This project aims to understand how novices perform their tasks. The researcher will perform an analysis of how novices investigate marketing campaigns. Eye tracking technology is applied to track attention and understand the obstacles and challenges a novice encounters. Thinking activities in creating reports and approaches of novices are analyzed by heat maps and gaze plots qualitatively. Utilizing the collected data from Tobii's eye tracking technology, allows for an in depth understanding of what a novice does and what challenges and obstacles are faced by a novice. This research will provide a greater understanding than merely analyzing a novice on the job. Rather the thought processes of a novice while doing various new tasks will be revealed. The data gathered will prove useful in creating future training materials for novice staff individuals going forward.

Y. Luo (Ed.): CDVE 2023, LNCS 14166, pp. 100–110, 2023.
https://doi.org/10.1007/978-3-031-43815-8_10

## 1.1 Objectives

The main objective of this project is to understand the process and phases of analytics in digital marketing in order to understand how a novice performs a given task. This research aims to study the following:

- Thinking patterns of novices when performing a task.
- Analyzing novice behavior in analytical business processes from given data.
- Analyzing the obstacles novices encounter when performing a given task.

## 1.2 Target Group: Novices in Digital Marketing

The target group of this research is aimed at novices who work in the field of digital marketing. The novice selected will have some basic knowledge of digital marketing and Google Ads and must have less than 1 year of experience working in the field. For this research, the business type where the novices' work is picked for analysis will be a fashion business for bags, which can be considered both fashion and utilitarian. The selected business sample is from a business based in Bangkok, Thailand.

# 2 Literature Review

## 2.1 Business Domain of Research

Currently, businesses utilize an online environment, such as e-commerce, with online shopping increasingly becoming a common habit for many individuals. As the e-commerce market grows, businesses will need to generate various digital marketing campaigns that appeal to online customers and attract them to their merchandise website [1]. In the fashion industry, for example, the fashion business is primarily consumer-based so that they must engage their best efforts to reach their consumer audience. In this case, this industry does a great amount of digital marketing, data collection, and statistical analysis. These methods can bridge the gap between technology and fashion [11]. Data analytics is becoming increasingly important to both fashion retailers and companies. In addition, fashion companies are offering personalized search options to tailor their goods to each consumer. This brings the industry towards digitization and a strong customer-centric strategy.

## 2.2 Human Behavior Analysis

Presently, gaze data is being used by researchers as experiments in various fields. These experiments utilize gaze to differentiate experts behavior from novices [2]. The concepts motivating these experiments are to "learn from the expert" and "train the novice" [3]. Since fields vary, experts have greater focus areas than novices, because they use their retina's visual foveal and parafoveal regions to see and process more accurately information from a visual stimulus, showing global processing behavior [3]. Training novices, therefore is essential, as it can result in improved performance, fewer errors, and an improved performance for the business marketing tasks. [4]. Considering the importance of digital marketing campaigns being visually appealing, it is valuable to investigate the obstacles novices face when performing digital marketing so that novices will be trained effectively overcome initial obstacles so as to gain an expert's level of judgment [13].

## 2.3 Data-Driven Organizations

In today's organizations and businesses, graphical displays of data are becoming increasingly popular, given that organizations tend to be data-driven. And innovations in how complex data sets can be analyzed [7]. Graphical displays can be considered an effective way of communicating quantitative data [8]. The ability to generate and interpret graph data is widely recognized as a core means [14].

## 2.4 Current Situation

In today's organization, most enterprises and growing businesses are always scaling up with their novice employees, including specialized training for creating new experts. Organizations, similarly, need a fast and effective way of training their employees [12]. Currently the training process of a novice to an expert can be time consuming and inefficient due to an unclear understanding of tasks by novices. This research thus focuses on understanding the obstacles a novice faces when performing tasks in the field of digital marketing. Taking into consideration that current marketing campaigns are analyzed giving different results, the problem with traditional retail analytics is that there are often factors that are overlooked or underestimated [8]. Previous studies have used idea maps and linkography to examine the interaction between actions in order to understand the design thinking process [9, 10]. In this research an advanced technology is utilized.

## 2.5 Tobii Technologies

There are 2 parts to the selected technologies of this research: hardware and software. The hardware performs data collection. The software performs in data analysis.

● **Hardware**

The hardware selected for this research is Tobii Glasses 3.
Figure 1 Shows Tobii Glasses 3 the wearable eye tracking glasses selected for this research. The glasses consist of two main components: the recording unit (1), and the head unit (2).

1. The recording unit allows for storage of the battery and SD card and allows the glasses to be connected to the computer. [5, 6]
2. The head unit contains eye tracking sensors on the lenses, allowing for accurate precision when tracking the wearer's eye movements.
3. Removable nose pads allow for adjusting the head unit to the wearer.
4. Rechargeable Li-ion batteries power the recording unit and head unit.
5. SD card is used to store recorded data.
6. Calibration card is used to calibrate the head unit every time before use.
7. Cleaning cloth is used to clean the head unit.

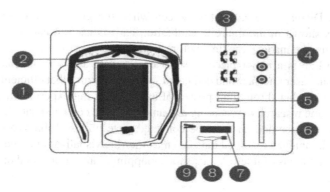

**Fig. 1.** Tobii Glasses 3

8. Head strap attaches to the head unit to keep it secure.
9. Cable clip is used to hold on to any dangling cables.

- **Software**

There are two Tobii software packages used in this research: 1) Glasses 3 Controller and 2) Tobii Pro Lab. The Glasses 3 Controller is used to connect and enable monitoring of the glasses on the recording screen, where Tobii Pro Lab enables analysis of the recorded data. Calibration of the glasses must be performed before each recording. The screen will display the battery life and memory available for the glasses on the top right of the controller screen. The screen will display the gaze point in a red circle; a calibration card must be used. The wearer will look directly at the point on the card once a check sound is heard, which means the calibration is complete [5, 6].

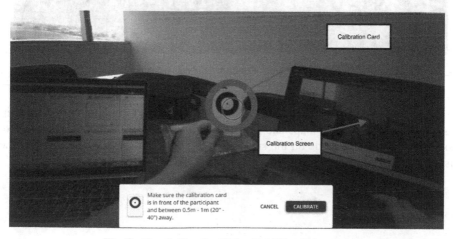

**Fig. 2.** Eye Calibration Using Tobii Pro Controller

Figure 2. Displays the calibration screen when the glasses are connected to the controller. As shown in the figure, a calibration card is used to calibrate the glasses. Calibration must be made every time before recording.

Tobii Pro Lab is a major piece of software for data analytics in this research. It provides a visual user interface and dedicated software features that efficiently guide and support the researcher through all phases of an eye tracking experiment, from testing and designing the research to recording and analyzing the collected data. Tobii Pro Lab allows the user to see and analyze the collected gaze points. Tobii Pro Lab includes features to help analyze recorded data, such as metrics visualization, creating times of interest, creating areas of interest, snapshots, mapping, gaze points, and data export [5, 6].

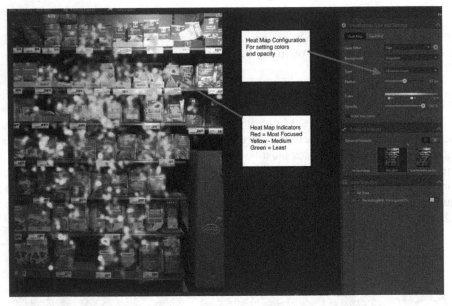

**Fig. 3.** Tobii Pro Lab Analysis Screen

Figure 3 Shows what the software looks like when performing analytics with it. It shows the different heat maps and gaze points from the eye tracking data collected. Configurations can be made on the side panel and heat maps can be displayed in the display.

# 3   Research Design

## 3.1   Research Setup

The research design collects qualitative data, including semi-structured interviews and eye-tracking behavior. The data collection of eye tracking behavior includes a novice being given a task that they need to complete. After being given a brief description of the task, the novice will perform the task and eye tracking data will be collected during the time they perform the task. These tasks will consist of different sources of information, such as marketing ads, marketing ad reports, and product reports. Using the data collected from the eye tracking analytics, including times of interest, that focuses on the judgments and obstacles of novice areas of interest of the novice working on the task and the overall gaze data and heat map behaviors.

1. Selected novices wear Tobii eyeglasses for eye tracking when collecting the data during the analysis phase.
2. Novices will be given 3 sets of tasks including Google Ads budget Analysis, Google Reports campaign analysis, and product reports analysis. Novices will perform these tasks and eye-tracking data is collected.
3. The datasets of the eyetracking samples will be used to analyze the situation faced by novices.

**Fig. 4.**  Recording Gaze Data Example

Figure 4 Shows the analytical screen from the collected recording data. This allows the researcher to understand the different gaze points and thought processes of the novice during the task.

## 3.2  Analysis Methods

The intent is to analyze the novice's behavior in understanding their thought process and obstacles that they may encounter. Features of the Tobii Pro Lab will be implemented. These features will include gaze points, heat maps, times of interest, and areas of interest.

During the research analysis process, the following steps are followed:

1. Segment the recorded data into sections for reports, ads, and product reports.
2. Upload the data into Tobii Pro segments and group them.
3. Utilize the feature on Tobii Pro to create times of interest.
4. Utilize the feature on Tobii Pro to create areas of interest.
5. From the times of interest and areas of interest, look at the gaze data.
6. From the times of interest and areas of interest, look at the gaze plots.
7. From the times of interest and areas of interest, look at the heat map.
8. Analytical conclusions can be drawn when significant behavior or obstacles are identified.

**Fig. 5.**  Gaze Plot Visualization on Tobii Pro Lab

Figure 5 Shows the gaze analysis screen, where researchers are able to understand and draw conclusions from the thought process of a novice through the different points. As shown in the figure, the order of eye movement can be tracked from the beginning to understand the whole process of the novice.

Figure 6 Shows the heat map analysis screen where researchers can further understand the heavy spots that a novice focuses on. This allows researchers to understand a novice's behavior on what they primarily focus their attention on and what they tend to overlook.

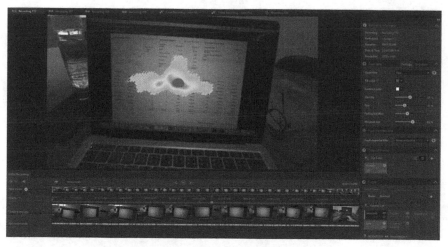

**Fig. 6.** Heat map Visualization on Tobii Pro Lab

# 4 Results and Analysis

## 4.1 Results

Data suggests that the novice relies heavily on one single spot rather than multiple points. The data collected from the experiment suggests that novices have a smaller area of focus than experts. Thus, novices tend to only look at certain aspects. This experiment demonstrates that a novice in the field of digital marketing with limited knowledge can face obstacles such as focusing heavily on a single spot, as the data can suggest. The data suggests that a novice relies heavily on a single spot on the screen rather than looking at the different aspects of the data presented.

## 4.2 Key Findings

The key findings can be drawn from gaze plots, gaze during the recorded data, and heat maps. The results of the findings and interpretation are as follows:

Figure 7 Shows the novice's gaze during the recording. The selected times of interest shows how the novice focuses mainly on a single area within the timeframe. This timeframe was selected due to the novice's significant focus on a single area of interest.

Figure 8 Shows the novice's gaze plots in the order that the novice sees the screen. The gaze plots show that the novice may struggle in finding a clear indication for analysis of this task. This shows how a novice might struggle when given a broad task.

Figure 9 Shows the heat map, which enhances the visualization of understanding on what a novice focuses. A novice was given the task of analyzing a budget. This clearly indicates the red spots being directly amplified on a single point of just the budget, signaling that the novice focuses heavily on a single point rather than from a big picture perspective.

From the findings drawn from the analysis the data suggests that novices choose to heavily focus on the specific point of the task. The data demonstrates that if a novice is

**Fig. 7.** Times of Interest with Gaze Data Recording

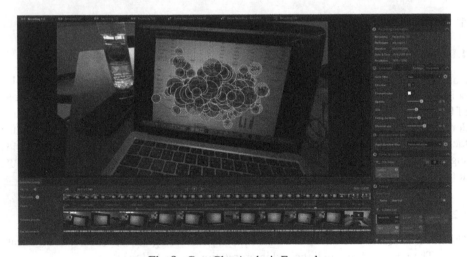

**Fig. 8.** Gaze Plot Analysis Example

given the task of budget analysis, they will only focus on costs. If a novice is given the task of campaign analysis, they tend to look at everything without specific focus points proving that this task is challenging.

**Fig. 9.** Heat map Visualization Analysis

## 5  Discussion and Conclusions

From the findings of the collected tracked eye movement and the analysis of the data, it can be suggested that novices are limited by their thought process or might only look at small sectors of data, which limits their ability to look at data from a top-down perspective or the big picture. The data collected suggests that eye movement of a novice when given a task they would directly focus on the main point of the given task. For example, when given the task to analyze the budget a novice would only focus on the budget and disregards other factors. Therefore, the data clearly shows that a novice would rely heavily on a single spec of data rather than putting multiple aspects they might feel overly challenged and unable to perform the task in a clear manner.

This research aims to collect data from the viewpoint of an expert for future research. Therefore, data from both novices and experts will be collected and compared. This will allow for this research to compare and understand the difference in thought processes and decision-making between a novice and an expert.

## References

1. Hartmann, J., De Angeli, A., Sutcliffe, A.: Framing the User Experience: information Biases on Website quality judgement. In: Proceedings of the SIGCHI Conference on Human Factors in Computing Systems: ACM, pp. 855–864 (2008)
2. APA PsycNet. (n.d.-b). https://psycnet.apa.org/record/2011-26946-004
3. Deveau, R., Griffin, S.J., Reis, S.: AI-powered marketing and sales reach new heights with Generative AI. McKinsey & Company (2023) . https://www.mckinsey.com/capabilities/growth-marketing-and-sales/our-insights/ai-powered-marketing-and-sales-reach-new-heights-with-generative-ai. Accessed 14 June 2023
4. Lazar, J., Norcio, A.: Training novice users in developing strategies for responding to errors when browsing the web. Int. J. Hum.-Comput. Interact. **15**(3), 361–377 (2003)

5. Discover the benefits of training your team with Eye Tracking. (n.d.). Tobii. https://www.tobii.com/resource-center/customer-stories/training-your-team. Accessed 14 June 2023
6. Kar, A.K., Dwivedi, Y.K.: Eye tracking unlocks learning and education insights. (n.d.). https://www.tobii.com/solutions/scientific-research/learning-and-education (2020)
7. Kar, A., Dwivedi, Y.K.: Theory building with big data-driven research – moving away from the "What" towards the "Why." Int. J. Inf. Manag. **54**, 102205 (2020). https://doi.org/10.1016/j.ijinfomgt.2020.102205
8. The Visual Display of Quantitative Information, 2nd Ed.: Edward R. Tufte: 9781930824133:Books. (n.d.). http://faculty.salisbury.edu/~jtanderson/teaching/cosc311/fa21/files/tufte.pdf
9. Zhu, M., Bao, D., Yu, Y., Shen, D., Yi, M.: Differences in thinking flexibility between novices and experts based on eye tracking. PLoS ONE **17**(6), e0269363 (2022). https://doi.org/10.1371/journal.pone.0269363
10. Michailidou, E., Harper, S., Bechhofer, S.: Visual complexity and aesthetic perception of web pages. In: Bringé, A. (ed.) International Conference on Design of Communication (2008). https://doi.org/10.1145/1456536.1456581 (2020)
11. Data is a techy domain, but can the fashion industry handle it? Forbes. https://www.forbes.com. Training Industry, Inc. (2019)
12. Seeing Through Another's Eyes: How Eye-tracking Technology Can Improve Training and Employee Safety. Training Industry. https://trainingindustry.com/articles/compliance/seeing-through-anothers-eyes-how-eye-tracking-technology-can-improve-training-and-employee-safety/
13. Pappas, I., Sharma, K., Mikalef, P., Giannakos, M.: A comparison of gaze behavior of experts and novices to explain website visual appeal. ResearchGate (2018c). https://www.researchgate.net/publication/325079849_A_Comparison_of_Gaze_Behavior_of_Experts_and_Novices_to_Explain_Website_Visual_Appeal
14. Bean, R.: Why becoming a data-driven organization is so hard (2022). https://hbr.org/2022/02/why-becoming-a-data-driven-organization-is-so-hard

# A Multilevel Industrial Internet Value Co-creation System Structure and Mechanism

Siwei Yang[1]([✉]), Shuangxi Huang[1], Yunjian Qiu[2], Xing Luo[1], and Xi He[1]

[1] Tsinghua University, Beijing, China
914823246@qq.com
[2] University of Southern California, Los Angeles, USA

**Abstract.** Industrial Internet is a new form of industrial organization that accelerates the reshaping and transformation of the industrial chain, making the structure of the industrial value chain increasingly complex. Under this context, traditional organizational theory and value theory are insufficient to support a comprehensive and systematic industry analysis. This paper integrates ecological theory and value co-creation theory to propose a multilevel and dynamic evolutionary value co-creation system architecture for Industrial Internet. It analyzes the key elements, value creation motivation and activities at different levels and provides decision methods and suggestions for government, Industrial Internet leaders and participants to make industrial policies.

**Keywords:** Industrial Internet · Value Co-creation · Symbiotic Evolution · Service Ecosystem

## 1 Introduction

The Industrial Internet is a new form of industrial organization managed by the government or Industrial Internet leaders (usually leading enterprises in the industry), relying on one or multiple information platforms and providing full-process, full-life cycle services to all types of industrial members in the industrial chain (Fig. 1).

The Industrial Internet's output to customers no longer solely consists of tangible goods, but also includes a significant amount of intangible services and added value. In terms of value creation, the involved parties have become more complex; suppliers, business partners, collaborators, and customers all participate in co-creating value [1]. In this context, traditional product-centric logic within industrial analysis is no longer sufficient to guide economic management activities, making it difficult for government or Industrial Internet leaders to formulate appropriate industrial policies.

In 2004, Vargo and Lusch [2] proposed a service-dominant logic for industrial analysis. With the continuous development of service-dominant logic research, service ecosystems with self-regulation and relative independence have become the focus of attention [3]. Service ecosystems study value creation and business collaboration from a macro perspective of complex network systems, is more suitable for conducting industrial internet analysis than traditional organizational and value theories [4].

Y. Luo (Ed.): CDVE 2023, LNCS 14166, pp. 111–122, 2023.
https://doi.org/10.1007/978-3-031-43815-8_11

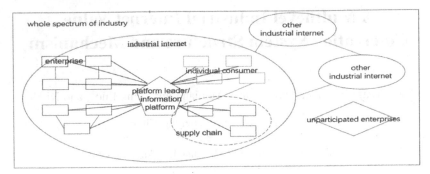

**Fig. 1.** Schematic diagram of industrial internet and industry.

Based on service ecosystem theory, this paper proposes a multilevel and dynamic evolutionary value co-creation system architecture, including the micro, meso, and macro levels, then briefly describes the decision model and methods for the Industrial Internet.

## 2  Related Research

### 2.1  Service Ecosystem Theory

The concept of the ecosystem was first proposed by Tansley in 1935, which refers to the entire population of organisms living in a specific area and all physical factors that form the environment for the biotic community. Vargo and Lusch [3, 4] combined the concept with service-dominant logic and proposed the concept of the service ecosystem. The core idea of the service ecosystem is that participants interact and create value through service exchange, resource integration, and institutional constraints in a dynamic and multi-level system [5]. The role distinctions of participants within the service ecosystem disappear, and all participants create value for themselves or others. Therefore, the service ecosystem not only focuses on achieving the benefits of oneself and partners but also focuses on the interests of all participants to promote the sustainable and healthy development of the system, which is consistent with the goal of Industrial Internet development.

### 2.2  Value Co-creation Theory

Value co-creation was first proposed by Prahalad and Ramaswamy [6] in 2000. Based on service-dominant logic, Vargo and Lusch [2] emphasize that service is the foundation of all economic transactions, customers are important participants in value co-creation, interaction and resource integration are key activities of value co-creation. Based on the service ecosystem perspective, Vargo and Lusch [4] in 2010 pointed out that value co-creation is the process of co-creating value by participants and participants (A2A) through resource integration and service provision in a complex network system. In this paper, value co-creation in the context of Industrial Internet refers to the process of multiple stakeholders co-creating value through effective interaction and resource integration.

# 3   Multilevel Architecture of Value Co-creation System

The value co-creation system architecture of the Industrial Internet follows the service ecosystem. It is seen as a collection of multiple levels, achieving value co creation through micro, meso, and macro level interactions [7]. The value creation activities and their relationships at the three levels are shown in Fig. 2.

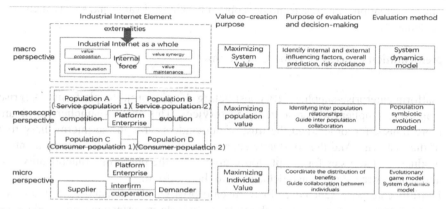

**Fig. 2.** The architecture of the industrial internet value co creation system, the purpose of value co creation, and the purpose of decision

The micro level is the lowest level, reflecting the structure and activities among several specific participating entitics; the meso level is the middle level, reflecting the structure and activities among several categories of stakeholders; the macro level is the highest level, reflecting the social structure and activities of the Industrial Internet as a whole. The definition of the structure and activities of each level is not fixed and absolutely independent, and the interaction of each interrelated level will evolve and change over time [8].

## 3.1   Value Co-creation Mechanism Analysis at the Micro Level

### The Driving Force for Achieving Value Co-creation

From a microscopic perspective, the industrial Internet value ecosystem is a complex business ecosystem composed of multiple stakeholders such as platform companies, suppliers, demanders, and other supporting members. The overall activity of the Industrial Internet can be viewed as a process of value co-creation among multiple sets of suppliers-platform-demanders.Driven by internal and external factors, different stakeholders interact and depend on each other to form a mutually beneficial and symbiotic relationship, and result in value co-creation and sharing through interactive cooperation and resource integration. The motivation for promoting the realization of value co-creation activities is essentially the demand for the value of all stakeholders.

The value demands of the platform enterprise include: revenue demands, demands for platform development, demands for platform social value. The value demands of suppliers include: revenue demands, demands for maintaining competitive advantages, demands for maintaining stable transaction relationships. The value demands of demanders include: functional demands through service, demands for cost-effectiveness, emotional demands in certain situations.

There are significant differences but also mutual influences and interactions among the value demands of the platform enterprise, suppliers, and demanders that drive the occurrence and implementation of value co-creation. Only through the implementation of value co-creation, can all stakeholders obtain maximized value and satisfy their own value demands.

**Implementation Process of Value Co-creation**

- Platform enterprise-suppliers. By constructing the platform, the platform enterprise empowers suppliers with resources and services. This enables suppliers to obtain more transaction orders and the trust of demanders through the intermediary role of the platform. And the constantly entering suppliers can provide complementary products and services for the platform, improving the platform's functionality and attracting more suppliers and demanders to the platform.
- Platform enterprise-demanders. Platform enterprise enables demanders to obtain various services and increase their ability to participate in service design, production, and consumption through resource empowerment and service empowerment. The integration of supplier behavior on the platform also increases the bargaining power of demanders. By comparison, demanders generate direct economic value for the platform enterprise through purchasing and consuming behavior.
- Suppliers-demanders. Suppliers can bring the most direct value to demanders by providing services. At the same time, suppliers and demanders establish stable and good transaction relationships through the platform. Suppliers can refer to demander's knowledge to improve services, while demanders can obtain services with higher cost-effectiveness through stable transaction relationships, achieving value creation and realization for suppliers and demanders.

### 3.2 Value Co-creation Mechanism Analysis at the Meso Level

**The Driving force for Achieving Value Co-creation**

The industrial internet value co-creation system at the meso level is similar to the concept of an ecosystem. All stakeholders are treated as customers of the industrial internet, not distinguished according to supplier or demander. Similar customers form a population. The purpose of value co-creation is the growth and development of the population (the population size in this context can be understood as the total value obtained by the population through the industrial internet). The driving force for achieving value co-creation are mainly determined by the characteristics of the industrial internet itself.

*Changes in the Carrier of Value Trigger Customer Habitation Behavior*

In the context of the industrial internet, value creation activities are concentrated on online and offline service processes, and the carrier of value has shifted from products to the service. Leveraging its characteristics of service integration, instant communication and extensive interaction, the industrial internet has become a fixed "habitat" for customers.

*Qualitative Changes Caused by Quantitative Changes in Customer Demand*
As the number of customers accessing the industrial internet continues to increase, integrated services targeting bulk users have emerged. Meanwhile, under the support of information technology, customers' personalized demands directly reach service providers, which not only effectively meet customer needs but also enhance the economic benefits of service providers. As a result, numerous customers and service providers work together around the industrial internet, forming various value co-creation models.

*The Competition Relationship Between Customers Transitions to Multi-Form Cooperation and Competition*
In the industrial internet, competition between same-type customers is no longer a zero-sum game but has transformed into a new relationship that is both competitive and cooperative. For example, multiple consumers can form an alliance to access high-value services through quantity advantages, while multiple service providers can collaborate on after-sales services through the platform, achieving a win-win situation. In this case, competition is no longer the focus of attention.

**Implementation Process of Value Co-creation**
Value co-creation activities at the mesoscopic level are similar to natural ecosystems, relying on the organic coordination of producers, consumers, and decomposers to form a cycle.

- Value Producers. The platform provides customers with a basic framework for habitat and interaction, and encourages customers to engage in value co-creation. The center-periphery structure loses its existence foundation in the information age. "Decentralization" stimulates individual autonomy and initiative to mobilize and allocate resources on a broader scale, matching diverse demands with supply, optimizing resource allocation, and enhancing overall efficiency.
- Primary Consumers. Customers' "consumption" behavior occupies a primary position in the material cycle and energy flow of the value co-creation system. They influence the innovation activities of service producers and the way platform enterprises construct and maintain the value ecosystem. Customer needs are the starting point of the value co-creation system. Meeting their needs with higher efficiency, better experience, and lower costs is the foundation for the development of the value ecosystem.
- Secondary Consumers. As secondary consumers, platform enterprises obtain data from customer consumption behavior, which becomes the basis for enhancing the competitiveness of the platform. This link is the most important feature that distinguishes the industrial internet value co-creation system from traditional organizational forms of value creation.

**3.3  Value Co-creation Mechanism Analysis at the Macro Level**

From a macro perspective, the development of the value co-creation system in the industrial internet is the result of continuous material exchange and energy flow among the various entities within the system. The system integrates resources to achieve a series of activities such as propositions, co-creating, acquisition and maintaining of value [9]. As a whole, the system coordinates and integrates resources from all parties under the co-action of internal and external environmental factors (Fig. 3).

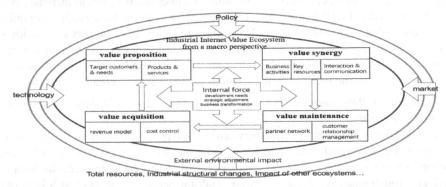

**Fig. 3.** The value stage and internal and external factors of industrial internet from a macro perspective.

- Value Proposition Stage. The value proposition reflects the industrial internet's ability to connect with customer needs. A clear and unique value proposition is the starting point for attracting target customers. The focus of this stage is to accurately position the market, tap into potential customer needs, upgrade and optimize the value of products and services, and maximize customer satisfaction.
- Value Synergy Stage. After proposing value propositions, the industrial internet needs to support the interaction and connectivity of suppliers and customers, reorganize business processes through shared complementary resources, and enhance interaction between customers by leveraging advantages in value integration and added value.
- Value Acquisition Stage. A fair value distribution mechanism is a powerful guarantee for the industrial internet to realize value transmission and acquisition. The value acquisition stage is the process by which members of the industrial internet realize their own value and benefits through collaborative value creation activities.
- Value Maintenance Stage. Value maintenance refers to the process in which members of the industrial internet form close interactive relationships through cooperation, ensuring the efficient and continuous optimization of value creation processes. Partners form mutually trustworthy and long-term stable relationships, which can improve the compatibility of platform interests and obtain sufficient complementary resource advantages.

    To sustainably develop the industrial internet value system, it is necessary to connect all participating entities closely, integrate heterogeneous resources through the platform, and conduct value creation activities around the value proposition. Meanwhile, the platform's development model is dynamically adjusted and optimized based on internal and external environmental conditions to effectively respond to changing business risks.

# 4  Decision of Value Co-creation System in Industrial Internet

## 4.1  Decision and Strategy at the Macro Level

**Purpose and Significance**

As mentioned in Sect. 3.1, platform enterprise, supplier, and demander all have incentives to participate in value co-creation activities. However, due to self-interest considerations, factors such as low cooperation benefits and additional losses may lead to non-cooperative strategies. The purpose of decision-making at the microscopic level is to enable platform enterprises to clarify the key factors that cause conflicts among the parties and evaluate the rationality of the parameters related to value distribution.

**Decision Methods**

There are many methods for evaluating the cooperation value distribution of the platform enterprise, supplier, and demander in microscopic scenarios, such as the contribution-based value distribution method, the risk-sharing based value distribution method and so on. However, those methods are greatly influenced by specific scenarios, and relevant research mainly focuses on the construction of corresponding evaluation indicator systems.

This paper selects an decision method based on evolutionary game theory, by constructing a value co-creation evolutionary game model and solving it to analyze factors that affect the willingness of stakeholders to participate in value co-creation. The advantage of this method is that it considers the trial-and-error, imitation, and learning ability of game subjects with limited rationality under incomplete information conditions, and the relevance between the indicator parameters and the scenarios is relatively weak. This paper refers to previous research results and proposes evolutionary game model parameters and benefit matrices for micro level decision of industrial internet, as shown in Tables 1 and 2.

Evolutionary game theory is often solved by constructing the Jacobian matrix based on the replicator dynamic equation. Based on the analysis of evolutionary game theory, the system dynamics simulation analysis method can be further used to construct a value co-creation evolutionary game SD model for the platform enterprise, supplier, and demand-side, and clarify the influence of different key factors on the stable state of the behavior strategies. The process of evolutionary game solving and dynamic simulation is not the main focus of this paper and will not be discussed in detail.

Through simulation, we obtained the following results:

- Initial willingness to cooperate is an important factor in facilitating cooperation. When any party chooses the "actively participate" strategy with a high initial probability, it can stimulate the participation enthusiasm of the other two parties and lead to the implementation of value co creation activities.
- The impact of key parameters on cooperation can be divided into three categories: an increase in the values of $R_i$, $E_i$, $J_i$, $P_2$, $P_3$, $F_1$, and $F_2$ will lead to an increase in cooperation willingness, while an increase in the values of $C_i$ and $I_i$ will lead to a decrease in cooperation willingness, and the standalone benefit $R_i$ has no effect on cooperation willingness.

**Table 1.** Relevant parameter setting and meaning

| Parameter | Description |
|---|---|
| $R_i$ | Individual income (i = 1 platform side; i = 2 supply side; i = 3 demand side, the same below) |
| $R_i'$ | Co-creation value gains from participating in value co-creation activities |
| $C_i$ | Cost of actively participating in value co-creation activities |
| $E_i$ | Additional gains from one party's passive participation |
| $I_i$ | Speculative gains caused by the active participation of the other two parties |
| $J_i$ | Additional losses caused by passive participation in value co-creation activities |
| $P_2$ | Rewards from platform enterprises to suppliers who actively participate in value co-creation activities |
| $P_3$ | Rewards from platform enterprises to demanders who actively participate in value co-creation activities |
| $F_1$ | Penalties paid by platform enterprises to actively participate in value co-creation activities according to prior contracts |
| $F_2$ | Penalty paid by the supplier to the platform enterprises actively participating in the value co-creation activities according to the prior contract |

**Table 2.** Benefit matrix

| Game strategy selection and gains | | Platform enterprise | |
|---|---|---|---|
| | | actively participate ($z$) | negative participate ($1 - z$) |
| Demander actively participate ($x$) | Supplier actively participate ($y$) | $R_1 + R_1' - C_1 - P_2 - P_3$ | $R_1 + I_1 - F_1 - J_1$ |
| | | $R_2 + R_2' - C_2 + P_2$ | $R_2 - C_2 + E_2 + F_1$ |
| | | $R_3 + R_3' - C_3 + P_3$ | $R_3 - C_3 + E_3$ |
| | Supplier negative participate ($1 - y$) | $R_1 - C_1 + E_1 + F_2 - P_3$ | $R_1 - J_1$ |
| | | $R_2 + I_2 - F_2 - J_2$ | $R_2 - J_2$ |
| | | $R_3 - C_3 + E_3 + P_3$ | $R_3 - C_3$ |
| Demander negative participate ($1 - x$) | Supplier actively participate ($y$) | $R_1 - C_1 + E_1 - P_2$ | $R_1 - J_1 - F_1$ |
| | | $R_2 - C_2 + E_2 + P_2$ | $R_2 - C_2 + F_1$ |
| | | $R_3 + I_3 - J_3$ | $R_3 - J_3$ |
| | Supplier negative participate ($1 - y$) | $R_1 - C_1 + F_2$ | $R_1 - J_1$ |
| | | $R_2 - J_2 - F_2$ | $R_2 - J_2$ |
| | | $R_3 - J_3$ | $R_3 - J_3$ |

Based on these results, we propose the following strategies for the platform enterprise at the microscopic level:

- Find ways to improve the initial cooperation willingness of each party. To achieve this goal, on the one hand, the platform ecological system's basic infrastructure design should be established and improved to create a good platform ecological environment. On the other hand, by improving the platform's data and business empowerment mechanisms, the enthusiasm of both suppliers and consumers participating in value co-creation activities can be enhanced.
- Reduce cooperation costs and increase punishment for speculative behavior. The platform enterprise can reduce cooperation costs and strengthen cooperation involved by improving interactive collaboration and resource sharing mechanisms. They can also strengthen supervision and establish a sound reward and punishment mechanism to guide, constrain, and regulate platform activities to ensure that dishonest participants are punished.

### 4.2 Decision and Strategy at the Meso Level

**Purpose and Significance**

The meso level industrial internet value co-creation system is composed of the platform enterprise and multiple customer populations. However, the development of a single population is not always optimal for the entire industrial internet. The purpose of the meso level decision-making is to identify the state and relationship between different populations as early as possible, guide cooperation among populations, and reduce malignant competition.

**Decision Methods**

There are many methods used to evaluate the evolution and competition trends between different populations in the mesoscopic scene, such as combination algorithms, deep learning methods, social network analysis methods. In this paper, the Logistic-based symbiotic evolution model is selected as the basis for evaluating the evolution trend. Compared with other methods, this modeling approach is relatively simple and consumes less computational resources while still effectively reflecting the influence of different symbiotic relationships on population development.

Although populations may not be distinguished as supplier or provider roles at the meso level, for ease of subsequent analysis and recommendations, we still chose a scenario with role attributes as the research object in the model construction and simulation phase. Based on the Logistic basic model, a symbiotic evolution model was constructed:

$$F(sp_1) = \frac{d(sp_1)}{dt} = p_1 sp_1 \left( 1 - \frac{sp_1}{N_{sp_1}} + r_{sp_1 u_1} \frac{u_1}{N_{u_1}} + r_{sp_{12}} \frac{sp_2}{N_{sp_2}} \right) \tag{1}$$

$$H(sp_2) = \frac{d(sp_2)}{dt} = p_2 sp_2 \left( 1 - \frac{sp_2}{N_{sp_2}} + r_{sp_2 u_1} \frac{u_1}{N_{u_1}} + r_{sp_{21}} \frac{sp_1}{N_{sp_1}} \right) \tag{2}$$

$$G(u_1) = \frac{d(u_1)}{dt} = q_1 u_1 \left( 1 - \frac{u_1}{N_{u_1}} + r_{u_1 sp_1} \frac{sp_1}{N_{sp_1}} + r_{u_1 sp_2} \frac{sp_2}{N_{sp_2}} \right) \tag{3}$$

This scenario includes two supply side populations $sp_1$ and $sp_2$ (with natural growth rates of $p_1$ and $p_2$) and one demand side population $u_1$ (with natural growth rate of $q_1$), N represents the maximum population size under a given situation, r represents the symbiotic coefficient between the two populations. According to different symbiotic coefficient values, we defined 5 symbiotic modes. The purpose of the simulation is to observe the scale and time when the population reaches stability under different initial values and symbiotic modes.

The symbiotic mode is shown in Table 3:

**Table 3.** Symbiosis mode of populations

| Value range | Symbiosis mode | Description |
|---|---|---|
| $r_{sp_i u_j} = 0, r_{u_j sp_i} = 0, r_{sp_{is}} = 0$ | independent development | the symbiosis coefficient is zero, all populations develop independently |
| $r_{sp_i u_j} > 0, r_{u_j sp_i} > 0, r_{sp_{is}} > 0$ | mutual benefit | the symbiosis coefficient between units is greater than zero, and all populations benefit |
| $r_{sp_i u_j} = 0, r_{u_j sp_i} > 0,$ $r_{sp_{is}} > 0$ or $r_{sp_i u_j} > 0,$ $r_{sp_{is}} = 0, r_{u_j sp_i} = 0$ | Partial symbiosis | one population benefit and the other don't be affected |
| $r_{sp_i u_j} < 0, r_{u_j sp_i} > 0$ $r_{sp_{is}} > 0$ or $r_{sp_i u_j} > 0$ $r_{u_j sp_i} < 0, r_{sp_{is}} < 0$ | parasitism | one population benefit and the other unit suffer losses |
| $r_{sp_i u_j} = 0, r_{u_j sp_i} = 0, r_{sp_{is}} = 0$ | competition | populations competes with each other |

Through simulation, we obtained the following results:

- Under the competition mode, when the symbiotic coefficient value is within the range of $[-1, 0)$, the evolution path of each population is basically consistent, and the final stable size is smaller than the maximum size under the independent development mode. When the symbiotic coefficient value is in the $(-1, -\infty)$, at least one population exhibits a gradually increasing trend and eventually reaches the maximum size; at least one population's evolution is greatly suppressed and eventually eliminated.
- Under the parasitism mode, the larger the absolute value of the symbiotic coefficient, the larger the final stable value of the parasitic population.
- Under the partial symbiosis mode, the evolution path of populations is basically consistent, but the stable values they reach are different. The larger the symbiotic coefficient, the faster the symbiosis evolution.
- Under the mutual benefit mode, the larger the symbiotic coefficient, the larger the stable equilibrium point of the final size, and the total size of all populations added together is the largest.

Based on the simulation results, we propose the following strategies for the platform enterprise at the mesoscopic level:

- Maintain reciprocal relationships between different populations. For example, the centralized procurement model, which has been applied to many supply chain systems, have achieved mutual benefit among populations that were originally in a competitive relationship.
- Avoid the occurrence of malignant competition within the system. Platform providers can reduce malignant competition among populations through incentive and guidance measures, such as rewards and preferential policies, or avoid this issue by building sub platforms and population migration.

### 4.3 Decision-Making at the Macro Level

The object of decision-making on the macro level is the entire ecosystem. The purpose is to identify the internal and external influencing factors of the system, including external policies, technologies, markets, competition, and internal factors such as platform investment, strategy, architecture and functions. Traditional methods such as SWOT, PEST, and the Five Forces model are also applicable to analyzing the industrial internet. If the static analysis method cannot meet the requirements, system dynamics can be considered for analysis.

## 5  Conclusion

This paper combines ecological theory with value co creation theory and proposes a multi-level value co-creation system architecture. The constituent elements of the industrial internet are described at three levels: micro, meso, and macro. Methodologies for decision-making at each level are proposed. This study provides a reference for platform enterprises to make decisions for industrial enterprises and for further research in this field.

Future research ideas:

- At the micro level, using fuzzy numbers to approximate the expected benefits and considering the impact of risks and reputation on game outcomes can make the evolutionary game scenario more realistic.
- At the meso level, combining deep learning methods or combination algorithms to predict population behavior can make decision-making for platform enterprises more targeted.

**Acknowledgement.** This work was supported by National Key R&D Program of China under Grant No. 2021YFF0901200.

# References

1. Pinho, N., Beirão, G., Patrício, L., Figueiredo, J., Nóbrega, L.: Understanding value co-creation in complex services with many actors. J. Serv. Manag. **25**, 470–493 (2014)
2. Vargo, S.L., Lusch, R.F.: Evolving to a new dominant logic for marketing. J. Mark. **68**, 1–17 (2004)
3. Vargo, S.L., Lusch, R.F.: It's all B2B… and beyond: toward a systems perspective of the market. Ind. Mark. Manag. **40**, 181–187 (2011)
4. Vargo, S.L., Lusch, R.F.: From repeat patronage to value co-creation in service ecosystems: a transcending conceptualization of relationship. J. Bus. Mark. Manag. **4**, 169–179 (2010)
5. Lusch, R.F., Vargo, S.L.: Service-Dominant Logic: Premises, Perspectives, Possibilities. Cambridge University Press, New York (2014)
6. Prahalad, C.K., Ramaswamy, V.: Co-opting customer competence. Harv. Bus. Rev. **78**, 79–90 (2000)
7. Linghu, K.R., Jian, Z.Q., Li, L.: Service ecosystem: origin, core concept and theoretical framework. Res. Dev. Manag. **30**, 147–158 (2018)
8. Frow, P., McColl-Kennedy, J.R., Hilton, T., et al.: Value propositions - a service ecosystem perspective. Mark. Theory **14**, 327–351 (2014)
9. Bocken, N.M.P., Short, S.W., Rana, P., Evans, S.: A literature and practice review to develop sustainable business model archetypes. J. Clean. Prod. **65**, 42–56 (2014)

# Cooperative Development of a Technical, Entrepreneurial Mindset in Manufacturing

Rene Bennyson[1]([⊠]) [iD], Lasse Christiansen[1,2] [iD], and Esben S. Laursen[1] [iD]

[1] University College of Northern Denmark, 9200 Aalborg, SV, Denmark
{reb,lch,esl}@ucn.dk
[2] Aalborg University, 9220 Aalborg E, Denmark

**Abstract.** This study focuses on the importance of developing technical and entrepreneurial capabilities to support the digital transformations in manufacturing, known as Industry 4.0 and Industry 5.0. Digital transformation creates new business opportunities through product and service development that demand new skills and capabilities from the workforce, such as analytical ability, problem-solving, ideation and innovation. However, these skills are not usually found in the manufacturing operators but are more closely associated with entrepreneurs.

The study proposes a cooperative learning approach to address this challenge that combines domain-specific technical skills (such as monitoring manufacturing data, programming, data analysis, and automation) with entrepreneurial skills. The approach aims to upgrade digital and entrepreneurial skills by co-designing learning programmes with industry stakeholders. Insights gained can be used to develop workforce capabilities and promote digital transformation.

The proposed concept involves collaboration between stakeholders in digitised manufacturing to build workforce capabilities. The goal is to generate a shared understanding of skill-building and learning programmes and to create a new foundation for decision-making.

This study highlights the need to combine core technical and contextual entrepreneurial skills to support industrial digitalisation and prepare the manufacturing workforce for new challenges. By adopting a cooperative learning approach, stakeholders can develop learning activities that enhance the workforce's digital capabilities, creating a more agile and responsive manufacturing industry.

**Keywords:** Further education · Entrepreneurship · Educational Co-design

## 1 Introduction

Entrepreneurial and innovation competencies are vital for industrial digitalisation [2]. The digital transformation of manufacturing has been labelled Industry

© The Author(s), under exclusive license to Springer Nature Switzerland AG 2023
Y. Luo (Ed.): CDVE 2023, LNCS 14166, pp. 123–134, 2023.
https://doi.org/10.1007/978-3-031-43815-8_12

4.0, which has a very technology-focused approach [19]. However, the source of the innovational power to change the manufacturing systems needs to be clarified. The new Industry 5.0 perspective relies on the same technologies, but is more focused on the workforce and how they aid the transition through manufactural innovation, [22]. However, traditional manufacturing education does not include these competencies [2].

One way to approach industry competency gaps is to include stakeholders at the front end of the educational development process in a two-pronged approach [5]. The critical competency gaps can then be identified and assessed in collaboration with industrial stakeholders [15] and capabilities to meet these demands identified with educational stakeholders [13]. While this process has been used to investigate technical competencies in higher education and technical upskilling, similar work is still needed for innovation competencies.

Stakeholder involvement in educational development can be achieved in many ways and at many levels. Involvement can be purely passive, where existing research and information are analysed, but it can also be more active [18]. Interviews with industry stakeholders and internal mapping at educational institutions can also be a viable approach, and so can adopting a co-design process among all relevant stakeholders [7]. A co-design process ensures that the skills are authentic and relevant.

This study lays a conceptual foundation for how co-design can improve entrepreneurial education as innovation competency moves from a contextual skill to a central core skill for technical professionals. As core skills, these competencies should be an output of education, compared to the more catalytic nature of the contextual competencies that can aid the other skills in both education and work-life. Hence, this study explores how a co-design approach in education could introduce entrepreneurial skills to support industrial digital transformation.

This study is based on the EU-supported EIT HEI Initiative, HEI4Future: Innovation Capacity Building for Higher Education. The main goal of the EIT HEI Initiative is to promote innovation and entrepreneurship in Europe. HEI4Future aims to develop innovation programmes with multi-disciplinary approaches.

## 2    Education for Entrepreneurship and Innovational Competencies

Research on entrepreneurship education has been conducted since the 19901990ss, primarily focused on starting companies after ending education [1]. These business-specific studies have been published in a limited number of journals targeting small and medium-sized enterprises and, to a lesser extent, education, resulting in a knowledge gap regarding education and its contribution to entrepreneurial success [1]. Didactical models can remain undeveloped, as can be seen, for example, in the learning factory concept [6].

There has been a shift in entrepreneurial education from teacher-guided instructional models to a more constructivist approach [8]. This shift shows that didactics have followed the general trend of turning to more open-ended and problem-based learning approaches. However, the field diverges between a narrow understanding of entrepreneurship, focused on startups, to a broader understanding [8].

Nabi et al. identified the following impact indicators for evaluating entrepreneurial education: attitude, skills and knowledge, perceived feasibility, and entrepreneurial intention [14]. Evaluation of upskilling has shown that attitude results are typically obtained more quickly and at a lower level than long-term measurements stemming from education [11]. 'Industrial process innovation led by educated employees can be hard to monitor especially for entrepreneurial education outside the startup domain [14].

Furthermore, macro, meso and micro level contexts are vital in entrepreneurship education [21] and are important for successful learning. At the micro level, stakeholder involvement across different levels is seen as important [21]; however, the span of control educators have over context elements is limited, and their insights can be outdated or non-existent. Hence, entrepreneurship education needs more industry stakeholder involvement.

## 3   Industry Impact

According to Jeanne Ross [17], successful digital transformation in a manufacturing company has the following benefits:

- Operational efficiency, enabling the company to optimise and streamline its internal processes.
- Data-driven decision-making, leveraging data analytics to make more informed and effective business decisions.
- Improved customer experience, where digital capabilities enable manufacturers to understand customer needs and preferences better and respond to them faster and more effectively.
- New business models, where digital transformation opens new revenue streams, as developing product-as-a-service models, or creating digital platforms.
- Enhanced innovation through digital capabilities, where manufacturers can accelerate innovation and develop new products and services faster.

Digital transformation enables manufacturers to transition to Industry 5.0, stay competitive in the marketplace, improve operations, and provide better customer service [17].

However, for digital transformation to succeed and for companies to benefit from the advantages that digital transformation brings, companies must become digital and digitised [16]. Digitising a company's operational activities leads to operational excellence, enabling the company to launch new products and improve service delivery, leading to the introduction of new business models and value creation [16].

While technical competency is necessary for operating digital technologies in industrial manufacturing, different competencies, such as entrepreneurship, are needed for digital transformation [10,17]. Although contextual to Industry 4.0 core technical skills, the skillset required to enable digital transformation goes beyond the traditional competencies of manufacturing operators. Entrepreneurial skills, such as identifying opportunities, assessing resources required, and taking action, are necessary to take advantage of the opportunities that Industry 4.0 presents [3]. These skills are considered contextual to technical manufacturing [12] and are usually found in management, who have research and development as their core competencies. It is well known that seeing new opportunities in manufacturing does not only come from the company's management level, as shown in Fig. 1. It can also come from the digital manufacturing operators. Having these operator competencies enhances digital transformation [17].

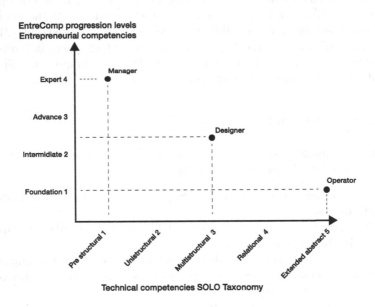

**Fig. 1.** Conceptual model showing the core skills of different professionals

Digital skills are no longer the only competencies driving digital transformation. From a digital perspective, new skills are necessary to support new value-creation opportunities. Entrepreneurship and innovation skills can help the workforce to cope with the new challenges they meet and foster new opportunities in their specific manufacturing setup.

The European Commission has developed a framework for entrepreneurial competencies, where different areas are identified to meet these challenges and generate new opportunities. The outcome of the identification of the skills within entrepreneurial competencies is *Ideas and opportunities*, *Resources* and *Into action*, further unpacked in Table 1. The EntreComp framework comprises 15 competencies in three areas [3] relevant to digital transformation. When a workforce possesses these competencies, they can identify and react to new opportunities that digitalisation offers [17]. This study suggests a conceptual model incorporating these entrepreneurial competencies into the core technical skills needed for industrial digital transformation.

**Table 1.** EntreComp competencies divided by area

| Ideas and opportunities | Resources | Into action |
| --- | --- | --- |
| Spotting opportunities, Creativity, Vision, Valuing ideas, Ethical and sustainable thinking | Self-awareness and self-efficacy, motivation and perseverance, mobilising resources, financial and economic literacy, and mobilising others | Taking the initiative, planning and management, coping with uncertainty, ambiguity and risk, working with others, and learning through experience |

As these competencies are considered contextual to digital transformation in a manufacturing company, transitioning from contextual to core skills seems necessary to ensure that skills are available when opportunities occur. This means people are moving their competence's positioning to become more entrepreneurial than their starting point, as shown in Fig. 2.

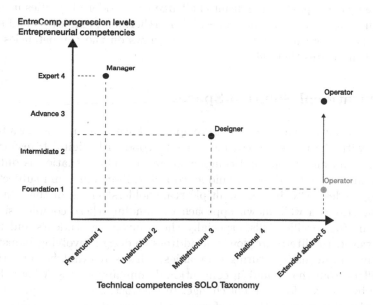

**Fig. 2.** Conceptual model showing where different professionals have their core skills with the new position of the operator.

There are several perspectives on the digital transformation of a company [9]. Employers and employees involved in digital transformation see and understand transformation and its benefits differently and, therefore, have different motivations for contributing to digital transformation [9]. Companies pursuing digital transformation achieve better collaboration among employees to enhance productivity, improved products and services to increase customer acquisition and satisfaction, the leveraging of digital technologies to minimise costs, streamlined business processes to improve operational efficiency, competitive advantages, and the ability to remain relevant and sustainable in the face of rapid technological advances [9]. From the employees' perspective, they would like to work with digital tools customised to their specific tasks, experience, and working styles, enabling them to work more effectively and efficiently [9]. There can be significant differences among organisations regarding digital transformation initiatives. While some organisations have developed a comprehensive strategy and a clear understanding of the benefits of digital transformation, others are still in the early stages of planning and need a clearer sense of their goals for digital transformation [9].

The different stages of digital transformation are complex and must be considered when setting goals and strategy for successful digital transformation. Identifying the skill set for digital transformation in specific situations is also challenging. In some cases, the workforce has the skills needed to see new opportunities. In contrast, other companies require new skills to mobilise resources to take action depending on where they are in the maturity stage of the digital transformation.

This situation reveals a new aspect of the challenge of succeeding with digital transformation. The complex and varied motivations and perspectives of employees and employers pose a significant challenge to consider all parties involved in digitalising manufacturing companies, [4]. Furthermore, employees and employers may need more insight into each other views on the competencies needed and what motivates them [4].

## 4    Educational Solution Space

There are various perspectives on developing educational programmes to equip students with the necessary competencies to cope with digital transformation, resulting in an ambiguous and complex situation. This situation is difficult to handle and can be described as unique, complex, ill-defined, and subjective [4].

Using co-design to include multiple stakeholders' views in the educational design process is a well-known approach to handling these complex situations on training for specific skills, especially those involving students and teachers [20]. However, the literature does not address co-design involving industry representatives from manufacturing companies. This is relevant because the situation differs from that found in conventional company setups, where the skills required by the workforce do not change. In contrast, the skills required for digital transformation mean the workforce needs a digital context-based skillset to advance in digital transformation. The aim is to generate a new foundation for decision-making in workforce skill-building and form new learning programmes.

The co-design model is derived from industrial collaborative educational design (ICoED) methodology [4, 15]. The ICoED model has eight dimensions, divided into an 8-step co-design process facilitating dialogues and reflections among the stakeholders to reveal each stakeholder's perception and generate a shared understanding. Moreover, a new solution to the problem of educational design is suggested in the discussion. The results show that the approach is also good for transforming tacit knowledge into suggestions for solutions. The ICoED methodology is based on co-design methodology used in design practice. The approach is considered effective for handling complex, ambiguous situations, such as that found in industrial digital transformation.

The co-design approach in the HEI4Future project is derived from ICoED methodology, where skills represented in the new co-design approach are technical skills traditionally found in Industry 4.0, such as manufacturing data monitoring, PLC programming, analysis of manufacturing data, and automation. The technical skills are combined with the entrepreneurial skillset to develop learning activities that will empower the workforce to seize opportunities and excel in industrial digitalisation. This combination fosters the development of competence from a conventional technical skillset to also include entrepreneurial skills. The HEI4Future Initiative has incorporated EntreComp skills as representing entrepreneurial competencies and, therefore, has a narrow scope in contrast to ICoED. The co-design process forces stakeholders to embrace the full potential of the entrepreneurial mindset, by combining core technical skills with contextual EntreComp skills to enable a more accurate alignment with the industry's challenges in digital transformation. Combining technical digital manufacturing skills with an entrepreneurial contextual mindset creates a framework for a shared understanding of the workforce's capability building in industrial digitalisation. Furthermore, each skill is considered at a training output level according to the EntreComp Progression Model [3], Fig. 3, to meet the industry requirements. Understanding the level of training and the core skill combination positively impacts the learning outcome.

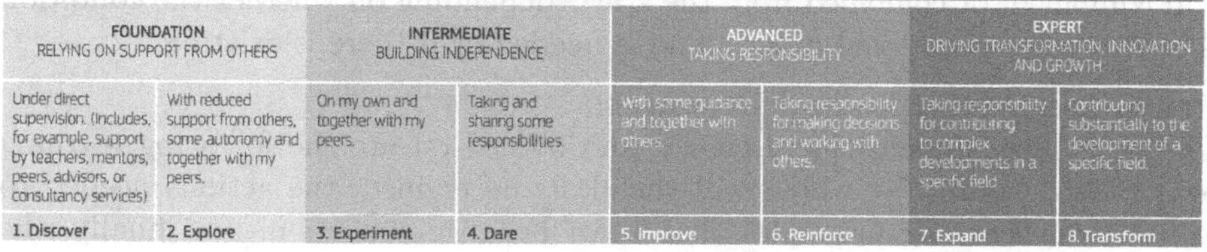

| EntreComp progression model | | | | | | | |
|---|---|---|---|---|---|---|---|
| **FOUNDATION** RELYING ON SUPPORT FROM OTHERS | | **INTERMEDIATE** BUILDING INDEPENDENCE | | **ADVANCED** TAKING RESPONSIBILITY | | **EXPERT** DRIVING TRANSFORMATION, INNOVATION AND GROWTH | |
| Under direct supervision. (Includes, for example, support by teachers, mentors, peers, advisors, or consultancy services) | With reduced support from others, some autonomy and together with my peers. | On my own and together with my peers. | Taking and sharing some responsibilities. | With some guidance and together with others. | Taking responsibility for making decisions and working with others. | Taking responsibility for contributing to complex developments in a specific field. | Contributing substantially to the development of a specific field. |
| 1. Discover | 2. Explore | 3. Experiment | 4. Dare | 5. Improve | 6. Reinforce | 7. Expand | 8. Transform |

**Fig. 3.** EntreComp progression model.

The core principle of co-design methodology is that it is a dialogue-based process, where all relevant aspects of educational design are discussed and agreed upon while working towards the final programme. Participants in the co-design method are representatives of the stakeholders relevant to industrial digitalisation, and those training the skills. In this study, three roles have been identified, namely, employee, employer and educator. Other roles may exist in specific industries, and, in those cases, involving them in the co-design process should be considered. The HEI4Future co-design process has seven dimensions of dialogues and discussions based on different topics that each participant of the co-design find relevant for the programme. The programme develops progressively as participants agree on relevant topics. Each participant reveals their understanding and motivation for industrial digitalisation as a base for their decisions. This generates shared agreements upon which the lecturers can develop specific educational courses.

The seven topic dimensions in the discussion and the decisions the participants have to make are illustrated in Figs. 4, 5, 6 and 7:

## Conditions
The prerequisites for understanding are industry, company and workforce specific. Moreover, conditions regard the educational institutions, students and accreditation.

**Fig. 4.** Topics of discussion are represented as cards in the HEI4Future co-design board.

## Contextual Skills Entrecomp & Core Technical Skills
The different skills are discussed with regard to the company or industry's specific situation and each stakeholder's (employer, employee or educator) view on the skills and level needed. These two dimensions are either discussed separately and combined, or combined from the start, depending on whether the condition is that a new educational programme is needed or if there is existing.

## Principles, Activities and Resources
The next three dimensions discussed and agreed on are the following learning principles: how and by whom will the skills be trained, the actions needed to execute the learning principles that have been agreed upon, and finally, the resources required to execute the activities aligned with the learning principles.

## Consolidation
The final dimension of the co-design process is consolidation, where all the decisions made about skills, learning principles, and activities are structured to ensure the best possible outcome of cooperative learning.

# 5  Discussion and Conclusion

The manufacturing industry is being transformed through digitalisation, which has the potential to improve operational efficiency, enable data-driven decision-making, improve customer experience, open up new business models, and enhance innovation. The emergence of Industry 5.0, which encompasses these trends, underlines the need for additional competencies beyond those found in Industry 4.0. These competencies, which include innovation and entrepreneurship, must be precisely defined to implement Industry 5.0 effectively. Co-design with relevant stakeholders is proposed to narrow the focus and identify critical competencies needed for Industry 5.0. However, companies must be digitised and digital to benefit from these advantages. Technical competencies are essential in digital transformation, but contextual competencies are also necessary for success. These competencies are usually found in management, with research and development as their core competencies. However, innovation in manufacturing can also come from digital manufacturing operators. Entrepreneurship and innovation skills are necessary to support new value-creation arising from digitalisation. The European Commission has identified 15 entrepreneurial competencies relevant to digital transformation, including ideas and opportunities, resources, and action. Possessing these competencies allows individuals to identify and capitalise on the new opportunities that digital transformation presents. Training in these competencies can help the workforce address new challenges and foster new opportunities.

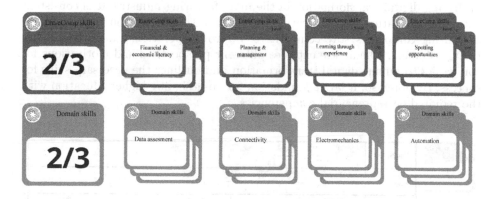

**Fig. 5.** EntreComp skills and core technical skills

This study examines the impact of digital transformation on the manufacturing industry through a multi-faceted analysis of the subject. In particular, it focuses on several benefits of digital transformation, including operational efficiency, data-driven decision-making, improved customer experience, new business models, and enhanced innovation.

In conclusion, this study provides a comprehensive analysis of the impact of digital transformation on the manufacturing industry. It contributes to the

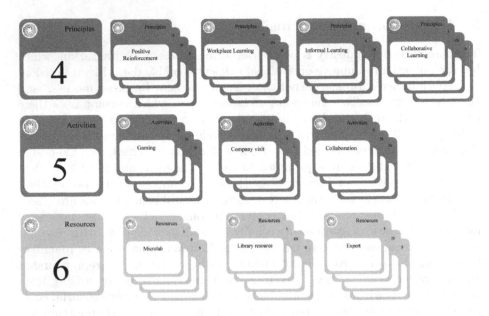

**Fig. 6.** Topics related to learning principles, course activities and resources.

existing literature by stressing the importance of becoming digital and digitised. Furthermore, it underscores the significance of contextual competencies in driving digital transformation in the manufacturing industry. It is consistent with prior literature, demonstrating that digital transformation can help manufacturing companies stay competitive, improve operations, and better serve their customers. The article explores different perspectives and motivations for companies to pursue digital transformation and outlines the necessary skills for success. By doing so, it lays a foundation for co-designing higher education with the required entrepreneurial competencies.

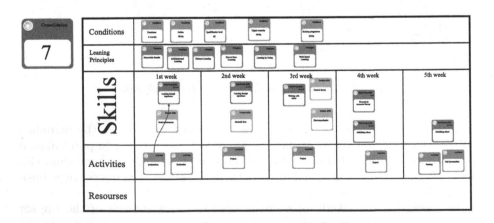

**Fig. 7.** The final board, where all the selected topics/cards are organised.

# References

1. Aparicio, G., Iturralde, T., Maseda, A.: Conceptual structure and perspectives on entrepreneurship education research: a bibliometric review. Eur. Res. Manag. Bus. Econ. **25**(3), 105–113 (2019)
2. Aslam, F., Aimin, W., Li, M., Ur Rehman, K.: Innovation in the era of IoT and industry 5.0: absolute innovation management (aim) framework. Information **11**(2), 124 (2020)
3. Bacigalupo, M., Kampylis, P., Punie, Y., den Brande, G.V.: Entrecomp: the entrepreneurship competence framework (2016)
4. Bennyson, R., Laursen, E.S.: Participatory design for worker training in an industrial context. In: Luo, Y. (eds.) Cooperative Design, Visualization, and Engineering. CDVE 2022. LNCS, vol. 13492, pp. 187–196. Springer, Cham (2022). https://doi.org/10.1007/978-3-031-16538-2_19
5. Christiansen, L., et al.: A framework for developing educational industry 4.0 activities and study materials. Educ. Sci. **12**(10), 659 (2022)
6. Enke, J., Glass, R., Metternich, J.: Introducing a maturity model for learning factories. Procedia Manuf. **9**, 1–8 (2017)
7. Geraldes, C.A., et al.: Co-design process for upskilling the workforce in the factories of the future. In: IECON 2021–47th Annual Conference of the IEEE Industrial Electronics Society, pp. 1–6. IEEE (2021)
8. Hägg, G., Gabrielsson, J.: A systematic literature review of the evolution of pedagogy in entrepreneurial education research. Int. J. Entrepreneurial Behav. Res. **26**(5), 829–861 (2020)
9. Hamburg, I.: Implementation of a digital workplace strategy to drive behavior change and improve competencies. Strategy Behav. Digital Econ. **2**(1), 19–32 (2019)
10. Hansen, A.K., Lassen, A.H., Larsen, M.S.S., Sorensen, D.G.H.: Competence considerations for industry 4.0 and future trends. In: The Future of Smart Production for SMEs: A Methodological and Practical Approach Towards Digitalization in SMEs, pp. 379–389. Springer, Cham (2022). https://doi.org/10.1007/978-3-031-15428-7_35
11. Kaufman, R., Keller, J.M.: Levels of evaluation: beyond kirkpatrick. Hum. Resour. Dev. Q. **5**(4), 371–80 (1994)
12. van Laar, E., van Deursen, A.J., van Dijk, J.A., de Haan, J.: The relation between 21st-century skills and digital skills: a systematic literature review. Comput. Hum. Behav. **72**, 577–588 (2017). https://doi.org/10.1016/j.chb.2017.03.010
13. Mahmood, K., et al.: Analysis of industry 4.0 capabilities: a perspective of educational institutions and needs of industry. In: Andersen, A.-L., Andersen, R., Brunoe, T.D., Larsen, M.S.S., Nielsen, K., Napoleone, A., Kjeldgaard, S. (eds.) CARV/MCPC -2021. LNME, pp. 887–894. Springer, Cham (2022). https://doi.org/10.1007/978-3-030-90700-6_101
14. Nabi, G., Liñán, F., Fayolle, A., Krueger, N., Walmsley, A.: The impact of entrepreneurship education in higher education: a systematic review and research agenda. Acad. Manage. Learn. Educ. **16**(2), 277–299 (2017)
15. Pors, A.L.K., et al.: Co-design of technical upskilling training program through early stakeholder involvement. In: CDVE 2022. LNCS, pp. 175–186. Springer, Cham (2022). https://doi.org/10.1007/978-3-031-16538-2_18
16. Ross, J.: Don't Confuse Digital with Digitization, pp. 1–197. The MIT Press (2019). https://lccn.loc.gov/2018034414

17. Ross, J.W., Beath, C.M., Mocker, M.: Designed for Digital. MIT Press (2019)
18. Sam, C., Dahles, H.: Stakeholder involvement in the higher education sector in cambodia. Stud. High. Educ. **42**(9), 1764–1784 (2017)
19. Schou, C., Colli, M., Berger, U., Lassen, A.H., Madsen, O., Møller, C., Wæhrens, B.V.: Deconstructing industry 4.0: defining the smart factory. In: Andersen, A.-L., et al. (eds.) CARV/MCPC -2021. LNME, pp. 356–363. Springer, Cham (2022). https://doi.org/10.1007/978-3-030-90700-6_40
20. Shrivastava, S., Bardoel, E.A., Djurkovic, N., Rajendran, D., Plueckhahn, T.: Co-creating curricula with industry partners: a case study. Int. J. Manage. Educ. **20**, August 2022. https://doi.org/10.1016/j.ijme.2022.100646
21. Thomassen, M.L., Williams Middleton, K., Ramsgaard, M.B., Neergaard, H., Warren, L.: Conceptualizing context in entrepreneurship education: a literature review. Int. J. Entrepreneurial Behav. Res. **26**(5), 863–886 (2020)
22. Xu, X., Lu, Y., Vogel-Heuser, B., Wang, L.: Industry 4.0 and industry 5.0-inception, conception and perception. J. Manuf. Syst. **61**, 530–535 (2021)

# A Comparative Study on Manipulator Development in Multi-robotic Systems

Özlem Çavuş[1](✉) , İnanç Şencan[1] , and Ozan Balcı[2]

[1] Architectural Design Computing Graduate Program,
Istanbul Technical University, Istanbul, Türkiye
{cavus19,sencani}@itu.edu.tr
[2] Research[x]Design, Department of Architecture, Katholieke Universiteit Leuven,
Leuven, Belgium
ozan.balci@kuleuven.be

**Abstract.** Robotic assembly of modular blocks has a great interest in multi-robotic studies in many disciplines. The existing studies primarily focus on context-specific tasks, especially in the self-assembly of robots, from an engineering perspective. However, considering a modular composition's entire design and fabrication process regarding mereological relationships is significant for the module's reuse in different pattern formations by mobile multi-robots. This study defines mobile robot swarms' adaptability to the assembly-disassembly-reassembly (ADR) process to any-time change of the 3D pattern being assembled. Hence, the robot's manipulator needs to be compatible with picking up, carrying, attaching, and detaching the modules in the ADR process. This study questions the effects of the ADR process on manipulator development in multi-robotic systems. It aims to customize and develop manipulator systems beyond the existing gripper for multi-robot systems. Accordingly, it introduces a new conceptual understanding of manipulators' taxonomy as friction-based and active and passive magnetic field-based end-effectors for the ADR process. Active indicates the use of electromagnets, whereas passive refers to using metal parts in the manipulator's body. A physical experiment is conducted based on the above-stated taxonomies whose manipulators are printed in the Creality Ender3 and mounted to a mobile robot with a differential drive. The process is observed to discuss the introduced magnetic end-effectors, the system's adaptability needs, and the pros and cons compared to the conventional gripper.

**Keywords:** Robotic Assembly · Disassembly · Swarm Robotics · Multi-robotic Systems · 3D Printing · Manipulator

## 1 Introduction

The deployment of mobile robot swarms in increasingly complex environments through an increased complexity in design requires the development of new algorithms and enhanced design tools [1]. Developing new tools in assembly with swarm robotic systems by designers requires understanding how the process works, how tools interact with the design object, the existing literacy, and its pros and cons. Within the swarm robotic systems, its manipulator is one of the most critical parts in articulating objects for assembly. A manipulator that can adapt to given functions is essential to accomplish different tasks during the entire (dis)assembly process.

This study defines mobile robots' adaptability to the assembly-disassembly-reassembly (ADR) process to any-time change of the 3D pattern being assembled. This holistic process is considered over tasks in object articulation. Hence, the robot's manipulator must be compatible with picking up, carrying, attaching, and detaching the modules in the ADR process. This study questions the effects of the ADR process on manipulator development in swarm robotic systems.

A gripper is a standard manipulator for grasping and manipulating objects in (dis)assembly. It allows mobile robots to pick up, hold, and release objects precisely, enabling them to perform tasks such as picking and placing objects, assembling parts, and manipulating tools or equipment. However, mobile swarm robots often operate in dynamic and unstructured environments, where objects may be moving, cluttered, or in challenging positions. Grippers need to handle such dynamic environments and adapt to changing conditions, which can be challenging due to uncertainties and complexities in the environment. In addition, many tasks require precise manipulation, such as picking up small or delicate objects, rotating objects, or performing intricate tasks. Designing grippers with sufficient dexterity and flexibility to handle such tasks can be challenging, especially in constrained spaces or with limited weight and size requirements. Also, grippers must be controlled in real-time to achieve precise and reliable grasping. However, controlling grippers in real-time can be challenging due to factors such as communication delays, computation limitations, and synchronization with other robotic components, which may impact the performance of the gripper. Therefore, the development of new manipulator systems is important for designers to allow design realization and flexibility.

This study aims to develop manipulator systems beyond the existing gripper. Accordingly, it first examines related background studies to stress its unique aspects. Then, research methodology and materials are presented to identify a case study based on physical experiments. The results and conclusion depict this study's contribution, limitations, and potential future research.

## 2    Background

A typical manipulator is a conventional gripper, and a gripper of a mobile robot is used for manipulation and pick and place tasks. The gripper design is an active research topic within robotics and production. For example, Bhatt and Chauhan [2] address the design of an impactive two-fingered gripper for a wheeled mobile robot that can be utilized in industry. With the increasing use of robotic arms in industry, grasping and picking, as a part of industrial processes, are of great importance. In the article [3], a robotic gripper with the ability to cylindrical object grasping is designed and fabricated. According to [3], a robotic gripper's ability to satisfy the form-gripping is a significant aspect to satisfy the efficient performance of robotic arms.

Gripper design in literature is extended using magnetic parts. Regarding this issue, Mao et al. [4] propose a design concept and 3D model of a magnetic gripper with two arms consisting of magnets that keep the gripper closing and open when there is an external magnetic field. According to Garcia and Mehrubeoglu [5], switchable magnets are more energy efficient than an electromagnet in mobile robotic applications because electromagnets require a constant state of power consumption, whereas switchable magnets only require power to change their state on or off. Loianno et al. [6] argue that the end effector is the core of the gripper, and an electromagnet creates strong magnetic contact with the ferrous object.

Achieving the desired global behavior in the assembly process is crucial, and this can be accomplished using various fastening systems, such as nuts and bolts, shear clips, or cable ties [7]. The approach employed in this context involves utilizing uncomplicated, passive magnetic connections to simplify the robot's end effector and facilitate the swift development of assembly strategies.

In developing manipulators, different techniques are adopted from distinct fields. While many computational techniques are adopted from other disciplines, approaches such as optimization cannot necessarily be directly ported into the open-ended design processes of architecture and form-making [8]. In architecture, we must question what data are collected, how we use it, and to what ends we are undertaking these investigations.

In contrast to the above-stated studies, this study focuses on the ADR process. It considers both the assembly and disassembly of modular compositions and the lifecycle of the assembly modules. It considers adaptability to the given tasks in developing manipulators. As a result, this study differs from the existing literature in terms of its context, focus field, gripper taxonomy, and depicted process.

## 3 Methodology

The gripper is one of the most used manipulators, manipulating objects based on friction. Apart from friction, one of the common manipulating principles is using magnetic fields. Hence, this study introduces a new conceptual understanding of manipulators' taxonomy as friction-based and active and passive magnetic field-based end-effectors for the ADR process (Fig. 1). Active indicates the use of electromagnets, whereas passive refers to the use of metal parts in the manipulator's body.

This study focuses on three basic tasks: pick, carry, and place the object. Table 1 lists these tasks together with their sub-categories. Accordingly, a stand-alone module indicates a module that is not in any structure and is scattered on the ground as a single module. On the other hand, a module within a 3D composition refers to a module attached to other modules and located within a 3D structure. Both picking and placing tasks are performed according to these two categories. In addition, robots carry the modules on the horizontal flat ground.

**Table 1.** The tasks for the case studies.

| Pick | Carry | Place |
|---|---|---|
| a stand-alone module | on the flat ground | a stand-alone module |
| a module within a 3D composition | | a module within a composition |

A physical experiment is conducted based on the above-stated taxonomies. Manipulators are printed in the Creality Ender 3 and mounted to mobile robot swarms with a differential drive. The physical experiment with mobile swarm robots depends on case studies. These case studies are performed to show design procedures in a customized manipulator's design and implementation concerning processes and tasks. In these case studies, experiments are conducted with differential drive mobile robots, magnetic modules printed in Creality Ender 3, and Arduino software.

The process is observed to compare the conventional gripper with the introduced magnetic end-effectors in terms of the system's adaptability needs, pros, and cons. It is design research as a systematic inquiry. Its purpose is knowledge of, or in, the embodiment of configuration, composition, structure, purpose, value, and meaning in the systems. It is also observational research to see how agents behave in a natural setting and how physical factors influence their behavior. In light of the physical experiments, the results discuss whether there is a countable and observable correlation among the cases.

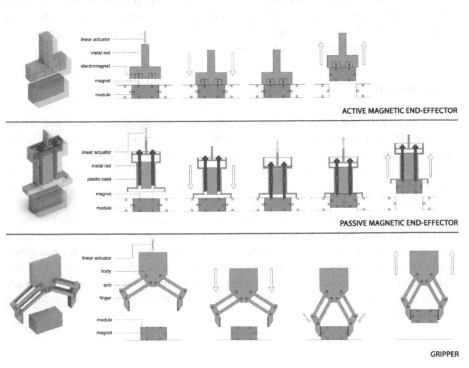

**Fig. 1.** Manipulators' diagram developed by the authors.

The case study comprises two physical experiments. The first experiment is a scenario in which manipulators are integrated into robots, and it tests manipulators on individual robots, while the second is a test on swarm robots. The first focuses on manipulators' basic movement, whereas the second concentrates on interaction within an environment. The case study explains the algorithms and tools (software and hardware) used in the experiments and the differences between the two experiments. Then, results are discussed and evaluated regarding limitations and their associated reasons.

## 3.1 Experiment Setup

Three types of manipulators (gripper, electromagnetic manipulator, passive manipulator) are mounted on three robots named RIZOBot to test their function (Fig. 3). RIZOBots are differential-drive mobile robots used to perform different swarm studies. These robots detect modules (Fig. 2) with infrared sensors located in front of them at the height of 10 mm from the ground and activate the manipulators in this sensing light.

The used gripper (Fig. 3a) is a generic conventional gripper with a 12 cm finger span and is controlled by a servo motor adapted from BCN3D-Moveo open-source robot arm project [9]. Sponge layers have been added to the gripper's fingers to increase the gripper's impact surface with modules and facilitate grip.

The created electromagnetic manipulator (Fig. 3c) is a manipulator with 12V electromagnets with a lifting power of 2.5 kg. It is placed on the robot to coincide with the magnets within the modules. When the manipulator is required to interact with the modules, the electromagnets are energized to activate. When the module needs to be detached, the power is cut off, and the module is separated from the manipulator.

The third and last manipulator, the passive manipulator (Fig. 3b), uses the magnetic attraction force just like the electromagnetic manipulator. However, it performs not by creating an extra magnetic field but by using the magnets already on the modules' surfaces. There is a metal plate 10 mm inside the contact surface of the manipulator with the module. Besides, a linear activator is controlled by the servo motor to which this plate is attached. When the manipulator is required to interact with the module, the linear activator lowers the metal plate by 12 mm, and this plate interacts with the module via sticking, lifting, etc. When the module is desired to be separated from the manipulator, the metal plate is pulled 12 mm up from the contact surface with the same linear activator, thus leaving the magnets in the module out of the affected area and ending the manipulator-module interaction. The linear activator design used in the manipulator is an adapted version of the project developed by [10] and shared as open source.

Of these three manipulators, the gripper and passive manipulator are raised with an L-type arm driven by a servo motor with an average torque of 10 kg-cm. On the other hand, the electromagnetic manipulator is lowered and lifted at a shorter distance than other manipulators, with a rope system driven by the same type of servo motor instead of an L-type arm due to its weight. The gripper and passive manipulator block the robot's distance sensors due to their size and need to be lifted to the robot's top. In contrast, the small volume of the electromagnetic manipulator only needs to be lifted until the module is landed from the ground or lifted 15 mm from the ground.

**Fig. 2.** Assembly modules. a: The digital model showing magnetic balls inside the module's surfaces. b: The physical model.

**Fig. 3.** RIZObots. a: The basic gripper. b: The passive magnetic manipulator. C: The active magnetic manipulator.

## 4    Case Study

The study was carried out with two experiments to analyze only the performance of the manipulators that are desired to be tested on mobile robots, independent of other factors.

RIZOBots are equipped with a light intensity sensor and programmed to collect the modules from the areas where the measurement is below the defined threshold value and leave them in the areas where the measurement is above the threshold value. Within the scope of the first experiment, the motion algorithms of the RIZOBots were disabled, and only for testing the manipulator, the actions of lifting, carrying, and dropping the module placed in front of the manipulator were performed and observed by manipulating the ambient light.

In the second experiment, the motion algorithm of RIZOBots was activated. Their interaction with randomly placed modules was observed on a flat surface of 2*3, 5 m, limited by 50 cm black fabric.

## 4.1 Experiment 1

In the first experiment, three different manipulator types mounted on RIZOBot with three identical features are respectively tested for picking, carrying, and placing, while the robots were stationary. Figure 4 illustrates these three manipulators in performing tasks step by step.

Firstly, RIZOBot with the gripper is located in an environment where the light intensity is below the threshold value. A module is placed in front of the robot with its short side perpendicular to the robot, and the gripper is activated. The module is tested by triggering the infrared sensor. Then, the light intensity of the environment is increased above the threshold value, and it is observed that the robot places the module on the ground and drops it. This cycle is repeated, and it is observed that the gripper has problems interacting with modules that are too close to the robot and not perpendicular to the robot.

After the gripper, the same test is performed with the passive manipulator. Unlike the gripper, the passive manipulator, which interacts with the modules with the long side perpendicular to the robot, succeeded in interacting with the modules standing at different angles and + −5 mm deviated positions against the robot. It presents a higher tolerance than the gripper.

Finally, the same tests are performed with the electromagnetic manipulator. The importance of the electromagnets' position in the manipulator's body design is highlighted in the tests. In case electromagnets are placed too close to the module's contact surface, they successfully pick the module. However, due to the electromagnets' material, the manipulator could not place and drop the modules. Since electromagnets are metals, they interact with the magnets within the modules even when the electromagnets are deactivated. In the tests where the electromagnets are placed far from the contact surface of the module, the magnetic field created by the electromagnet fails to remove it. By learning from these results, the electromagnets placed inside the manipulator body at a certain distance (3 mm in this experiment set) successfully perform both the picking and the placing in the experiments. Besides, the module orientation and position tolerance are much higher than the passive manipulator and gripper. That results from the magnetic field of the magnets in the manipulator and the electromagnets.

## 4.2 Experiment 2

The tests performed in the first experiment are carried out with 3 RIZOBots with the same manipulators in the second experiment as illustrated in Fig. 5. 3 RIZOBots are operated simultaneously in the experiment area, limited by a black fabric 50 cm high and illuminated with a single-point light source. Its interaction with the modules in the area is observed. RIZOBots are programmed to pick the modules in the dark areas and areas with light intensity below the defined threshold and drop the modules in the areas with light intensity above the defined threshold. In cases where RIZOBots with obstacle avoidance algorithm detects the modules while moving without collision with each other. All three manipulators have difficulty carrying the modules they interact with. Since most of the modules detected by the robots are not perpendicular to the robot's front face, all three manipulators pick the modules from the ground. However, in most scenarios, they move without being able to pick up the module. As a result of unsuccessful interactions with the modules they encountered in the dark area, manipulators without any control mechanism could not pick the modules. However, assuming they do not carry the modules when they enter the light area, they successfully drop the modules they do not carry. The intended goal could not be achieved because there was no module in the manipulator. In the experiment that lasted for thirty minutes, the all manipulators interacted with the module. They could carry and drop the module.

## 4.3 Results and Discussion

Fifty iterations per manipulator were done in the first experiment. The results of the experiments are shown in Tables 2 and 3. By observing the results of the experiments, the gripper could easily grasp the module but only from its short side due to the finger span. The passive manipulator had a higher chance to release the modules when aligned with the manipulators and had a higher module orientation tolerance than the gripper. Twelve grasping actions done by the passive manipulator were not ideal because the magnetic field aligned the module in the wrong orientation. This situation was fixed later by using free-rotating magnets in the modules. With the active manipulator, the modules stuck to the manipulator when the electromagnets were positioned lower in the active manipulator. When electromagnets were positioned at a higher level inside the manipulator's end effector, the modules were not lifted due to decreased magnetic field effect. The critical factor of such a manipulator design was the positioning of the electromagnets.

In the second experiment, the manipulators interacted with the modules with the infrared sensor detecting the modules in the experiment environment. The robots were released into the experiment area, and their behavior was observed. According to these observations, the robots grasped the modules but failed to detach most of them. While moving according to the swarm behavior, the modules could be dropped because of a collision. Despite the modules falling, the robots acted as if they had not fallen and continued accomplishing the task. Supporting the system with image processing may be a solution to make the system more effective.

The errors caused by the actions of the manipulators were kept, while the issues caused by the navigation logic of the robots were ignored. As a result, the data observed from the second experiment were similar to the first experiment. This result shows that the manipulators can work when attached to a mobile body. However, their design needs to ensure the organized operation of the tool and the manipulator.

**Table 2.** The success rate of pick and place in experiment 1.

| Number | Passive Manipulator | | Active Manipulator | | | Gripper |
|---|---|---|---|---|---|---|
| | Right orientation | Wrong orientation | Low | High | Midle | Horizontal |
| iterations | 38/50 | 12/50 | 50 | 50 | 50 | 50 |
| pick | 36 | 0 | 44 | 5 | 39 | 41 |
| place | 36 | 0 | 10 | 5 | 36 | 41 |

**Table 3.** The success rate of pick and place in experiment 2.

| Number | Passive Manipulator | Active Manipulator | Gripper |
|---|---|---|---|
| interactions | 44 | 37 | 40 |
| pick | 41 | 35 | 24 |
| place | 31 | 27 | 21 |
| collision | 10 | 8 | 3 |

**Fig. 4.** Experiment 1.

**Fig. 5.** Experiment 2.

## 5 Conclusion

Multi-robot systems based on swarm behavior involve unpredictable situations in complex systems. Designing manipulators for these systems requires integrity of prototyping from earlier phases of design processes. However, prototyping is mainly conducted after the design is finished, although architectural design processes are getting more intertwined. Making the computational methods and approaches used in the initial design stages transparent can enhance designers' control over the process. Transparent computational methods and approaches allow designers to create prototypes and test their design concepts before the final design is completed. This allowance enables designers to iterate and refine their designs based on feedback and insights from prototyping, leading to more informed decision-making and improved control over the design process.

This study has limitations, mainly from the number of robots and tasks used in the experiments. Although the experiment set tests the applicability of the design idea regarding manipulators, with a limited sample size, the results may not accurately represent real-world scenarios. Increasing the sample size can improve the study's statistical power and provide more robust and reliable results. In addition, varying the tasks in an experiment can help explore the manipulators' range of capabilities and limitations under different conditions. Building patterns with more than two layers, for example, could provide insights into the robots' performance in more complex and challenging tasks. This insight can enhance the study's external validity and increase its applicability to real-world scenarios. By varying the tasks and increasing the number of robots, researchers can better control for potential confounding factors affecting the study results. For example, different robot designs or configurations, variations in environmental conditions, or differences in task difficulty levels can impact the study outcomes.

This study would contribute to developing robotic manipulators that can be used in various architectural scenarios, such as restoration in extreme conditions and structural (dis)assembly of formworks in dangerous places for human workers. Even if this study mainly concentrates on pattern formation with manipulators attached to mobile robots, its scope can also be extended to the painting, cleaning, inspection, environmental monitoring, and construction tasks in the long term.

## References

1. Ntzoufras, S., Oungrinis, K.A., Liapi, M., Papamanolis, A.: Robotic swarms in architectural design-a communication platform bridging design analysis and robotic construction. In: Proceedings of the 38th eCAADe Conference - Volume 2, TU Berlin, Berlin, Germany, pp. 453–462 (2020). https://doi.org/10.52842/conf.ecaade.2020.2.453
2. Bhatt, N., Chauhan, N.R.: Design of a two fingered friction gripper for a wheel mobile robot. In: Advanced Computing and Communication Technologies, pp. 195–203. Springer, Singapore (2016)
3. Samavati, F.C., Feizollahi, A., Sabetian, P., Moosavian, S.A.A.: Design, fabrication and control of a three-finger robotic gripper. In: 2011 First International Conference on Robot, Vision and Signal Processing, pp. 280–283. IEEE (2011)
4. Mao, Y., Yuan, S., Wang, J., Zhang, J., Song, S.: Modeling and control of an untethered magnetic gripper. In: 2021 IEEE International Conference on Robotics and Automation (ICRA), pp. 7274–7280. IEEE (2021)
5. Garcia, A., Mehrubeoglu, M.: Switchable magnets as a power-efficient alternative for electromagnets in a mobile robotic system. In: 2020 IEEE Green Technologies Conference (GreenTech), pp. 212–216. IEEE (2020)
6. Loianno, G., et al.: Localization, grasping, and transportation of magnetic objects by a team of mavs in challenging desert-like environments. IEEE Robotics and Automation Letters 3(3), 1576–1583 (2018)
7. Jenett, B., Abdel-Rahman, A., Cheung, K., Gershenfeld, N.: Material–robot system for assembly of discrete cellular structures. IEEE Robotics and Automation Letters 4(4), 4019–4026 (2019)
8. Tamke, M., Özkar, M., Tunçer, B., Gattegno, N., Peters, B.: IJAC 2017: special ACADIA edited issue. Int. J. Archit. Comput. 15(1), 3–5 (2017)
9. BCN3D-Moveo. https://github.com/BCN3D/BCN3D-Moveo. Accessed 27 Oct 2022
10. Linear Servo Actuators. https://www.thingiverse.com/thing:3170748. Accessed 27 Oct 2022

# Evaluation System and Efficient Improvement of Reverse Logistics for Shared Bicycle

Chengchong Gao[✉], Yunxia Wang, Ying Dong, Hongxi Yuan, and Zhiliang Wang[✉]

School of Mechanical Engineering, Nanjing Institute of Technology, Nanjing 211167, China
{gaocc,wang-yunxia,wwangzzll}@njit.edu.cn, nlgdaisy@163.com,
183651070@qq.com

**Abstract.** With the rise in popularity of shared bicycles, a growing number of defective shared bicycles are constantly abandoned indiscriminately and leads to a relatively serious impact on the city traffic and the environment. As such, the establishment of a recycling system for faulty bicycles becomes imperative, with the key challenges lying in selecting an appropriate recovery method and reducing recycling costs. This study focuses on the reverse logistics of shared bicycle recycling and employs the Analytic Network Process (ANP) to develop an evaluation system and address the associated evaluation indicators. Building upon this foundation, an optimization model for minimizing reverse recovery costs is proposed, and the minimum recovery cost is calculated using the LINGO software. Then a more complete recycling model and evaluation system are established. The effectiveness and practicality of the model and evaluation system are demonstrated through illustrative examples.

**Keywords:** Life Cycle · Shared Bicycle · Reverse Logistics · Evaluation System · Recovery Modes

## 1 Introduction

In recent years, shared bicycles have gained popularity due to their convenience and the compatibility with low-carbon and environmentally friendly lifestyles [1].

The introduction of ofo shared bicycles in China in 2016 marked the global advent of dockless shared bicycles and spurred the growth of the sharing economy in China [2]. However, the innovative way parking anytime and anywhere results in the disordered and scattered placement of the shared bicycles, even hinders traffic, pose challenges for the recycling and disposal of faulty bicycles. Relevant research on reverse logistics for shared bicycles has not received sufficient attention so far. In 2017, Recognizing the adverse environmental and societal impacts caused by abandoned shared bicycles, some scholars pointed out that the shared bicycles' recovery should be considered [3, 4]. Over the past two years, these concerns have been further validated as the once-promising development of shared bicycles has faced decline, which highlights the urgency of addressing shared bicycle recycling as a pressing social issue [5, 6].

Y. Luo (Ed.): CDVE 2023, LNCS 14166, pp. 147–157, 2023.
https://doi.org/10.1007/978-3-031-43815-8_14

Therefore, this paper intends to establish the evaluation system of shared bicycle's reverse logistics based on the Analytic Network Process (ANP). It seeks to explore the critical factors affecting reverse logistics and, in particular, examine the key factor of recycling cost to enhance the efficiency of shared bicycle reverse logistics.

## 2 Establishment of the Evaluation System for Shared Bicycle's Reverse Logistics

### 2.1 Recovery Mode of Fault Sharing Bicycles

The recycling of waste materials or products and transportation problems encountered in the recycling process are integral components of reverse logistics. Due to the increasing accumulation of various wastes, there is an imminent need to protect the environment and enhance resource utilization, so as to drive the development of reverse logistics. The establishment of an efficient reverse logistics recycling system can effectively facilitate the comprehensive circulation and optimal utilization of waste resources, minimize resource wastage, and improve environmental benefits.

When it comes to the recycling of faulty shared bicycles, enterprises have two approaches at their hands. The first approach involves enterprises directly handling the recycling of faulty bicycles, wherein the shared bicycle enterprises themselves are responsible for the recycling process. The other is that enterprises are indirectly involved in the recycling of shared bicycles, i.e., the businesses of recycling faulty bicycles are outsourced to third-party logistics companies [7]. Depending on the level of involvement of the enterprises, the recycling of shared bicycles can be classified into three operational modes: self-operation, joint operation, and outsourcing. The choice of recovery mode for faulty shared bicycles determines the efficiency of reverse logistics.

### 2.2 Evaluation System Model Building Based on ANP

Proper evaluation of different recovery modes is a prerequisite for establishing an efficient reverse logistics system. This paper tries to apply ANP method to evaluate the reverse logistics system of shared bicycles [8]. First, according to the practical operation of shared bicycles' reverse logistics, the key factors influencing the reverse logistics system are identified for evaluating the three recovery modes. These factors encompass four dimensions: economy, society, technology, and resources, which serve as the primary evaluation indicators. Furthermore, the economy factor is expanded to include four subfactors: reclamation cost, operation cost, logistics cost, and scale of logistics recovery. Society factor also contains four subfactors: support from supply chain members, social morals and cultural influence, compliance with laws and regulations, and relative ecological benefits.

Technology factor contains three subfactors, namely, degree of specialization, competitive edge, and degree of management informatization. Lastly, the technology and resource dimension consists of two subfactors: product recovery and recycling rate. Collectively, these 13 subfactors constitute the second-level evaluation indicators. The conceptual model of the reverse logistics evaluation system is depicted in Fig. 1.

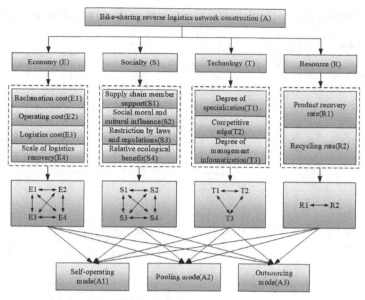

**Fig. 1.** Evaluation System Model of Reverse Logistics Network for Shared Bicycles

## 2.3  Evaluation System Model Application by Super Decisions

In the process of constructing the index system, it is also necessary to understand the mutual influence relationship among the evaluation indicators, specifically the management of feedback and dependence. Thus, an investigation was conducted to examine the interactions among the evaluation indicators at all levels, and the relationships between the influencing factors were determined through a questionnaire survey, as presented in Table 1.

The table above provides a clear depiction of the interrelationships among the evaluation indicators at all levels and the mutual influence within each level of evaluation indicators. It was selected to illustrate the interrelationship between the secondary influencing factors, and allow for an intuitive understanding. Based on this table, an ANP structure diagram of the shared bicycle recycling scheme was developed, as depicted in Fig. 2.

This conceptual model is used to evaluate the above three recovery modes. First, through a questionnaire survey, data about the importance of each first-level and second-level evaluation indicators was acquired.

Due to the complex principle and calculation process of ANP, Super Decisions software was used to assist the calculation. The evaluation system model and importance data were inputted into the software. After corresponding operations were carried out on SD software, the weight of each evaluation indicator was determined, as shown in Fig. 3. The simulation solution for the reverse logistics network in the context of shared bicycles was achieved. A1, A2 and A3 represent the respective weights of the three recycling modes, as depicted in Fig. 2. A1, corresponding to self-operation mode, is 0.29117. A2, corresponding to the joint operation mode, holds a weight of 0.31482. A3 corresponding

**Table 1.** Questionnaire on the correlation of indicators of shared bicycle recycling schemes

| | Affected factors | A | | | E | | | | S | | | | T | | | R | |
|---|---|---|---|---|---|---|---|---|---|---|---|---|---|---|---|---|---|
| factors | | A1 | A2 | A3 | E1 | E2 | E3 | E4 | S1 | S2 | S3 | S4 | T1 | T2 | T3 | R1 | R2 |
| A | A1 | | | | √ | √ | √ | √ | √ | √ | √ | √ | √ | √ | √ | √ | √ |
| | A2 | | | | √ | √ | √ | √ | √ | √ | √ | √ | √ | √ | √ | √ | √ |
| | A3 | | | | √ | √ | √ | √ | √ | √ | √ | √ | √ | √ | √ | √ | √ |
| E | E1 | √ | √ | √ | | √ | √ | √ | √ | | | | √ | √ | √ | √ | √ |
| | E2 | √ | √ | √ | | | √ | √ | √ | | | | √ | √ | | √ | √ |
| | E3 | √ | √ | √ | | | | | √ | | | | | | | | |
| | E4 | √ | √ | √ | √ | √ | | | √ | | | | √ | | | √ | |
| S | S1 | √ | √ | √ | √ | | | | | | | | √ | √ | | | |
| | S2 | √ | √ | √ | | | | | √ | | √ | | | | | | |
| | S3 | √ | √ | √ | | | | | | | | √ | | | | | |
| | S4 | √ | √ | √ | | | | | √ | √ | | | | | | √ | √ |
| T | T1 | √ | √ | √ | √ | | | | √ | | | | | √ | √ | | |
| | T2 | √ | √ | √ | | | √ | | √ | | | | √ | | √ | | √ |
| | T3 | √ | √ | √ | √ | | | | √ | | | | √ | √ | | | |
| R | R1 | √ | √ | √ | | √ | √ | | | | | | √ | | | | |
| | R2 | √ | √ | √ | √ | | √ | | | | | | √ | √ | | | |

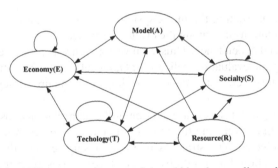

**Fig. 2.** ANP structure diagram of shared bicycle recycling scheme

to the outsourcing mode is 0.39400. It is evident that the optimal operational scheme for reverse logistics in bicycle-sharing enterprises is the outsourcing mode, followed by the joint operation mode, and ultimately the self-operation mode.

In the second-level evaluation indicators, the four largest indicators are denoted as S1, R1, T1, E1, respectively. Specifically, E1 corresponds to the recycling cost with a value of 0.40626, R1 corresponds to the product recovery rate with a value of 0.62148, S1 represents the support of supply chain members with a value of 0.69975, and T1 represents the degree of specialization with a value of 0.51806. These four indicators should be emphatically considered in the construction of reverse logistics network for shared bicycles. Product recovery rate mainly involves product recycling policy, support of supply chain members mainly depends on supply contracts, degree of specialization mainly involves recovery team construction. These factors are categorized as subjective factors in the realm of reverse logistics, and recycling cost as reverse logistics' objective factor will be further discussed in the subsequent section. The optimization model of recycling cost will be built and recovery operation for faulty shared bicycles in an administrative region of Nanjing will be took as the optimization calculation examples. It is noteworthy that this region encompasses 14 initial collection sites, 4 recycling centers, and 1 recycling treatment plant, all sections are operated by the designated recovery enterprise.

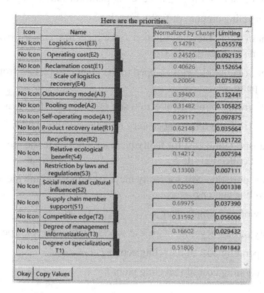

**Fig. 3.** Weights of Evaluation Indicators

# 3 Calculation of Shared Bicycles' Recycling Cost

## 3.1 Establishment of Recycling Cost Optimal Model

### 3.1.1 Decision Variables

The parameters involved in the optimal model of recycling cost for shared bicycles are defined at Table 2.

The decision variables are defined as follows.

$$Z_{ij} = \begin{cases} 1, & \text{Ship a faulty bike from initial collection site } i \text{ to recovery center } j; \\ 0 \end{cases}$$

$$W_{jk} = \begin{cases} 1, & \text{Ship a faulty bike from recovery center } j \text{ to recovery plant } k. \\ 0 \end{cases}$$

**Table 2.** The Cost Model Parameters and Their Meanings

| Parameters | Meanings of Parameters |
|---|---|
| $i$ | Initial collection site of the faulty bicycle |
| $j$ | Recycling center for faulty bicycles |
| $k$ | Recycling plant for faulty bicycles |
| $C_j$ | The fixed cost of setting up a recycling center for faulty bicycles |
| $C_k$ | The fixed cost of setting up a recycling plant for faulty bicycles |
| $q_i$ | Daily recycling amount of faulty bicycles |
| $n_{ij}$ | Amount of faulty bicycles shipped to the recycling center $j$ from the initial collection site $i$ per day |
| $n_{jk}$ | Amount of faulty bicycles shipped to the recycling plant $k$ from the recycling center $j$ per day |
| $d_{ij}$ | Distance from the initial collection site $i$ to the collection center $j$ |
| $d_{jk}$ | Distance from the recycling center $j$ to the recycling plant $k$ |
| $t_{ij}$ | Unit transportation cost for faulty bicycles shipped to the recycling center $j$ from the initial collection site $i$ |
| $t_{jk}$ | Unit transportation cost for faulty bicycles shipped to the recycling plant $k$ from the recycling center $j$ |
| $l_j$ | Capacity of recycling center $j$ |
| $A_k$ | Capacity of the recycling plant $k$ to process faulty bicycles per day |
| $e_j$ | Daily operating cost of recycling center $j$ |
| $e_k$ | Daily operating cost of recycling plant $k$ |

### 3.1.2 Objective Function

The total recycling cost of faulty bicycles comprises three components: transportation cost, operation cost, and fixed cost. The detailed analysis is presented as follows.

Transportation cost refers to the expenses incurred during the transportation process and encompasses the cost of shipping faulty bicycles from the initial collection sites to the recycling centers (including the cost of searching for faulty bicycles) and from the recycling centers to the recycling plants, as shown in Eq. 1.

$$Zt = \sum_j \sum_i d_{ij} t_{ij} n_{ij} Z_{ij} + \sum_k \sum_j d_{jk} t_{jk} n_{jk} W_{jk} \tag{1}$$

Operation cost refers to the sum of daily costs required to maintain operation of recycling centers and recycling plants, as shown in Eq. 2.

$$Zo = \sum_j e_j + \sum_k e_k \tag{2}$$

Fixed cost refers to the fixed investments related to the establishment of recycling centers and recycling plants, as shown in Eq. 3.

$$Zf = \sum_j C_j + \sum_k C_k \tag{3}$$

Therefore, the total recycling cost of faulty bicycle is:

$$\min Z = \sum_j \sum_i d_{ij} t_{ij} n_{ij} Z_{ij} + \sum_k \sum_j d_{jk} t_{jk} n_{jk} W_{jk} + \sum_j e_j + \sum_k e_k + \sum_j C_j + \sum_k C_k \tag{4}$$

### 3.1.3  Constraint Conditions

$$\begin{cases} \sum_i n_{ij} \leq l_j \\ \sum_j n_{jk} \leq A_k, k = 1 \\ \sum_j \sum_i Z_{ij} \geq 1, i = 1, ..., 14 \\ \sum_k \sum_j W_{jk} \geq 1, j = 1, ..., 4 \\ \sum_j \sum_i n_{ij} = q_i, i = 1, ..., 14 \\ \sum_i \sum_j n_{ij} = \sum_k \sum_j n_{jk} \\ Z_{ij} = 1, \forall n_{ij}, d_{ij} > 0 \\ Z_{ij} = 0, \forall n_{ij} + d_{ij} = 0 \\ W_{jk} = 1, \forall n_{jk}, d_{jk} > 0 \\ W_{jk} = 0, \forall n_{jk} + d_{jk} = 0 \end{cases} \tag{5}$$

Equation 5 was divided into 10 sub formulas. Among these sub-formulas, the first formula signifies that the daily shipment of faulty bicycles to the recycling center must not exceed its capacity. The second formula indicates that the daily shipment of faulty bicycles to the recycling plant should also not surpass its capacity. The third formula ensures that at least one of the initial collection sites dispatches the faulty bicycles to the recycling centers. The fourth formula guarantees that at least one of the recycling centers transfers the faulty bicycles to the recycling plants. According to the 5th formula, the amount of recycled bicycles of an initial collection site is defined as the amount of faulty bicycles shipped to the recycling center from this initial collection site. The 6th formula shows the amount of recycled bicycles of a recycling center is defined as the amount of faulty bicycles shipped to the recycling plant from this recycling center. The 7th and the 8th state that when either the quantity condition or the distance condition is met, the faulty bicycles at initial collection site i will be transported to recycling center j. Likewise, according to the last two formulas, when either the quantity condition or the distance condition is satisfied, the faulty bicycle at recycling center j will be transported to recycling plant k.

## 3.2 Analysis of Recycling Cost

There are 14 initial collection points, 4 recycling centers and 1 recycling plant in Qixia District of Nanjing. The precise positioning of these facilities is depicted on a location distribution map, as illustrated in Fig. 4. The initial collection points are labeled as points 1 to 14, while the recycling centers are denoted as centers 1 to 4. According to the location of the four cycle recycling centers, the average value method was used to determine the specific location of the recycling plant, which was (longitude 118.950701°, latitude N32.114837°).

**Fig. 4.** Initial collection points and recycling center distribution

There are 4 recycling centers R1, R2, R3 and R4 and one recycling plant P1 in the above example, and their fixed investment costs and unit operation costs are shown in Table 3.

**Table 3.** Investment Costs and Operation Costs for Recycling Centers and Recycling Plant

| Recycling Nodes | Fixed Investment Costs (CNY) | Unit Operation Costs (CNY PER BICYCLE) |
| --- | --- | --- |
| $R_1$ | 100000 | 200 |
| $R_2$ | 110000 | 280 |
| $R_3$ | 130000 | 300 |
| $R_4$ | 120000 | 220 |
| $P_1$ | 2000000 | 2000 |

The daily amount of recovery bicycles at each initial collection site was shown in Table 4. Table 5 displays the unit freight charge for transporting defective bicycles from the initial collection sites to the recycling centers. The unit freight charge includes the cost of searching for faulty bicycles through the application (APP) as well as the transportation cost.

**Table 4.** Daily Amount of Recovery Bicycles at Each Initial Collection Site

| $C_1$ | $C_2$ | $C_3$ | $C_4$ | $C_5$ | $C_6$ | $C_7$ | $C_8$ | $C_9$ | $C_{10}$ | $C_{11}$ | $C_{12}$ | $C_{13}$ | $C_{14}$ |
|---|---|---|---|---|---|---|---|---|---|---|---|---|---|
| 10 | 70 | 85 | 15 | 25 | 20 | 105 | 55 | 75 | 30 | 30 | 40 | 20 | 20 |

**Table 5.** Unit Freight Charge for Shipping Faulty Bicycles from Initial Collection Sites to Recycling Centers

| Centers | $C_1$ | $C_2$ | $C_3$ | $C_4$ | $C_5$ | $C_6$ | $C_7$ | $C_8$ | $C_9$ | $C_{10}$ | $C_{11}$ | $C_{12}$ | $C_{13}$ | $C_{14}$ |
|---|---|---|---|---|---|---|---|---|---|---|---|---|---|---|
| $R_1$ | 5 | 7 | 7 | 5 | 4 | 4 | 6 | 6 | 7 | 4 | 5 | 5 | 4 | 5 |
| $R_2$ | 4 | 7 | 7 | 4 | 5 | 4 | 6 | 6 | 7 | 5 | 4 | 5 | 5 | 5 |
| $R_3$ | 6 | 5 | 6 | 6 | 6 | 5 | 4 | 4 | 6 | 5 | 5 | 4 | 6 | 4 |
| $R_4$ | 7 | 4 | 4 | 7 | 6 | 6 | 5 | 5 | 4 | 6 | 6 | 5 | 7 | 5 |

The daily processing capacities of R1, R2, R3 and R4 are 200, 500, 400 and 300 vehicles, respectively. The unit transportation cost for shipping faulty bicycles from the four recycling centers to recycling plant P1 are 7 CNY, 7 CNY, 6 CNY, and 8 CNY, respectively. Also, the daily processing capacity of the recycling plant is 700 vehicles.

The distances between the initial collection sites and the recycling centers, as well as the distances from the recycling centers to the recycling plants, have been obtained based on the selected paths. These distances are presented in Table 6.

**Table 6.** Distances between Initial Collection Sites and Recycling Centers and Distances between Recycling Centers and Plants

| Path | Distance (km) | Path | Distance (km) | Path | Distance (km) | Path | Distance (km) | Path | Distance (km) | Path | Distance (km) |
|---|---|---|---|---|---|---|---|---|---|---|---|
| $C_1$-$R_1$ | 1.2 | $C_4$-$R_1$ | 1.44 | $C_7$-$R_2$ | 1.95 | $C_{10}$-$R_4$ | 0.68 | $C_{13}$-$R_4$ | 1.2 | $R_2$-$P_1$ | 1.07 |
| $C_2$-$R_3$ | 1.48 | $C_5$-$R_4$ | 1.69 | $C_8$-$R_2$ | 1.19 | $C_{11}$-$R_1$ | 1.5 | $C_{14}$-$R_2$ | 2.18 | $R_3$-$P_1$ | 6.75 |
| $C_3$-$R_3$ | 1.65 | $C_6$-$R_4$ | 2.27 | $C_9$-$R_3$ | 0.8 | $C_{12}$-$R_2$ | 1.01 | $R_1$-$P_1$ | 4.98 | $R_4$-$P_1$ | 3.98 |

The LINGO software was used to calculate the transportation cost, operation cost, fixed cost and total recycling cost associated with faulty bicycles. According to Fig. 5, the daily transportation cost Zt amounts to 7800.2 CNY, the daily total operation cost Zo is 3000 CNY, the fixed investment cost Zf is 2460000 CNY, and the total recycling cost Z sums up to 2467906 CNY. Assuming that the investment cost can be recovered within one year, considering the presence of 251 working days per year, the daily fixed investment cost is estimated to be 9800.8 CNY. Thus, the total daily recycling cost reaches 20601 CNY. Based on the above data, it can be observed that the daily fixed investment cost represents the largest proportion within the total cost, followed by the transportation cost. Therefore, effective management of the facility, along with an increase in the recycling rate of faulty bicycles and waste resources, can significantly contribute to the recycling of investment costs. In addition, reasonable bicycle parking can reduce the workload of finding faulty bicycles, and can also reduce the cost of bicycle transportation and recycling.

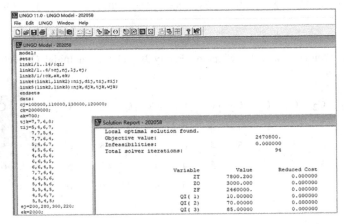

**Fig. 5.** LINGO Program and Results

## 4 Conclusion

According to faulty bicycles recycling, in order to select proper recovery mode and improve operational efficiency, the following research has been carried out in the paper.

(1) Based on ANP, this study identifies four main aspects: economy, society, technology, and resources, as the first-level evaluation indicators. The 13 s-level evaluation indicators are extracted. And then, the evaluation system of shared bicycles' reverse logistics is built to evaluate the three recovery modes.

(2) Through a questionnaire survey, the importance of each first-level and second-level evaluation indicators was acquired by the established evaluation system of shared bicycles' reverse logistics. The findings indicate that the outsourcing mode is optimal and the four most significant second-level indicators are recycling cost, product recovery rate, support of supply chain members, and degree of specialization, respectively.

(3) The cost optimization model of the faulty bicycles recycling is presented and applied to a case study. Based on the calculation results, various approaches for reducing recycling costs are identified, such as improving plant operations, increasing the recycling rate of faulty bicycles, enhancing the utilization rate of waste resources, and implementing more efficient parking strategies.

Applying the proposed method and the established model to the recycling of faulty shared bicycles in the future, the waste of resources can be minimized, both economic and ecological benefits gained.

**Acknowledgments.** The project was supported by the Open Research Fund of NJIT Institute of Industrial Economy and Innovation Management (No. JGKB202204), Philosophy and Social Science Research Project of Jiangsu Universities (No. 2020SJA0442).

# References

1. Liu, Z., Jia, X., Cheng, W.: Solving the Last Mile Problem: Ensure the Success of Public Bicycle System in Beijing. Procedia - Social and Behavioral Sci. **43**, 7378 (2012)
2. Gao, M., Xu, Q., Xi, X.: Exploration on the Development mode of shared bikes under the background of "Internet +". Technology Wind, (14), 78-79 (2019)
3. Xue, Y.: Research on Fault Shared Bike Recycling based on Reverse Logistics. Chang'an University, Si'an (2019)
4. Chang, S., Song, R., et al.: Shared bike fault vehicle recovery model. J. Jilin University (Engineering Edition) **48**(06), 1677–1684 (2018)
5. Xu, J.: Analysis of the problems and countermeasures of shared bicycle recycling management in China. Science and Technol. Economic Guide **26**(29), 184-185 (2018)
6. Ma, Z.: Analysis of the existing problems and countermeasures existing in the process of reverse logistics of shared bikes. Logistics Technol. **38**(04), 10-13 (2019)
7. Liu, X., Chen, T., et al.: Evaluation of reverse logistics recovery mode selection based on network analysis method. J. University of Electronic Science and Technol. China (Social Science edition) (03), 32–35+58 (2007)
8. Liu, T., Xiang, Z.: Research on reverse logistics operation mode decision-making based on ANP. Logistics Technol. (11), 114-116 (2007)

# Skeleton-Based Fall Detection Using Computer Vision

Can Thi Hoa Mai, Duong Thi Phuong Dung, Pham Le Anh Duc,
and Phan Duy Hung$^{(\boxtimes)}$

Computer Science Department, FPT University, Hanoi, Vietnam
{maicthhe150645,dungdtphe150041,ducplahe150572}@fpt.edu.vn,
hungpd2@fe.edu.vn

**Abstract.** Falling is one of the biggest public health issues that can cause many serious long-term repercussions for patients and their families. In this paper, we propose an appropriate model for fall detection using graph convolutional networks. Recently, most problems related to human action recognition, including fall detection, can be handled by applying the spatio-temporal graph convolutional model using 2D or 3D skeletal data. We take advantage of the transfer learning technique from the NTU RGB + D consisting of 60 daily actions to extract features for fall detection tasks efficiently. Besides, to highlight critical frames in the original sequence, we suggest using a temporal attention module consisting of two parts: (1) an average global pooling, and (2) two fully connected layers. We conduct the test on two datasets, leading to a 3.12% increase in the TST dataset and a 2.67% improvement in the FallFree dataset. Notably, concerning the FallFree dataset, the model's accuracy is up to 100%.

**Keyword:** Fall detection · human action recognition · spatio-temporal graph convolutional networks · transfer learning · attention mechanism

## 1 Introduction

Falling is the second-largest cause of unintentional injury fatalities after road traffic injuries. Besides, it also leads to more years of disability in life than traffic accidents, drowning, burns, and poisoning combined [1]. Falling accidents not only cause direct consequences for the patient but also greatly affect family members. To reduce and prevent falls and their related consequences, a variety of methods have been developed to monitor and detect falls as soon as possible and then alert related personnel about patients. Especially for families that often have elderly people or children at home alone, fall detection becomes an important task in both healthcare and daily life.

Much research and application about fall detection has been performed and has obtained good results. Three main types of fall detection methods are video-based, ambience device-based, and wearable device-based. In the wearable device-based approach, several parts of the human body have sensors mounted, while in the ambient device-based method, the sensors are installed in the living space of the followed person, such as wall, floor, bed, etc. Take the Apple Watch as an example. In series 4, Apple gathered data from 2,500 people wearing this product and had more than 250,000 days of data for fall detection [2]. The main sensors applied to detect falls are an accelerometer that can measure a higher amount of gravity (16–32 Gs), a 24/7 enabled gyroscope that can measure rotational speed, and a gyroscope that can visualize the different ways it does this through three axes in space. However, not everyone can afford or feels comfortable wearing the device all the time. Therefore, a video-based approach, including RGB-based and skeleton-based, from indoor cameras for fall detection applications is being widely developed. Compared to the RGB-based approach, the skeleton-based method has the huge advantage of not only having a lower computational cost but also being unaffected by changes in the surrounding environment. Extracting skeleton points from video helps to recognize human action in general and detect falls in particular.

Recently, there have been leaps and bounds in human action recognition research, from CNN and RNN to graph convolutional networks (GCN). GCN includes two types: spectral and spatial. While spectral GCN transforms graphs into the spectrum domain and employs the graph Fourier transform, spatial GCN gathers information from nearby nodes [3]. In 2018, Yan et al. presented a spatio-temporal graph convolution network (ST-GCN) that is much more advanced than old methods by learning both space and time in the data. Each human skeleton's spatial characteristics are extracted using a GCN, and the same joint's continuous time edge is subjected to a time convolution network [4]. The original ST-GCN is created by ST-GCN blocks that alternately apply temporal and spatial graph convolutions to a skeleton graph [3]. Finally, the action class is predicted by fully connected layers and a classifier using Softmax. In the last few years, many researchers have made great improvements based on ST-GCN. With respect to the fall detection problem, Oussema Keskes et al. introduced a general vision-based system using ST-GCN [5]. With the advantages of transfer learning, the system showed effectiveness when having good performance, with the accuracy of some experiments reaching 100%.

During the research, we found out that the attention mechanism, which helps the model assign different weights for each input to represent different levels of importance of the input sequences [6], may be useful for detecting falls. Especially for fall detection problems where some critical frames have abrupt changes in action [7], it is expected that the attention mechanism aids the model in reasonably weighing the sequence of skeletal frames. Attention mechanisms for computer vision can be classified as soft attention and hard attention [8]. Soft attention computes a weighted input from input features so that it is a differentiable function, and the weights of the network can learn from forward and backward propagation [9]. On the other hand, Xu et al. [8] use attention scores to select a single feature, such as via the argmax function, which makes it not differentiable, and therefore, it is often supported by using reinforcement learning. With respect to soft attention, there are three well-known types: channel, spatial, and temporal attention [9, 10]. In image processing, each channel contains specific information about distinct objects. Via CNN, the number of channels may change in every layer and generate new information. A novel model called SEnet (Squeeze and Excitation Networks) is presented by Hu et al. [11] to highlight channels to which we need to pay attention. However, channel attention usually ignores some important features of spatial attention. For that reason, mixed attention is now studied and applied in many computer vision applications.

For example, in [12], Woo et al. introduce the hybrid of spatial and channel attention. Recently, Zhu et al. [7] used the collaboration of channel attention and temporal attention. They are supposed to learn the correlations among channels in the time dimension and extract information about keyframes by adding a squeeze-and-excitation (SE) block with the temporal gated unit and attention block, respectively. We can apply that idea to fall detection, which needs to pay attention to frames with significant changes to recognize the action [7].

In summary, both fields of research show good performance and potential for the problem of fall detection. However, there is not much existing research that combines these two techniques using skeletal data. The main contribution of this paper is to build a model to find an appropriate method for fall detection. The combination of ST-GCN with temporal attention was applied, in which ST-GCN automatically learns not only spatial but also temporal patterns from skeletal data while the attention mechanism helps to improve the extraction of spatiotemporal features of a skeleton sequence by considering different importance levels of frames. As an additional contribution, transfer learning is applied to leverage the available knowledge from human action recognition to help with fall detection. We tested our recommended model to verify its performance. The study experimented on two datasets, TST v2 and FallFree, and then compared with several methods for the best results with up to 100% accuracy.

## 2  Methodology

Our proposed fall detection pipeline is illustrated as Fig. 1 and consists of two phases: training and fine-tuning on the two fall datasets; applying temporal attention and classifying.

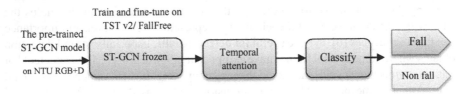

**Fig. 1.** The structure of the fall detection model.

In the first phase of the pipeline, we use the ST-GCN model to train and fine-tune two fall datasets. The key idea of ST-GCN is to model the spatiotemporal relationships between various components of the input data by means of GCNs. Each human joint in a skeleton sequence is typically represented by 2D or 3D coordinates in each frame. In [4], Yan et al. used a skeleton sequence with $N$ joints and $T$ frames that has both intra-body connectivities ($E_S$) referring to the relationships between different joints in the same frame, and inter-frame connectivity ($E_F$) referring to the relationships between the joint positions in different frames. They constructed an undirected spatial-temporal graph $G = (V, E)$, in particular, $V$ denoting the set including all joints in a skeleton sequence: $V = \{v_{ti} | t = 1, \ldots, T; i = 1, \ldots, N\}$ and edge set $E$ consists two parts: 1)

$E_S = \{v_{ti}, v_{tj} | (i,j) \in H\}$, where $H$ is the group of the human body's naturally linked joint pairs; and 2) $E_F = \{v_{ti}v_{(t+1)i}\}$. The graph CNN is sort of different from the normal CNN where we just use weights of a kernel to map with the fixed neighbors of the current pixel. In graph CNN, for each node, it is necessary to define its neighbor nodes and label the weight coefficient for each of them. In [4], three proposed methods for the graph labeling process are uni-labeling partition, distance partition, and spatial configuration partition. In this work, they used just a 1-neighbor set of joint nodes for each current node to convolve. For each neighbor node around the root $v_{tj}$, they define function $l_{ti}$ to map it with a unique label. Based on the following partitioning strategies illustrated in Fig. 2, the GCN is implemented to extract from both temporal and spatial features. Then, extracted features are provided into the classifier layer to predict the class of action.

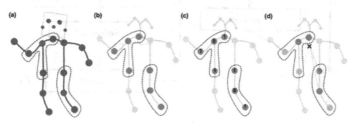

**Fig. 2.** (a) An illustration of an input skeleton frame; (b) Uni-labeling partition; c) Distance partitioning; (d) Spatial configuration partitioning [4].

Also in this phase, we perform transfer learning regarding two fall datasets. Yan et al. [4] provide the pre-trained ST-GCN model on some datasets, so Keskes et al. [5] suggested a method that can exploit the huge data for human action recognition, including fall samples, into fall detection problem and prove that it is effective on the FallFree and TST v2 dataset. The model has four components: a batch normalization layer, ST-GCN networks which is a list of 10 layers of ST-GCN units, a learnable mask for the learned edge importance weight, and a fully connected layer. According to [5], they froze the first 9 layers of the ST-GCN networks and changed the number of classes in the output layers to 2 (fall and non-fall). The data was split based on the cross-subject method. Inspired by that idea, we decide to apply the pre-trained ST-GCN model on the NTU RGB + D dataset, then carried out new training and fine-tuning with TST v2 and FallFree datasets as the first step in our pipeline for detecting falls.

As noted above, not all frames have the same level of importance when recognizing human actions. Particularly in fall detection, some frames have sudden changes in movement, and it is important to pay more attention to those frames. Therefore, inspired by [13], we propose to involve a temporal attention mechanism in our problem to highlight critical frames and detect falls more accurately in the second phase. As depicted in Fig. 3, our temporal attention module includes an average pooling layer and two fully connected layers. The average pooling layer takes an input of C × T × V, in which C denotes the number of channels, T is the number of frames and V denotes the number of nodes of the input. This layer compresses and extracts global information from each frame. This layer also helps to downsize the number of parameters when fitting in the FCN [2].

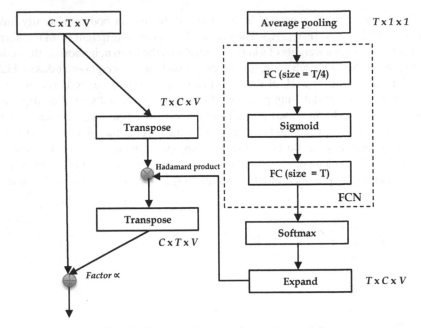

**Fig. 3.** Structure of temporal attention module.

Then, data is fed into two fully connected layers (FC) that generate T features to learn the appropriate weights of each input frame [13]. The output of the second FC layer is applied to the Softmax to compute a distribution of weights. In the original model [13], the authors use the Sigmoid to calculate the weight matrix and exploit it as the relationship between frames. However, if very large or small values appear frequently in the data, the sigmoid then returns all weights of approximately 1 or 0. This will give us senseless value for emphasizing essential frames, so we decide to employ softmax instead. The distribution of weights (attention scores) for each frame is mapped into the range (0, 1) to show different levels of importance in the whole frame sequence. We multiply this weight distribution with the initial input to adjust attention scores for each frame. Finally, it is scaled by factor $\alpha$ and added back to the input information.

## 3   Experiments and Results

### 3.1   Data Collection

The TST v2 dataset and the FallFree dataset are used to train and evaluate the model. The pre-trained ST-GCN model on the NTU RGB + D dataset [4] was utilized to extract features for the specific task of fall detection more efficiently. The data statistics are listed in Table 1.

The TST fall detection dataset v2 [14] was published in 2015. It provides three kinds of data: depth, skeletal, and acceleration data. It is split into two groups: activities of daily living (ADL) and the fall. There are four actions in each category. Sitting, grasping,

**Table 1.** Data statistics

| Dataset | # Actions | # Subjects | # Fall samples | # Samples |
|---------|-----------|------------|----------------|-----------|
| NTU RGB + D | 60 | 40 | 276 | 56880 |
| TST v2 | 5 | 11 | 132 | 264 |
| FallFree | 10 | 2 | 208 | 391 |

walking, and lying belong to the ADL category, while the front fall, the backward fall, the lateral fall, and the ends-up sitting fall in the fall category. The monitoring device was placed about 1.5 m from the floor and 2 m from the tracked people. Each action was simulated by 11 actors between the ages of 22 and 39, and with heights ranging from 1.62 to 1.97 m. They performed all actions three times. Consequently, the total number of samples in this dataset is 264, and each category is composed of 132 samples.

Alzahrani et al. [15] introduced the FallFree dataset in 2017. There are five types of data stored in FallFree: color, skeleton, depth, infrared, and body index. The dataset contains 79 actions, equivalent to 391 samples. True fall, pseudo fall, and ADL are the three major categories corresponding to 208, 115, and 68 samples, respectively. First, the true fall category is made up of forward, backward, and sideways falls. Second, falls with recovery or falls due to syncope are included in the pseudo-fall category. And the last category, ADL, is composed of daily life movements. Two actors performed the actions in three separate rooms with dissimilar lighting prerequisites. They were 30 and 35 years old, with heights of 1.50 and 1.68 m respectively. The tracking device was placed on a table at a distance of 1 m from the floor and facing the subject being followed. With a field of view (FOV) of 70 degrees horizontally and 60 degrees vertically, the camera covers the room and the subject.

This paper only uses the 3D skeletal data of the dataset for training and testing due to the advantages of storage capacity and training time. In this data type, each skeleton is represented by 25 joint points. These skeletons are all provided by the authors, so extracting the skeletons again from the raw video is not necessary.

## 3.2 Experiments

We tested the problem on an NVIDIA GTX 1650 with Cuda 12 and Python 3.9. We divided the data into training and test sets using the cross-subject method. The TST v2 dataset was split into two subsets. The training set contains videos that were performed by 7 actors: 1, 3, 5, 7, 9, 10, and 11. The videos of the 4 remaining actors were a test set. In FallFree, while the first person simulated all actions four times, the other did so once. Due to theirs characteristics, the videos of the first and the second subjects were used for training and testing, respectively. After pre-processing, the length of each sequence is set to 300 frames. Through the experiments, we chose the factor $\alpha$ in the attention module as 0.5 for the highest result (Table 2).

**Table 2.** The parameter of ST-GCN model

| Parameter | Value |
|---|---|
| base_lr | 0.1 |
| batch_size | 8 |
| num epoch | 50 |
| optimizer | SGD |
| weight_decay | 0.0001 |

## 3.3 Result and Analysis

We have tested two cases as suggested in the pipeline, and the results are listed below (Table 3).

**Table 3.** Results of our proposed method on two fall datasets

| Dataset | Accuracy | Sensitivity | Specificity | F1-score | ROC AUC |
|---|---|---|---|---|---|
| TST v2 | 89.58% | 97.22% | 85% | 87.5% | 91.11% |
| FallFree | 100% | 100% | 100% | 100% | 100% |

**Table 4.** Comparison of our method and other methods on the TST v2 dataset

| Method | Algorithms | Evaluation method | Accuracy |
|---|---|---|---|
| Keskes et al., 2021 [5] | Pre-trained ST-GCN | Cross subject | 100% |
| [5]* | Pre-trained ST-GCN | Cross subject | 86.46% |
| Our method | Pre-trained ST-GCN and attention mechanism | Cross subject | 89.58% |

* The result we obtained after implementing the method in[5]

In Table 4, our approach is inferior to others on the TST v2 dataset. In the process of implementing the idea of the method [5], we did not achieve the results they published on the TST v2 dataset (this did not happen with the FallFree dataset). Compared to their 100% accuracy, we only received an accuracy of 86.46%. Their study does not mention how the datasets were preprocessed. Thus, discrepancies between our results and theirs may occur since the way we preprocessed the data was not the same as theirs. After combining the attention mechanism we proposed, the accuracy of our model increased by 3.12%.

As shown in Table 5, our method was compared with two models on the FallFree dataset. Compared to the model in [15], our accuracy is 0.5% higher. Our approach adopted the idea of [5], which uses the pre-trained ST-GCN model, in addition to the attention mechanism. It resulted in our model having 2.67% better accuracy.

**Table 5.** Comparison of our method and other methods on the FallFree dataset

| Method | Algorithms | Evaluation method | Accuracy |
|---|---|---|---|
| Alzahrani et al., 2019 [15] | NCA for feature selection, RF classifier | 70% of data for training, 30% for testing | 99.5% |
| Keskes et al., 2021 [5] | Pre-trained ST-GCN | Cross subject | 97.33% |
| Our method | Pre-trained ST-GCN | Cross subject | 100% |

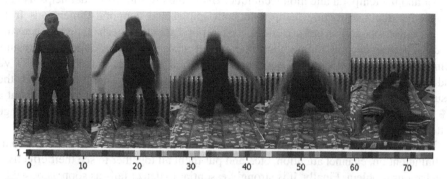

**Fig. 4.** The falling process and the distribution of attention weights for 75-frame sequence.

As can be seen in Fig. 4, from frame 20 to frame 45, the areas that have brighter colors mean "when to pay attention", since, in those frames, changes in movement occur very quickly. The falling action is fast and can last just one second, so the number of frames to focus on is about 30. Frames before the fall starts and after it ends have little difference, thus obtaining a lower score and a darker color in the distribution map.

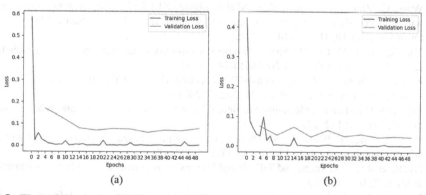

(a)                                                    (b)

**Fig. 5.** The training and validation loss graph in cases: (a) without and (b) with our proposed attention mechanism on the FallFree dataset.

In Fig. 5, the "distance" between the blue line and the orange line in the case with the attention mechanism is lower than in the case without the attention mechanism. The training loss shown in Fig. 5b in the rear epochs is more stable than in the remaining cases. In Fig. 5a, the validation loss values are approximately around 0.1 in later epochs, while in Fig. 5b, the entire orange line is completely below the 0.1 value. It can be seen that the attention technique reduces loss and makes the learning process more effective.

## 4 Conclusion and Future Works

This paper proposes a model for fall detection by combining the pre-trained ST-GCN model and the temporal attention technique. Using the pre-trained model helps us gain knowledge about extracting features in both spatial and temporal dimensions from human action recognition tasks. Besides, the temporal attention mechanism enhances the model's performance by highlighting important frames in a video. Experiment results demonstrate the effectiveness of our proposed method when performed on the TST v2 and the FallFree datasets. Especially in the experiment with the FallFree dataset, the result is extremely good when obtaining an accuracy of 100%. It also leads to about a 3% improvement in the TST v2 dataset. The work is also a good reference for image pattern recognition problems [16–20].

In the future, we want to do more experiments on different kinds of attention, such as spatial attention, channel attention, etc., and put them all together to see their effectiveness for our problem. Finally, it is strongly essential to detect falls as soon as possible, hence, our next goal is to develop the current model into a real-time fall detection application that can detect falls promptly and send an urgent warning to their relatives.

## References

1. Falls. https://www.who.int/news-room/fact-sheets/detail/falls. Accessed 01 Mar 2023
2. Verger, R.: The Apple Watch learned to detect falls using data from real human mishaps, Popular Science.https://www.popsci.com/apple-watch-fall-detection/. Accessed 01 Mar 2023
3. Wang, Q., Zhang, K., Asghar, M.A.: Skeleton-based ST-GCN for human action recognition with extended skeleton graph and partitioning strategy. IEEE Access: Practical Innovations, Open Solutions **10**, 41403–41410 (2022)
4. Yan, S., Xiong, Y., Lin, D.: Spatial Temporal Graph Convolutional Networks for Skeleton-Based Action Recognition. arXiv:1801.07455 (2018)
5. Keskes, O., Noumeir, R.: Vision-based fall detection using ST-GCN. IEEE Access: Practical Innovations, Open Solutions **9**, 28224–28236 (2021)
6. Soydaner, D.: Attention Mechanism in Neural Networks: Where it Comes and Where it Goes. arXiv:2204.13154 (2022)
7. Zhu, Q., Deng, H., Wang, K.: Skeleton action recognition based on temporal gated unit and adaptive graph convolution. Electronics **11**(18), 2973 (2022)
8. Xu, K., et al.: Show, Attend and Tell: Neural Image Caption Generation with Visual Attention. arXiv:1502.03044 (2015)
9. Yang, X.: An overview of the attention mechanisms in computer vision. J. Phys: Conf. Ser. **1693**(1), 012173 (2020)
10. Guo, M.-H., et al.: Attention Mechanisms in Computer Vision: A Survey. arXiv:2111.07624 (2021)
11. Hu, J., Shen, L., Albanie, S., Sun, G., Wu, E.: Squeeze-and-Excitation Networks. arXiv:1709. 01507 (2017)

12. Woo, S., Park, J., Lee, J.-Y., Kweon, I.S.: CBAM: Convolutional Block Attention Module. arXiv:1807.06521 (2018)
13. Kim, J., Li, G., Yun, I., Jung, C., Kim, J.: Weakly-supervised temporal attention 3D network for human action recognition. Pattern Recognition. **119**(108068) (2021)
14. Gasparrini, S., et al.: Proposal and experimental evaluation of fall detection solution based on wearable and depth data fusion. ICT Innovations 2015, Springer International Publishing, pp. 99–108 (2016)
15. Alzahrani, M.S., Jarraya, S.K., Salamah, M.A., Ben-Abdallah, H.: FallFree: multiple fall scenario dataset of cane users for monitoring applications using Kinect. In: Proceedings of the 13th International Conference on Signal-Image Technology & Internet-Based Systems (SITIS), pp. 327–333 (2017)
16. Hung, P.D., Kien, N.N.: SSD-Mobilenet implementation for classifying fish species. In: Vasant, P., Zelinka, I., Weber, GW. (eds) Intelligent Computing and Optimization. ICO 2019. Advances in Intelligent Systems and Computing, vol 1072. Springer, Cham. https://doi.org/10.1007/978-3-030-33585-4_40 (2020)
17. Hung, P.D., Su, N.T., Diep, V.T.: Surface classification of damaged concrete using deep convolutional neural network. Pattern Recognit. Image Anal. **29**, 676–687 (2019)
18. Hung, P.D., Su, N.T.: Unsafe construction behavior classification using deep convolutional neural network. Pattern Recognit. Image Anal. **31**, 271–284 (2021)
19. Duy, L.D., Hung, P.D.: Adaptive graph attention network in person re-identification. Pattern Recognit. Image Anal. **32**, 384–392 (2022)
20. Su, N.T., Hung, P.D., Vinh, B.T., Diep, V.T.: Rice Leaf disease classification using deep learning and target for mobile devices. In: Al-Emran, M., Al-Sharafi, M.A., Al-Kabi, M.N., Shaalan, K. (eds) Proceedings of International Conference on Emerging Technologies and Intelligent Systems. ICETIS 2021. Lecture Notes in Networks and Systems, vol 299. Springer, Cham (2022)

# Deep Regression Learning for Collaborative Electronically Assisted Astronomy

Olivier Parisot[✉]

Luxembourg Institute of Science and Technology (LIST), 5 Avenue des
Hauts-Fourneaux, 4362 Esch-sur-Alzette, Luxembourg
olivier.parisot@list.lu

**Abstract.** Observing deep sky is a fascinating activity, and the democratization of automated telescopes for the general public makes the practice of Electronically Assisted Astronomy even more accessible. In this paper, we show how Deep Regression Learning can be useful for supporting collaboration between astronomers to obtain better images.

**Keywords:** Electronically Assisted Astronomy · Computer Vision ·
Deep Regression Learning

## 1 Introduction

Electronically Assisted Astronomy (EAA) consists in combining optical instruments and dedicated cameras to observe planets and faint deep sky objects like nebulae, galaxies and stars clusters. EAA enables admiring through screens hundreds of faint celestial targets that are invisible through direct observation: sensors are much more sensitive than the human eye to capture faint signal [10, 11]. EAA is ideal for observers with poor visual acuity, for viewing sessions with family/friends and for public outreach events [8]. It is also an effective approach to observe the night sky in geographical areas impacted by light pollution (cities, suburbs, etc.).

Recently, robotic portable telescopes have appeared on the market, making sky observation much more accessible. With these instruments, all the steps are automatized and transparent for the end-user: tracking, focus, capture, storage, lightweight image processing, and then display. Thus, they can be driven by users with different parameters (exposure time and gain for each unit shot).

These instruments have numerous advantages, in particular for scientific methodology: they work in a reproducible way, so it is easier to aggregate the data obtained with such devices. Each image obtained will have exactly the same resolution (in arc seconds per pixel): thus, combining the images of a given target taken with several automated telescopes is very easy, since it is enough to align and stack the images.

In this paper, we propose a Deep Regression Learning approach to help astronomers when they collaborate by combining images obtained during EAA sessions. The rest of this article is organized as follows. Firstly, related works

Y. Luo (Ed.): CDVE 2023, LNCS 14166, pp. 168–173, 2023.
https://doi.org/10.1007/978-3-031-43815-8_16

about collaboration in astronomy and images quality assessment are briefly presented (Sect. 2). Then, a Deep Regression Learning approach is described (Sect. 3). Finally, the results of preliminary experiments are discussed (Sect. 4) and we conclude by opening some perspectives (Sect. 5).

## 2    Related Works

There are several ways to collaborate in EAA. The first is to share the equipment needed to capture images. Indeed, astrophotography can be expensive and some equipment can be very specialized: telescopes, cameras, mounts, filters, etc. [7]. Pooling these different instruments within a group or a club allows to make possible combinations that would be impossible for the observer. Collaboration can also take the form of exchange of knowledge, skills, via discussion forums or dedicated exchange platforms.

Another more concrete way of collaboration consists in collecting and merging data obtained during different observation sessions. The more time a telescope spends observing a target, the higher the signal-to-noise ratio of the resulting data. This is because the signal from the target (such as light from a distant galaxy) accumulates over time, while the noise from various sources (such as thermal fluctuations in the instrument) remains roughly constant. More precisely, accumulating data with several telescopes during different nights allows to obtain a larger quantity of images which can then be filtered, aligned and stacked. Collaborative observing programs are often used to study objects that require long integration times, such as faint galaxies or distant quasars. By combining observations from multiple telescopes or instruments, astronomers can obtain more complete data sets and make more robust measurements. As an example, a recent discovery was made during an amateur-professional collaboration, when a cloud near the Andromeda galaxy (Messier 31) was discovered [1].

In astronomy, the cumulative integration time refers to the total amount of time an object or region of the sky has been observed by a telescope or instrument. In other words, it is the sum of all the individual exposure times that were taken during a given period. This parameter has a direct impact on the quality of the final stacked image, and especially on the Signal-to-Noise Ratio (SNR): this metric is the ratio of the strength of the astronomical signal to the level of the noise in an image. It is usually measured in seconds, minutes or hours, depending on the duration of the observation. It can vary considerably depending on the type of observation, the sensitivity of the instrument and other factors. For example, some observations may require only a few minutes of integration time, while others may require several hours or even days to achieve the desired SNR level. In the case of a celestial targets like NGC7023 (Fig. 1), 30 min of data acquisition allows to obtain a detailed image of the nebula.

(a) Cumulative integration time: 4 min.  (b) Cumulative integration time: 40 min.

**Fig. 1.** Two stacked images of NGC7023 (aka Iris Nebula) obtained after different cumulative integration times with a robotic telescope [9]: the second one has a better Signal-to-Noise Ratio.

## 3    Approach

Deep Regression Learning is frequently applied in numerous computer vision tasks [6]. In this paper, we propose to train a model for estimating the cumulative integration time of astronomical images for which this value is not known, or when images have been obtained after the multiple combinations of images captured during parallel EAA sessions.

We have built a training dataset with astronomical images and an associated cumulative integration time by applying the DIQA generic methodology [3]. As original source, we have used the MILAN Sky Survey, a large set of deep sky images obtained with a Stellina robotic telescope during EAA sessions [9]. The Stellina observation station is based on an apochromatic ED doublet with an aperture of 80 mm and a focal length of 400 mm - focal ratio of f/5. The data acquisition is performed via a Sony IMX 178 CMOS sensor with a resolution of 6.4 million pixels (3096 × 2080 pixels). A light anti-pollution filter is placed in front of the camera sensor. The station also has a fully automated mount, and also an integrated field rotator that adapts to the target. Each Stellina image will have exactly the same resolution: thus, integrating together the images of a given target taken with several automated telescopes is very easy, since it is enough to align and stack the images.

The training dataset was defined as follows:

- For each deep sky object referenced in the MILAN Sky Survey, we have generated several stacked RGB images from raw images: each generated image corresponds to different cumulative integration time, i.e. images for 5 min, then 10 min, etc.
- Random crops were realized to obtain 224 × 224 patches (this resolution corresponds to the input shape for many Deep Learning algorithms).
- At the end, 10000 224 × 224 images of different cumulative integration time were selected. This is the value to estimate.

Thus, a Python prototype was developed to train a Deep Regression model from this dataset. Image preprocessing was realized with well-known open-source packages like *openCV*[1] and *scikit-images*[2].

We have used AutoKeras, a package to launch numerous training pipelines on-the-fly (model architecture selection, preprocessing steps, algorithms setting, training, model evaluation and then comparison) [2] To find the best configuration: AutoKeras is based on pre-defined pipelines, then incrementally refines the best one by making small mutations (as a genetic algorithm would do) [2]. Step by step, the pipeline leading to the best model is thus optimized up to a user-defined limit (i.e. number of trials).

To train a Deep Regression model for our task, the training was realized with the following hardware: 40 cores and 128 GB RAM (Intel(R) Xeon(R) Silver 4210 CPU @ 2.20GHz) and NVIDIA Tesla V100-PCIE-32GB. NUMBA was used to optimize the CPU/GPU usage during the image processing phases [4].

## 4    Preliminary Experiments

We have thus obtained different models with various architectures, but the best one corresponds to a network based on ResNet50. Recent work has shown that this architecture is often efficient for *Deep Regression* tasks [5].

| Layer (type) | Output Shape | Param # |
|---|---|---|
| input_42 (InputLayer) | [(None, 224, 224, 3)] | 0 |
| cast_to_float32_21 | (None, 224, 224, 3) | 0 |
| resnet50 (Functional) | (None, 7, 7, 2048) | 23587712 |
| dropout_20 (Dropout) | (None, 7, 7, 2048) | 0 |
| flatten_21 (Flatten) | (None, 100352) | 0 |
| regression_head_1 (Dense) | (None, 1) | 100353 |

The leading model has a R-squared score of 0.53, a Mean Absolute Error of 7.80 and a Root Mean Squared Error of 9.86. In practice, the predcitions are quite good for most of images (Fig. 2).

We therefore used the trained to evaluate the cumulative integration time of images obtained after aggregating captures of the same target with a similar robotic instrument. Let's take the example of two images of NGC2264, captured with two Vespera telescopes during the same night. The first image has a cumulative integration time of 33 min, the second one 190 min. We have combined them by following different approaches [12], and we have observed that only one aggregation method provided an image with a better predicted cumulative integration time (Fig. 3).

---

[1] https://pypi.org/project/opencv-python/.
[2] https://pypi.org/project/scikit-image/.

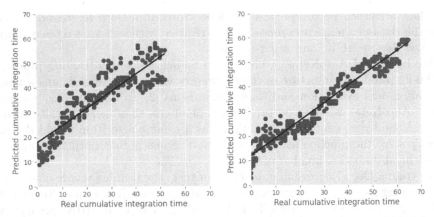

(a) NGC2174 (Monkey Head Nebula). (b) NGC7000 (North America Nebula).

**Fig. 2.** Regression plots for sequences of images for two deep sky objects, data extracted from the MILAN Sky Survey [9].

**Fig. 3.** Image obtained by aggregating two captures of NGC2264 (Cone Nebula).

# 5   Conclusion and Perspectives

This paper presented an approach to automatically estimate the cumulative integration time of astronomical RGB images captured during EAA sessions. A Python prototype was developed, a Deep Regression Learning model was trained and preliminary results were shown. The model can be used to guide astronomers and observers during collaborative observations to assess the benefits of acquiring data in parallel with robotic telescopes and then combining the resulting images of the same deep sky targets.

In future work, we will extend this Regression Learning task by applying eXplainable AI approaches that are relevant to images processing.

**Acknowledgments.** This research was funded by the Luxembourg National Research Fund (FNR), grant reference 15872557. Tests were realized on the LIST AIDA platform, thanks to Raynald Jadoul and Jean-François Merche.

# References

1. Drechsler, M., et al.: Discovery of extensive [o iii] emission near m31. Res. Notes AAS **7**(1), 1 (2023)
2. Jin, H., Chollet, F., Song, Q., Hu, X.: Autokeras: an automl library for deep learning. J. Mach. Learn. Res. **24**(6), 1–6 (2023)
3. Kim, J., Nguyen, A.D., Lee, S.: Deep CNN-based blind image quality predictor. IEEE Trans. Neural Netw. Learn. Syst. **30**(1), 11–24 (2019). https://doi.org/10.1109/TNNLS.2018.2829819
4. Lam, S.K., Pitrou, A., Seibert, S.: Numba: a LLVM-based python JIT compiler. In: Proceedings of the Second Workshop on the LLVM Compiler Infrastructure in HPC, pp. 1–6 (2015)
5. Lathuilière, S., Mesejo, P., Alameda-Pineda, X., Horaud, R.: A comprehensive analysis of deep regression. IEEE Trans. Pattern Anal. Mach. Intell. **42**(9), 2065–2081 (2019)
6. Milicevic, M., Batos, V., Lipovac, A., Car, Z.: Deep regression neural networks for proportion judgment. Future Internet **14**(4), 100 (2022)
7. ÓBrien, M.: A brief overview of deep-sky imaging equipment. In: A Deep Sky Astrophotography Primer. The Patrick Moore Practical Astronomy Series, pp. 7–12. Springer, Cham (2023). https://doi.org/10.1007/978-3-031-15762-2_2
8. Parisot, O., Bruneau, P., Hitzelberger, P., Krebs, G., Destruel, C.: Improving accessibility for deep sky observation. ERCIM News 2022(130) (2022)
9. Parisot, O., Hitzelberger, P., Bruneau, P., Krebs, G., Destruel, C., Vandame, B.: MILAN sky survey, a dataset of raw deep sky images captured during one year with a Stellina automated telescope. Data in Brief **48**, 109133 (2023). https://doi.org/10.1016/j.dib.2023.109133
10. Parker, G.: Making Beautiful Deep-Sky Images. TPMPAS, Springer, Cham (2017). https://doi.org/10.1007/978-3-319-46316-2
11. Redfern, G.I.: Astrophotography is Easy! TPMPAS, Springer, Cham (2020). https://doi.org/10.1007/978-3-030-45943-7
12. Woodhouse, C.: Image calibration and stacking: two strategies that go hand-in-hand to remove mean errors and reduce the noise level in the final image. In: The Astrophotography Manual, pp. 203–212. Routledge (2017)

# A Deeping Learning Based Framework and System for Effective Land Use Mapping

Xiaojin Liao[1], Xiaodi Huang[1], and Weidong Huang[2]([⊠])

[1] Charles Sturt University, Albury, NSW 2640, Australia
{xliao,xhuang}@csu.edu.au
[2] University of Technology Sydney, Ultimo, NSW 2007, Australia
weidong.huang@uts.edu.au

**Abstract.** This paper proposes and implements a novel framework that uses deep learning to classify and visualise satellite land images. The proposed framework uses deep learning to accurately detect features in satellite images, automating the extraction of useful information from large datasets. It involves building and training a deep learning module using various algorithms and settings to improve geographic data processing. Overall, this paper contributes to the field of spatial image processing and highlights the potential benefits of deep learning in land-use mapping and related applications. The implementation of this technology can increase agricultural productivity, improve natural disaster management, and protect the environment.

**Keywords:** Deep learning · Classification · Visualisation

## 1 Introduction

Advances in remote sensing technologies have made satellite imagery a valuable source of information for land use mapping. The collection of raw data is exploding, and the big-geospatial data from various sources has grown into petabytes and increases by terabytes in size every day [1]. However, it is difficult query and search on them before the raw data has been marked and categorised. For example, to query how many hectares of banana or apple plantations are in the area, or what sort of drought level or flood level currently is? There is no direct answer from those raw images.

Land use mapping analysing these images to extract meaningful information. The demand for data and information is growing, and the science department needs to provide more data, faster data, and models. With the increase in size and complexity of the raw data, the acquisition of them has been exponential as compared to the development of processing systems that can process the data in real time [2].

Deep learning (DL) has been identified as a potential technique for improvement and efficiency. There is the feasibility of using deep learning to identify the land use of satellite images to reduce the intensive manual effort required and to achieve results in a shorter time [3]. In our research, we attempted to design a novel framework that considers the spatial information contained in the data for land cover classification.

Y. Luo (Ed.): CDVE 2023, LNCS 14166, pp. 174–180, 2023.
https://doi.org/10.1007/978-3-031-43815-8_17

## 2  Design of the Framework

### 2.1  Design Requirements

To successfully implement a deep learning framework for land use mapping, it is important to carefully consider design requirements. Here we outline the key requirements for our framework. Firstly, our framework will be optimized for speed, efficient, and accuracy. Secondly, it designed to be security and raw data privacy, ensuring flexible and robust to handle incomplete data. Finally, it will support incremental training with localized data to accommodate changes in land use and new data sources. By meeting these requirements, our framework will provide a comprehensive solution for land use mapping with deep learning.

### 2.2  Design of the Framework

Our deep learning framework is flexible to accommodate various data sources and land use mapping requirements. We use a modular design approach, where each module performs a specific task, such as data pre-processing, model training, and inference. This design approach allows us to swap modules easily and tailor our framework to different use cases.

In the following, the main techniques used in the framework are explained.

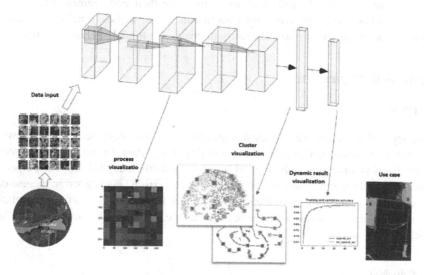

**Fig. 1.** Proposed deep learning algorithms and methods framework

The proposed framework is illustrated in Fig. 1. It consists of four parts: preprocessing, training, classification, and visualisation. Land images are represented by using the embedding method first, and the downstream tasks are then as follows:

1. classify the different land uses by using their similarities and distances in the embedding space;

2. visualise the intermediate abstract results of an image by DL;
3. visualise the classified results;
4. allow users to interact with the system.

We also apply state-of-the-art DL CapsNet algorithms to build the system. The input data of the system is the available historical spatial images and timeline data. Based on this historical data, the model can learn the features of land changes over seasons and years.

Furthermore, the visualisation techniques are applied to illustrate the different results of the modelling in various stages and outputs. Our system allows users to interact with it in a friendly way. Users may use visualisation to find the information needed.

### 2.3  Input Data

Within our framework, the input data can be various datasets, map data and high-definition satellite images. Some of the well-known public datasets we tested include: EuroSAT database [4], BigEarthNet [5]. Certain map engine data can also be used as input data for the framework, for example Google Earth Engine and Digital Earth Australia.

Customised satellite image dataset is the core dataset of our experiments. The Wet Tropic Natural Resource Management (NRM) Region Map is used to build this customised satellite image data.

To enable Federated Learning, clients must have their own training dataset. This dataset should be representative of the data that the client wishes to train the model on and should be of sufficient size and quality to enable the model to learn effectively.

## 3  Applied Algorithms

### 3.1  CNN

Efficiency and accuracy are a critical requirement for our deep learning framework. CNN has an excellent performance in processing image data. In our previous research finding, CNN algorithm have both good accuracy and efficiency [6]. So, our purpose is to use CNN to train and generate land use labels. Its texture bias is good in the use case of plantation classification from the satellite images [7] because classifying vegetation from satellite images mostly uses the texture feature, instead of the shapes of the land block.

### 3.2  CapsNet

The state-of-the-art CapsNet model which Hinton published in 2017 [8], has been used and analysed. We did extensive experiments on adjusting and fine tuning the CapsNet model with our Land Use Mapping (LUM) dataset. We are going to add more attributes (like historical data, different season images, temperature, rainfall data) to our dataset to further experiment and analyse this CapsNet model. This will further enhance the robustness of the framework.

### 3.3 Federated Learning

Preserving the security and privacy of raw data is a critical requirement for our deep learning framework. Federated Learning is a distributed machine learning technique that allows a model to be trained on data distributed across multiple devices, without having to transfer the raw data to a central server.

When data is privacy sensitive or large in size, it is preferable not to log it to the data centre purely for the purpose of model training. Federated Learning approach that allows multiple parties to train a model collaboratively without sharing their data. Each client has a local training dataset that is never uploaded to the server. Federated Learning enables training of local models with data distributed across multiple locations on individual machines or servers.

Experiments show that Federated Learning can be made practical, as FedAvg trains high-quality models using relatively few rounds of communication, as demonstrated by results on a variety of model architectures: a multi-layer perceptron, two different convolutional NNs, a two-layer character LSTM, and a large-scale word-level LSTM [9]. Other experiments also confirming that, applying Fedcrated Learning in a realistic setting is possible without affecting the user experience [10].

## 4 Visualisation

Data visualisation and visual analytics excel at knowledge communication and insight discovery by using encoding to transform abstract data into meaningful representations. The visualisation technique enabled projection from a model's learned feature space back to the pixel space. This technique and results give insight into what types of features deep neural networks are learning at specific layers and serve as a debugging tool for improving a model [11].

TensorBoard can visualise the network architecture, which is a great tool to help optimise the algorithm. A visual design based on charts is also incorporated to reveal intuitively raw sequential input that is related to the hidden states [12]. Looking at live activations that change in response to user input helps build valuable intuition about how ConvNets works [13].

Within the various stages of processing data, we use various visualisation methods based on the statistical method.

## 5 Experimental Evaluation

In the experiments, we examine the benefits and challenges of using Federated Learning for spatial classification and discuss some of the potential applications of this technology in the field of environmental sensing and monitoring.

In the land use mapping, Federated Learning allows multiple organizations or individuals to collaborate to train a model on their different datasets without the need to share raw data. With the advent of Federated Learning, it is now possible to create land cover groups using a distributed approach that enables data to reside on local devices, such as smartphones or sensors, and to allow models to be trained without the need to share raw data. This method can improve the accuracy of land cover classification models while dealing with privacy problems.

Here we present some of the experiment results of the evaluation of the framework on different datasets based on our experiment with Federated Learning after loading the custom dataset. Figure 2 shows the data distribution of clients.

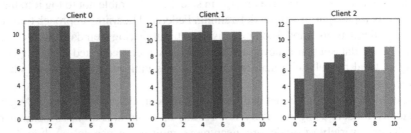

**Fig. 2.** The data distribution of the Federated Learning client data

We see in Fig. 3 that the random sample input data matches the label.

**Fig. 3.** Random sample input data matches the label

Using distribution, confusion metrics and other visualisation methods will make it much easier to analyse the data and help find a better model to process and debug data.

The Fig. 4 screenshot shows the performance of the Federated Learning in our framework in terms of accuracy, speed, and scalability.

There are some standard metrics of performance in these deep learning applications. For performance evaluation, we used accuracy, precision, recall and F1- (sensitivity, specificity, and overall accuracy) [14].With five rounds of client training, we can see the improvement of accuracy and the loss have been reduced.

Visualisation is used to display how the data is being processed, changed, and output results. In Fig. 5 we use matplotlib in Python to do the visualisation. It is the most widely used library for plotting in Python. Here are some visualisation output sample images from our current framework:

The two images in Fig. 6 show the input satellite image and the classified and marked image output by the framework.

```
INFO flwr 2023-02-01 09:48:03,027 | app.py:200 | app_fit: losses_centralized []
INFO:flwr:app_fit: losses_centralized []
INFO flwr 2023-02-01 09:48:03,033 | app.py:201 | app_fit: metrics_centralized {}
INFO:flwr:app_fit: metrics_centralized {}
History (loss, distributed):
        round 1: 0.0351541582606403
        round 2: 0.013042470899801215
        round 3: 0.010716904526151634
        round 4: 0.009950676676843904
        round 5: 0.0085489459640673 4
```

**Fig. 4.** The output of the Federated Learning

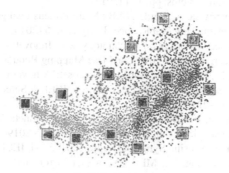

**Fig. 5.** Stacked encoder for unsupervised autolearning results (Small squares are thumbnails of class samples)

**Fig. 6.** Input image and a marked output image

## 6 Conclusion

In this research, we used deep learning in classifying and visualising satellite land images. As such, we propose a novel framework. The framework starts with building and training a DL module. After training the attributes of land images, the downstream tasks such as classification, and visualisation are based on these trained models.

The framework is applied and built with some DL algorithms that apply various settings in the process of satellite images. This provides a better way of doing geographic data processing. Implementing innovative AI and DL technology in spatial image processing can increase agricultural productivity, help better manage natural disasters and protect the environment. The final DL framework can help government science departments and researchers to develop and use the relevant applications and classes to better manage resources, make decisions and improve environmental protection.

# References

1. Eldawy, A., Niu, L., Haynes, D., Su, Z.: Large scale analytics of vector+raster big spatial data. Proceedings of the 25th ACM SIGSPATIAL International Conference on Advances in Geographic Information Systems, pp. 1–4 (2017)
2. Alkathiri, M., Jhummarwala, A., Potdar, M.B.: Multi-dimensional geospatial data mining in a distributed environment using MapReduce. J. Big Data **6** (2019)
3. Department of Science, Information Technology and Innovation (DSITI): DSITI89267 Building Machine Learning Capability: Land Use Mapping Request for quote (2017)
4. Helber, P., Bischke, B., Dengel, A., Borth, D.: Eurosat: A novel dataset and deep learning benchmark for land use and land cover classification. IEEE J. Select. Top. Appl. Earth Obs. Remote Sens. **12**, 2217–2226 (2019)
5. Sumbul, G., Charfuelan, M., Demir, B., Markl, V.: Bigearthnet: A large-scale benchmark archive for remote sensing image understanding. In: IGARSS 2019–2019 IEEE International Geoscience and Remote Sensing Symposium, pp. 5901–5904. IEEE (2019)
6. Liao, X., Huang, X., Huang, W.: ML-LUM: a system for land use mapping by machine learning algorithms. J. Comput. Lang. **54**, 100908 (2019)
7. Geirhos, R., Rubisch, P., Michaelis, C., Bethge, M., Wichmann, F.A., Brendel, W.: ImageNet-trained CNNs are biased towards texture; increasing shape bias improves accuracy and robustness. arXiv preprint arXiv:1811.12231 (2018)
8. Sabour, S., Frosst, N., Hinton, G.E.: Dynamic routing between capsules. Adv. Neural Inf. Process. Syst. **30**, 3859–3869 (2017)
9. McMahan, B., Moore, E., Ramage, D., Hampson, S., Arcas, B.A.: Communication-efficient learning of deep networks from decentralized data. Artif. Intell. Stat. 1273–1282 (2017)
10. Konečný, J., McMahan, H.B., Yu, F.X., Richtárik, P., Suresh, A.T., Bacon, D.: Federated learning: strategies for improving communication efficiency. arXiv preprint arXiv:1610.05492 (2016)
11. Hohman, F., Kahng, M., Pienta, R., Chau, D.H.: Visual analytics in deep learning: an interrogative survey for the next frontiers. IEEE Trans. Visual Comput. Graph. **25**, 2674–2693 (2018)
12. Yu, R., Shi, L.: A user-based taxonomy for deep learning visualization. Vis. Inform. **2**, 147–154 (2018)
13. Yosinski, J., Clune, J., Nguyen, A., Fuchs, T., Lipson, H.: Understanding neural networks through deep visualization. arXiv preprint arXiv:1506.06579 (2015)
14. Wieland, M., Pittore, M.: Performance evaluation of machine learning algorithms for urban pattern recognition from multi-spectral satellite images. Remote Sens. **6**, 2912–2939 (2014)

# Video and Audio Linkage in Recommender System

Le Dinh Huynh[1], Phan Quang Huy[1], Phan Duy Hung[1(✉)], and Vu Thu Diep[2(✉)]

[1] FPT Univerisity, Hanoi, Vietnam
{huynhld3,hungpd2}@fe.edu.vn, huypqhe141762@fpt.edu.vn
[2] Hanoi University of Science and Technology, Hanoi, Vietnam
diep.vuthu@hust.edu.vn

**Abstract.** Among the enormous volume of data available, the recommender system assists users in locating useful information that meets their needs. Video and audio recordings are complex media and linking datasets that satisfy defined requirements is becoming an increasingly significant, but challenging endeavor. As part of this paper, we propose a data linkage approach for matching audio recordings to related music videos. A cooperative method was introduced utilizing the Elasticsearch search engine primarily for preprocessing. Data features were further aggregated using text data matching scores, date and time features, popularity scores, and data completeness scores. We automated the machine learning process using PyCaret, which gave us more time for analysis and less time for coding. Experiments demonstrate that this method can generate a ranking of significant features and performance tracking that improves the efficacy of data linking.

**Keywords:** Data Linkage · Recommender System · Elasticsearch · PyCaret · Cooperative Engineering

## 1 Introduction

Nowadays, the recommender system is becoming more widespread and is an essential feature in many systems including e-commerce [1, 2], entertainment [2, 3], education [4, 5], and several more. The personalized recommendation has been classified into approaches: Popularity [6], Collaborative Filtering (CF), Content-based Filtering (CBF), and Hybrid approaches [1]. The idea of Popularity is to suggest the most popular things. It is simple and effective. CF models can be classified into memory-based and model-based approaches. Model-based techniques attempt to uncover user-item interactions to provide suggestions, whereas memory-based approaches work directly with the interactions. Using the preferences of one specific user and the available item information, CBF models create a user model (user profile) and produce suggestions. Hybrid recommender systems use a fusion technique to integrate two or more of the prior approaches. Ordinarily, the initial implementation was only performed on CF due to data limitations.

Since recommender systems have been considered for large-scale multimedia content like music, podcasts, or videos in recent years, numerous approaches to the task of metadata linking have been proposed. In 2018, Molina [7] built Netflix's recommendation system and surveyed it with Popularity, CF, CBF, and Hybrid Approaches. They achieved very good performance with new users and cold-start challenges. A second study on CF for podcast recommendations was conducted by scientists and researchers from Spotify and Cornell University in 2020 [8]. The authors proposed 9 podcast recommendation models, including both cross-domain CF models and hybrid demographic-based CF approaches. The work further developed a cross-domain transfer method based on a range of available features on popular music streaming services that represent a user's source profile. These features included:

- Demographics: age, country, gender.
- Metadata: genre, artists.
- Music Taste Embeddings: 40-dimensional vector representations of tracks.
- Podcast Interests: podcast watchlist.

In the same year, Yashal et al. [9] gained their interest in a recommendation system for multimedia based on pure CBF models or hybrid systems that combine CBF with CF and Context-aware models. The survey includes several prior recommender system approaches enriched by metadata.

More and more people can access the entertainment industry through various media platforms. Once information is gathered and integrated from various sources to create a cross-platform recommendation system for multimedia content. This poses several practical problems for data engineers. The sub-problem being addressed in this study is data linkage, which is a task that can be automated but was previously done by humans. It is used to create connections between media contents.

To sum up, this paper proposed a Machine Learning approach to rank audio recordings that match the input video programs in terms of metadata. To perform this task, it includes preprocessing step, embedding model, and evaluating model. This study optimized CBF-based by cooperating with Elasticsearch engine [10], PyCare low code machine learning [11], Boruta Feature Selection, and SMOTE Imbalance Handling Technique.

We proceed with the methodology in Sect. 2. Section 3 defines the implementation. Experiments and results are presented in Sect. 4. We conclude in Sect. 5.

## 2 Methodology

### 2.1 Dataset

Our dataset consists of 2 main groups: music video (MV) and audio recording. Celebrities own MVs. The song is represented by an audio file. MV contains some basic information in Table 1.

A recording has 9 attributes (Table 2).

There are MVs, Celebrities, Recordings, Songs, Artists and Edition Album. Their relationship is shown in Fig. 1 below.

Data is processed in two ways: manually and automatically by an Elasticsearch query, and is enriched and cleaned by:

**Table 1.** Music Video attributes

| No | Name | Abbreviation | Description |
|----|------|-------------|-------------|
| 1 | Title | title | Latin or non-Latin name of MV |
| 2 | Celebrity | celebs | celebrity name is written using a Latin script |
| 3 | Celebrity Type | celebType | celebrity personality types |
| 4 | Duration | duration | video length in milliseconds |
| 5 | Original Air Date | oriAirDate | the date of a broadcast or scheduled broadcast |

**Table 2.** Recording attributes.

| No | Name | Abbreviation | Description |
|----|------|-------------|-------------|
| 1 | Recording Name | recordingName | identify of recording |
| 2 | Artist Name | artistName | name of the artist normally written using a non-Latin script |
| 3 | Sort Name | sortName | name of the artist written using a Latin script |
| 4 | Name Variant | nameVariants | pseudonym or any related name |
| 5 | Original Air Date | oriAirDate | the date of a broadcast or scheduled broadcast |
| 6 | Artist Type | artistType | same as celebType |
| 7 | Duration | duration | recording length in milliseconds |
| 8 | Release Year | releaseYear | official release year |
| 9 | Number of Edition | numEdition | the total number of copies |

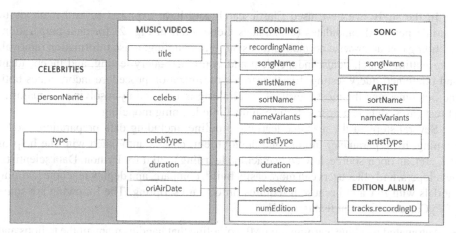

**Fig. 1.** Aggregated attributes for MVs, Recording, Celebrities, Artist, Edition Album and Song.

- Elasticsearch Match Query: customize Elasticsearch query by combining a set of *multi_match*, *most_fields* and *fuzziness*.
- Join characters Normalization: use replacement normalizes all *"Featuring"*, *"Ft."*, *"Feat."*, *"Feat"*, *"Ft"*, *"And"*, *"&"*, *";"*, *":"*, *"|"*, *"/"* with *","* for *RecordingName* and *ArtistName*.
- Accent and Mark Normalization: remove extra space, mark and accent.
- Noise characters Normalization: create a synonym dictionary (artists with abbreviations or special characters) and remove noise information in brackets.
- ID Standardized using TMSID: to distinguish between multiple types of content, standardized by the original entertainment media distributor.

## 2.2 Workflow

As a fast, extensible, and widely used search engine that works with JSON queries and responses, Elasticsearch Search Engine is highly regarded [12]. Elasticsearch was first created as a straightforward search engine, but it is constantly improved depending on the incredibly diverse uses and complexity of users. Users can conduct various full-text searches, among which are *simple search, fuzzy search* and *aggregating*. With the use of a match query, Elasticsearch is a helpful tool for both individuals and businesses [12–14]:

- Simple Search: Elasticsearch's full-text search that includes faceted navigation which informs how the results are distributed.
- Fuzzy Search: Users can perform spelling-errors lenient search with sensible use to reduce CPU expensiveness.
- Instant Autocomplete Search: Elasticsearch has a wide range of capabilities that can help provide autocomplete search.
- Data Analytics: Elasticsearch's aggregations of mass data are generated by Elasticsearch Kibana for analytical searches and data analytics.
- Data Uploads: Several common ways to ingest data into Elasticsearch Service.

In the study, we have used Elasticsearch and have explored several methods to conduct potential candidates (Candidates Generation in Fig. 2) for data preparation, including character-wise normalization, synonym handling, noise information removal, reformatting search fields, independent and combined query testing, and independent and combined query testing. Elasticsearch's optimization procedure incorporates both the outcomes and the most prevalent data linking issues, and by resolving the majority of test cases, data is prepared for use in machine learning modeling.

Several steps in the machine learning pipeline, including data preparation, model training, hyperparameter tuning, and deployment, can be automated with the help of PyCaret, an open-source, low-code machine learning toolkit for Python. Data scientists, developers, and other users can more easily build, compare, and deploy machine learning models with PyCaret because it requires little to no scripting. The following are some of PyCaret's important features [15]:

- Automated machine learning (autoML) pipeline that handles many of the tedious and time-consuming tasks involved in building machine learning models.
- Interactive user interface that allows users to build, compare, and deploy models with just a few lines of code.

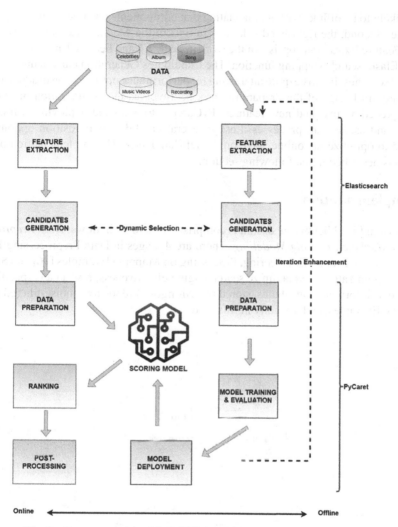

**Fig. 2.** Our proposed workflow is linked with Elasticsearch and PyCaret.

- Preprocessing functions for handling missing values, feature scaling, and categorical data.
- Hyperparameter tuning functions for optimizing model performance.
- Tools for model interpretation, feature importance analysis, and model visualization.
- Support for multiple file formats and data sources, including CSV, Excel, SQL databases, and cloud storage services.

The overall workflow is described in Fig. 2 above. The last component Ranking and Postprocessing is not described in detail since we are more interested in the recommender model construction process. There are a few things worth noting here. First, it instead introduces the idea that some components are more likely to be online while others are more likely to be offline, without mandating that components must be offline, online, or nearline. Second, the right-hand side flow initials to the Machine Learning Modelling Flow. Feature Extraction consists of the work in Sect. 2.1 and Feature Engineering based on the Elasticsearch Mapping function. The Candidates Generation can conduct various full-text searches. It will be quite interesting for performance optimization to adjust in this step. The third stage of the Preparation process involves the vectorization of features in the preceding part and new features. PyCaret automates the deployment, training, testing, and assessment processes. Lastly, several candidate composition options can be used to optimize the online stage on the left-hand side. The implementation of this section is described in the following section.

## 3  Implementation

As shown in Fig. 3 below, the design is comprised of two main flows: *Data Preprocessing* and *Machine Learning Modelling*. There are 4 stages in Data Preprocessing Flow: Data Ingestion, Feature Engineering, Processing on Mapping Examples [16] and Search Engine Optimization. To maximize search engine effectiveness, raw data is specifically ingested as information attributes, stored in a MongoDB repository, noise-filtered using Mapping Examples, and textually normalized.

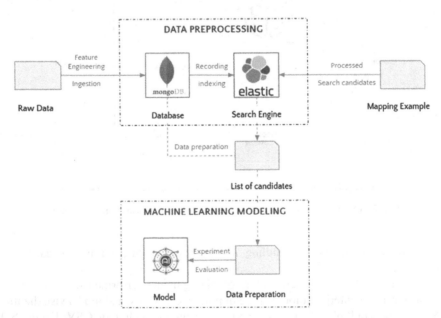

**Fig. 3.** Flow representation of the proposed metadata linking method.

As an initial step in the Machine Learning Modeling Flow, the preprocessed dataset is divided into new datasets for training and testing. Each audio recording candidate has a feature vector that contains both existing fields and newly available attributes. Two configurations are tested based on the selection of Boruta features and classic features, and an integrated assessment process is implemented. The study utilizes PyCaret, SMOTE techniques to address the issue of overfitting, Z-score normalization for the calculation of performance scores, and Logistical Regression as a pilot model. Finally, the feature-related ranking and performance-tracking process identify the most important fields and attributes to link metadata between music video and audio recordings.

In Feature Engineering, there are 4 processing steps: name, datetime, popularity scores, and data completeness.

*Name Processing* utilizes the FuzzyWuzzy method to perform partial ratio and token set ratio approaches. The evaluation value of features is calculated between 0.00 and 1.00. Attributes such as *songName*, *artistName*, *recordingName*, *sortName*, and *nameVariants* are applied to this processing method (Fig. 4).

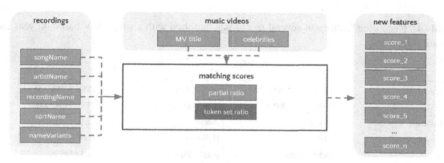

**Fig. 4.** Name processing method using partial ratio and token set ratio.

The sample data is in Table 3.

**Table 3.** Recording and MV features of a recording match scores

| artistName | recordingName | MV_title | partial ratio | token set ratio |
|---|---|---|---|---|
| Alanis Morissette | You Oughta Know [Alternate Take] | Alanis Morissette: You Oughta Know | 0.62 | 0.6 |

*DateTime Processing* generates new features regarding differences in release year and duration of music videos and recordings. *UpdateDate* and *orgAirDate* are MV features processed in this step, whereas *releaseYear* is the only recording feature. In this manner, *abs_diff_year* and diff_*yearRecording* are produced employing the formula (1) and (2).

```
diff_yearRecording = releaseYear - origAirDate        (1)
```

```
abs_diff_yearRecording = abs(diff_yearRecording)        (2)
```

Accordingly, MV with *mv_duration* feature and recording with *recording_duration* feature altogether outputs *diff_duration* and *ratio_duration* in (3) and (4).

```
diff_duration    = recording_duration - mv_duration      (3)
```

```
ratio_duration = recording_duration / mv_duration      (4)
```

Sample data can be found in Table 4.

**Table 4.** Recording features of several recordings matched with a single MV based on year and duration features.

|  | #1 | #2 | #3 |
|---|---|---|---|
| recordingID | GN5ZJ6CVJR1G5VD | GN92CGHKP6GHT8R | GN9S3V3GG44NJ25 |
| TMSID | SH023955430000 | SH023955430000 | SH023955430000 |
| artistName | Adele | Adele | Adele |
| recordingName | Hello | Hello | Hello |
| title | Adele: Hello | Adele: Hello | Adele: Hello |
| recording_duration | 254613 | 57253 | 136960 |
| MV_duration | 360 | 360 | 360 |
| diff_duration | −105.387 | −302.747 | −223.04 |
| ratio_duration | 0.0118 | 0.0027 | 0.0063 |
| releaseYear | 2015 | 2016 | 2010 |
| oriAirYear | 2015 | 2015 | 2015 |
| diff_yearRecording | 0 | 1 | -5 |
| abs_diff_yearRecording | 0 | 1 | 5 |

*Popularity Scores* are made up of *popularity_USA_recent, popularity_USA_alltime, popularity_CAN_alltime, popularity_CAN_recent* and *popularity_mean*. *Popularity_mean* is the average of the previous 4 points. The sample row is in Table 5.

*Data Completeness:* We wish to rank each candidate according to a variety of criteria, including *externalIDs, productCodes, genresid, origins, eras, artistTypes, moods, styles* and *tempos*. A recording can only obtain a maximum score of 9 if it is completely devoid of information. The score will be 1 if it just has one piece of information. The score is inversely correlated with the quantity of information in the recording. After then, the recordings will be sorted according to their ratings, with the recording with the highest rating receiving a *top_totalValue* of 1.

**Table 5.** Popularity features of a recording based on popularity scores in the USA and Canada.

| Features | Value |
|---|---|
| recordingID | GN5ZJ6CVJR1G5VD |
| TMSID | SH023955430000 |
| artistName | Adele |
| recordingName | Hello |
| title | Adele: Hello |
| popularity_USA_recent | 0.31131 |
| popularity_USA_alltime | 0.27874 |
| popularity_CAN_recent | 0.31813 |
| popularity_CAN_alltime | 0.22195 |
| popularity_mean | 0.282533 |

## 4  Experiment and Result

The data set is characterized by a highly imbalanced dataset, with a 5% positivity and 95% positivity ratio. The correlation of the data is presented in Fig. 5. The dataset contains a total of 2,603 true positive cases (52,076 recorded). To balance the dataset, 19 true negative cases were added for each positive case. The dataset has been partitioned into two sets; 10,000 additional cases were tested and 42,000 additional examples were trained. This partitioning of the dataset allows for a precise evaluation of the performance of unobserved data to ensure that the results are reliable and reliable. It is important to note that a balanced dataset does not lead to a bias towards one group over another, as is often the case with imbalanced data sets. The oversimplification of the minority class by the SMOTE algorithm is used to achieve a balanced dataset. The Boruta feature selection step is performed and the data is normalized using the Z-score function. A single classifier is used and a Stacking model is employed with adjustable thresholds.

To evaluate the quality of the linkage process, we compute 3 common metrics accuracy, precision and recall defined ((5), (6), (7)) as function of true positive (TP), false positive (FP), true negative (TN) and false negative (FN).

$$accuracy = (TP + TN) / (TP + TN + FP + FN) \qquad (5)$$

$$recall = TP / (TP + FN) \qquad (6)$$

$$precision = TP / (TP + FP) \qquad (7)$$

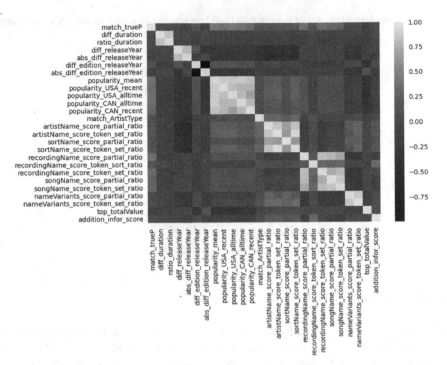

**Fig. 5.** Features correlation graph.

Table 6 compares and displays the experimental outcomes of various models, including XGBoost, CatBoost, LightGBM, Random Forest, Decision Tree, AdaBoost, Logistic Regression, SVM, KNN, Naive Bayes, Ridge, and our Stacking Classifier. During training, XGBoost had the highest accuracy score while logistic regression had the highest recall score. Therefore, the stacking model was produced by merging these two models to get a balanced score between recall and precision. The outcomes were determined by averaging the 10-fold cross-validation outcomes.

It is conceivable to combine models that specialize in optimizing either recall or precision. A stacked model with a better-balanced performance may be created by combining a Logistic Regression model with a high recall of **0.978** but a low precision of **0.5444** with an XGBoost model with a high precision of **0.776**. It is possible to achieve the appropriate balance between recall of **0.7965**, precision of **0.7622** and accuracy of **0.9771** by adjusting the hyperparameters of the individual models with the stacking classifier.

**Table 6.** Models performance

| Model | Accuracy | Recall | Precision |
|---|---|---|---|
| XGBoost | **0.9794** | 0.8396 | **0.776** |
| CatBoost | 0.9786 | 0.8496 | 0.761 |
| LightGBM | 0.9769 | 0.8509 | 0.7389 |
| Random Forest | 0.976 | 0.8622 | 0.7227 |
| Decision Tree | 0.9694 | 0.789 | 0.6705 |
| AdaBoost | 0.9633 | 0.8822 | 0.5961 |
| Logistic Regression | 0.9569 | **0.978** | 0.5444 |
| SVM | 0.9523 | 0.984 | 0.5188 |
| KNN | 0.949 | 0.9281 | 0.501 |
| Naive Bayes | 0.9287 | 0.9048 | 0.5648 |
| Ridge | 0.8966 | **0.9953** | 0.496 |
| Stacking Classifier (Ours – default) | 0.9787 | 0.8901 | 0.7441 |
| Stacking Classifier (Ours – adaptive tuning) | 0.9771 | 0.7965 | 0.7622 |

## 5 Conclusion

We demonstrated a data-linking approach for matching audio recordings to relevant music videos. A cooperative strategy has been put forward, mostly utilizing the Elasticsearch search engine for preprocessing. The machine learning pipeline was automated using PyCaret. The recommender system boosts the efficacy of data linking by up to 0.9771 accuracy, 0.7622 precision, and 0.7965 recall.

The suggested workflow is a beneficial element related to the design of both online and offline systems. It is also a good case study for high-performance recommender system. Section 2.1 and Sect. 3 introduce preprocessing methods that are useful for metadata processing and linkage data problems, including but not limited to other data mining pursuits. Without much effort, Candidate Generation adjustment produces positive variations in the system with the trained model.

## References

1. Hung, P.D, Huynh, L.D: E-Commerce recommendation system using Mahout. In: IEEE 4th International Conference on Computer and Communication Systems (ICCCS), Singapore, pp. 86–90 (2019). https://doi.org/10.1109/CCOMS.2019.8821663
2. Quan, V.H., Hung, P.D.: Heterogeneous neural collaborative filtering for a business recommender system. In: Al-Emran, M., Al-Sharafi, M.A., Al-Kabi, M.N., Shaalan, K. (eds.) Proceedings of International Conference on Emerging Technologies and Intelligent Systems. ICETIS 2021. Lecture Notes in Networks and Systems, vol 322. Springer, Cham (2021). https://doi.org/10.1007/978-3-030-85990-9_9

3. Hung, P.D., Son, D.N., Diep, V.T.: Building a recommendation system for travel location based on user check-ins on social network. In: Joshi, A., Mahmud, M., Ragel, R.G. (eds.) Information and Communication Technology for Competitive Strategies (ICTCS 2022). ICTCS 2022. Lecture Notes in Networks and Systems, vol. 623, pp. 713–724. Springer, Singapore (2023). https://doi.org/10.1007/978-981-19-9638-2_62

4. da Silva, F.L., Slodkowski, B.K., da Silva, K.K.A. et al: A systematic literature review on educational recommender systems for teaching and learning: research trends, limitations and opportunities. Educ. Inf. Technol. **28**, 3289–3328 (2023). https://doi.org/10.1007/s10639-022-11341-9

5. Rivera, A.C., Tapia-Leon, M., Lujan-Mora, S: Recommendation systems in education: a systematic mapping study. In: Rocha, Á., Guarda, T. (eds.) Proceedings of the International Conference on Information Technology & Systems (ICITS 2018). ICITS 2018. Advances in Intelligent Systems and Computing, vol. 721, pp. 937–947. Springer, Cham (2018). https://doi.org/10.1007/978-3-319-73450-7_89

6. Islam, F., Arman, M.S., Jahan, N., Sammak, M.H., Tasnim, N., Mahmud, I.: Model and popularity based recommendation system- a collaborative filtering approach. In:13th International Conference on Computing Communication and Networking Technologies (ICCCNT), Kharagpur, India, pp. 1–5 (2022). https://doi.org/10.1109/ICCCNT54827.2022.9984348

7. Molina, L.E: Recommendation System for Netflix (2018)

8. Nazari, Z., et al.: Recommending podcasts for cold-start users based on music listening and taste. In: Proceedings of the 43rd International ACM SIGIR Conference on Research and Development in Information Retrieval (SIGIR 2020). Association for Computing Machinery, New York, NY, USA, pp. 1041–1050 (2020). https://doi.org/10.1145/3397271.3401101

9. Deldjoo, Y., Schedl, M., Cremonesi, P., Pasi, G.: Recommender systems leveraging multimedia content. ACM Comput. Surv. **53**(5), 38 Article 106 (September 2021) (2020). https://doi.org/10.1145/3407190

10. Elasticsearch. https://www.elastic.co/elasticsearch. Accessed 22 May 2023

11. PyCaret. https://pycaret.org. Accessed 22 May 2023

12. Elastic Docs: Query DSL. https://www.elastic.co/guide/en/elasticsearch/reference/current/query-dsl.html. Accessed 22 May 2023

13. Elasticsearch features. https://www.elastic.co/elasticsearch/features. Accessed 22 May 2023

14. Using the Elastic Stack for Business Intelligence at Liefery. https://www.elastic.co/blog/using-the-elastic-stack-for-business-intelligence-at-liefery. Accessed 22 May 2023

15. Data preprocessing. https://pycaret.gitbook.io/docs/get-started/preprocessing. Accessed 22 May 2023

16. Mapping.    https://www.elastic.co/guide/en/elasticsearch/reference/current/mapping.html. Accessed 22 May 2023

# Visual Design with Representation of Patterns Using Composition Graphs

Ewa Grabska(⌂) [ID] and Agnieszka Mars [ID]

Department of Design and Computer Graphics, Faculty of Physics, Astronomy and Applied Computer Science, Jagiellonian University, Krakow, Poland
{ewa.grabska,agnieszka.mars}@uj.edu.pl

**Abstract.** This paper concerns the computer-aided process of designing architectural objects in the form of 3D primitive configurations following the general-to-detail principle. Design objects are represented by labeled specific graphs called composition graphs (CP-graphs) with nodes that have bonds to which edges are attached. The problem of grouping 3D design primitives in patterns with the possibility of their multiple uses is considered. This paper aims to show how to create equivalents of patterns at the level of CP-graphs and what possibilities this type of graph structure gives.

**Keywords:** Pattern · Composition Graph · Hierarchical Node

## 1 Introduction

This paper describes a support design system by computer where designs are configurations of 3D-visual components created by the designer on the monitor screen with the use of a given graphic editor. In most cases, for a given number of the same primitives and given types of relationships between them, designers can generate different configurations depending on their aesthetic preferences. Both partial and complete design solutions are represented in the form of such configurations being elements of a visual language created by the designer. At the level of the computer system, knowledge about this language is automatically obtained during the design process and presented using graph data structure modeled by composition graphs (CP-graphs). Composition graphs (CP-graphs) were proposed as a basis for both computer model representation during the design process and generative procedure [1, 2].

According to the recommendations in designing a designed object is created from top to bottom. A common solution used in computer-aided design is to allow the designer to group 3D-design components in patterns with the possibility of their repeated use. This paper aims to show how to create equivalents of patterns at the level of CP-graphs and what possibilities this type of graph structure gives. Creating patterns is one of the important features of intelligent computer systems called *semantic interoperability*, which can be achieved by adding metadata, ultimately combining each piece of data into a controlled structure [3].

© The Author(s), under exclusive license to Springer Nature Switzerland AG 2023
Y. Luo (Ed.): CDVE 2023, LNCS 14166, pp. 193–201, 2023.
https://doi.org/10.1007/978-3-031-43815-8_19

This paper is organized as follows. Section 2 introduces CP-graph representations of architectural objects, which are based on the extended Biederman model of human vision. Then, the concept of hierarchical CP-graph nodes representing patterns at the level of design structures is defined. In Sect. 3 the system of CP-graph rewriting rules which takes into account the design process of creating patterns is presented. The conclusion summarizes the research presented.

## 2   Architectural Objects and Composition Graphs (CP-Graphs)

In this paper, a three-dimensional form of an architectural object will be created by the designer as a configuration of three-dimensional primitives. The proposed approach can be used to generate building forms in virtual city generators. Our running simple example will concern the design process of an architectural object shown in Fig. 1. CP-graphs will be used as an internal representation of the architectural objects.

### 2.1   Volumetric Representation of Architectural Objects

We are inspired by a volumetric representation, which was proposed by Irving Biederman, both as a model of human vision and as a computer model in which 3D objects are constructed from three-dimensional building blocks of objects with two binary relations between the object's blocks: *end-to-side*, i.e., complete adjacency between the larger face of one solid to the smaller face of another solid, and *end-to-end*, i.e., complete adhesion of the solid faces to each other [3]. In the volumetric presentation of architectural objects proposed here, we add a third relation: *side to side*, i.e., partial adhesion of the solid faces to each other.

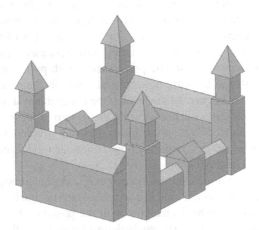

**Fig. 1.** An architectural object

Figure 2 presents all 3D primitives used by the designer to create the object in Fig. 1. Exemplary, there exists *end-to-side* relation between primitives *t1* and *r4* whereas *end-to-end* between primitives *b1* and *r1*, and *side-to-side* relation between *b1* and *t2*.

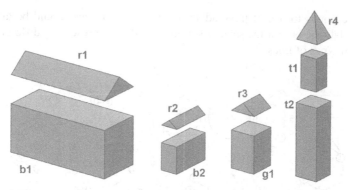

**Fig. 2.** Primitives used by the designer to create the object in Fig. 1.

## 2.2 Composition Graphs (CP-graphs)

Composition graphs (CP-graphs) are proposed as a basis for computer model representation during the design process. They are labeled graphs with nodes equipped with explicit connection elements for edges called bonds. Edges labeled with the name of a relation are attached to the bonds corresponding to the relation arguments.

Formally, Let $\sum$ be an alphabet.

**Definition 2.1**

A **labelled composition graph (CP-graph) over** $\sum$ is a tuple.

$$C = (V, E, B, bd, s, t, lb), \text{ where}$$

- $V, E, B$ are pairwise disjoint sets, whose elements are called *nodes*, *edges* and *bonds*, respectively;
- $bd : V \rightarrow B^+$ is a function such that defines a sequence of different bonds for each node and $\forall b \in B \exists! v \in V : (b \epsilon bd(v)))$, i.e., each bond is assigned to exactly one node;
- $s, t : E \rightarrow B$ are functions of which at least one is not surjective, and assign to edges *source* and *target* node bonds, respectively, in such a way, that $\forall E \exists v_1, v_2 : s(e) \epsilon bd(v_1) \wedge t(e) \epsilon bd(v_2) \wedge v_1 \neq v_2$;
- $lb : V \cup B \cup E \rightarrow \sum$ isalabelingfunction an edge, node and bond labeling function.

Denote elements of a CP-graph $C$ by $(V_C, E_C, B_C, bd_C, s_C, t_C, lb_C)$ and by $\Gamma(\Sigma)$ the set of all labelled CP-graphs over $\Sigma$.

Let us consider the architectural object shown in Fig. 1; it consists of 28 design components being 3D primitives shown in Fig. 2. This object is represented by its CP-graph in Fig. 3. For each node labeled by the name of primitive, the graphic code for any of its bonds is a small circle placed on the border of the node. Bonds are numbered and represent the faces of solids. Object nodes are equipped with two types of bonds: source bonds and target bonds; directed edges are drawn from source bonds to target bonds ( *end-to-side* relation). For two symmetrical *end-to-end* and *side-to-side* relations, we have only one bond type representing both source and target bonds. Each edge in

Fig. 3 corresponds to one of three adjacency relations. Edges should be labeled with names of relations, but for the sake of simplicity, edges representing different relations are different types of lines.

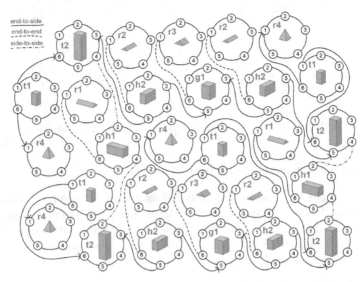

**Fig. 3.** CP-graph representing the architectural object shown in Fig. 1

The bonds connected by edges, that represent the arguments of the relations are called *internal* bonds. CP-graph bonds that are neither source nor target bonds are called *free* bonds and represent potential connections at the higher level hierarchy.

### 2.3 Patterns and Hierarchical CP-Graph Nodes

A common solution used in computer-aided design is to allow the user to group design components and treat such groups as patterns with the possibility of their repeated use. Thanks to the introduction of internal and free bonds, the CP-graph representing the pattern can be treated as a hierarchical node, where only its bonds selected from free bonds can be source and target bonds of edges for the higher level hierarchy.

Let's define for a given CP-graph $C \epsilon \Gamma(\Sigma)$ the sets $In(C) = s_C(E) \cup t_C(E)$ and $Free(C) = B_C \setminus In(C)$ which determine the sets of internal bonds and set of free bonds, respectively.

**Definition 2.2** Let $C \epsilon \Gamma(\Sigma)$. By a CP-graph **object pattern** for $C$, we understand a tuple.

$n(C) = (w, l, bd_{ext}, ch, C))$.
where.

- $w$ is a node called a hierarchical node that is not element of $V_C$,
- $l \in \Sigma$ is a label of $w$ that is not element of $lb(V \cup B \cup E)$,
- $bd_{ext}:\{w\} \to Free(C)^+$ is a function such that defines a sequence of different bonds called *external* bonds for $w$,
- CP-graph $C$ is a descendant of $w$ assigned by a function $ch: \{w\} \to C$.

In other words, a CP-graph object pattern for $C$ is a hierarchical labeled one-node CP-graph with its descendant being $C$ and with the sequence of external bonds selected from set $Free(C)$ of free bonds.

Let us consider two exemplary patterns from Fig. 4 occurring in the architectural object shown in Fig. 1. The pattern from Fig. 4a is repeated twice, while the one from Fig. 4b is repeated four times.

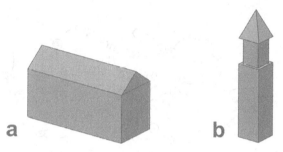

**Fig. 4.** Two exemplary patterns of the architectural object are shown in Fig. 1.

Figure 5a and b, show two possible representations of CP-graph object patterns that are hierarchical nodes for the patterns in Fig. 4a and b, respectively.

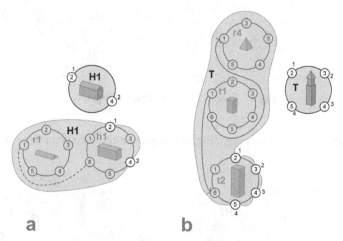

**Fig. 5.** Two possible representations of hierarchical nodes for patterns from Fig. 4.

For example, in a more detailed representation of a hierarchical node representing the tower in Fig. 5b, we have the node labeled T with the CP-graph as a descendant. This

CP-graph is created automatically during the design process of the pattern consisting of three three-dimensional primitives. The designer sets up these three primitives using the end-to-side relationship twice. Out of 14 free bonds, four are selected to be used as external bonds. After creating a hierarchical node in the later phase of the design process, the pattern will be treated as a primitive and can be represented by a hierarchical CP-graph node marked with an icon representing the pattern.

**Definition 2.2.** By a **hierarchical CP-graph** we understand a CP-graph of which at least one node is a CP-graph object pattern.

Figure 6 presents a hierarchical CP-graph with two hierarchical nodes for the architectural object shown in Fig. 1.

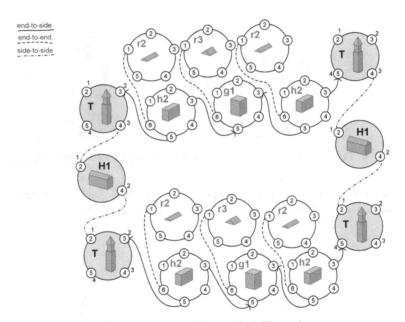

**Fig. 6.** Example of hierarchical CP-graph.

In the next step, the following CP-graph object pattern can be created (Fig. 7).

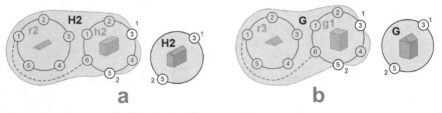

**Fig. 7.** Two CP-graph object patterns.

Using these CP graph object patterns, a successive hierarchical CP graph shown in Fig. 8 from the hierarchical CP graph in Fig. 5 can be created.

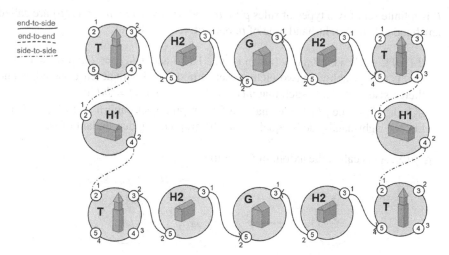

**Fig. 8.** A hierarchical CP-graph at the next level of the hierarchy.

## 3 Generative Procedures

The examples presented so far have been intended to highlight human-computer interaction using CP-graphs that allow categorizing knowledge during the conceptual design process where concepts and meanings are generated based on the human mind's ability. With the advance in modern information technology, a data structure based on graphs provides a fundamental principle to represent a design object, while graph rewriting i.e., the technique of creating a new graph out of an original graph algorithmically, is an adequate description of the design process actions [5, 6].

In the approach presented in this paper, during the design process, the designer selects successive 3D primitives and decides how to connect them. The rule rewriting system based on a CP-graph allows reflection of the designer's actions. The CP-graph shown in Fig. 3 and hierarchical CP-graphs shown in Figs. 6 and 8 describe design structures at different levels of the hierarchy. All these CP-graphs can be generated automatically with the use of CP-graph rules.

A CP-graph rule is a pair of CP-graphs in which the first element of the pair is called the left-hand side of the rule, and the second – is its right-hand side. The application of a graph rule to a given CP-graph is obtained by removing (a subgraph) isomorphic to the left-hand side of the rule and replacing it with its right-hand side, and then connecting the edges of this right-hand side with the rest of the host graph, according to the so-called embedding rule. Now, we are ready to formally define rewriting rules for CP-graphs.

Let $\gamma(\Sigma) \subset \Gamma(\Sigma)$ be the subset that contains all CP-graphs with one-element sets of nodes, and $\gamma^h(\Sigma)$ be a set of all hierarchical nodes.

**Definition 2.3.** By a **context-free CP-graph rewriting rules** over $\Sigma$, we understand a system $.G = (P, s)$, where

- $P$ is a finite set of two types of rules $p : l(p) \to r(p))$ where $l(p)$ and $r(p)$ are called left-hand-side and right-hand-side of $p$, respectively, such that

  - if $l(p) \in \gamma(\Sigma)$. i.e., $V_{l(p)} = \{w\}$ and $r(p) \in \Gamma(\Sigma)$ and $\#V_{r(p)} = 2$ and $E_r \neq \varnothing$, i.e., $r(p)$ is a CP-graph with two-element set of nodes and with at least one edge, and there exists $v \in V_{r(p))}$, such that $lb(v) = lb(w)$ and $bd(v) = bd(w)$,
  - if $l(p) \in \gamma^h(\Sigma)$ i.e., $l(p) = w$ that is a CP-graph object pattern and $r(p) = h(w)$, i.e., the right-hand-side is equal to the CP-graph being descendant of $w$.

- $s \in \gamma(\Sigma, A)$ is called the axiom of CP-graph.

**Fig. 9.** An example of a rule reflects the action of the designer.

Let's consider two examples of the CP-graph rules for the pattern in Fig. 3a. The first of them shown in Fig. 9 reflects the action of the designer creating the pattern, while the second (Fig. 10) is additional information about the design structure in the case of hierarchical CP-graphs from Figs. 6 and 8.

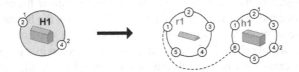

**Fig. 10.** An example of a rule for the hierarchical CP-graph.

## 4 Conclusion

In this paper, CP-graphs have been used to introduce the concept of hierarchical nodes representing patterns at the level of design structures. The idea of patterns defined by hierarchical CP-graph nodes without the formal model described here was used to develop an interactive computer system called Virtual City Creator (VCC) for computer games [7]. It turned out that CP-graphs with their internal and free bonds are a convenient tool for creating patterns. In generative design, patterns can be created using the rules of a graph grammar or a shape grammar [8]. In these rules, the whole pattern is added. The problem is to "secure" the pattern so that other rules do not add components to it in undesirable places. This can be solved by markers or terminal symbols. The use of output bonds in the proposed method is a simpler and more precise solution.

Must also be taken into account that in the design structure represented by a labeled CP-graph, labels assigned to nodes and bonds identify their corresponding components and component fragments, respectively, while labels of edges connecting bonds are names of relations. Whereas the cognitive process by labeling functions is associated with a structure that organizes elements, interrelating them, and, if we focus only on the logical structure, this can affect the meaning of the interpretation used in the initial phase of the creative design process, including for creating patterns.

The next topic related to patterns at the CP-graph semantic level associated with attributes and their values assigned to nodes and bonds, and establishing and determining instances is worth considering in further research.

# References

1. Grabska, E.: Graph and designing. In: Schneider, H.J., Ehrig, H. (eds.) Proceedings of the International Workshop on Graph Transformations in Computer Science, vol. 776, pp. 188–202 Springer, Heidelberg (1993). https://doi.org/10.1007/3-540-57787-4_12
2. Grabska, E.: Theoretical concepts of graphical modeling part two: CP-graph grammars and languages. Mach. Graph. Vis. 2(2), 149–178 (1993)
3. Arena, D.N.: Towards semantics-driven modelling and simulation of context-aware manufacturing systems, Ph.D. thesis, Swiss Federal Institute of Technology Lausanne (2019)
4. Biederman, I.: Recognition-by-components: a theory of human image understanding. Psychol. Rev. 94, 115–147 (1987)
5. Rozenberg, G. (ed.): Handbook on Graph Grammars and Computing by Graph Transformation. World Scientific River Edge NJ USA (1997),
6. Vilgertshofer, S., Borrmann, A.: Adv. Eng. Inform. 33, 502–515 (2017)
7. Mars, A., Grabska, E., Bielański, J., Mogiła, P., Mogiła, M.: Reference architectural model of buildings for virtual city creator. In: Abualdenien, J., Borrmann, A., Ungureanu, L.C., Hartmann, T. (eds.) Proceedings of the EG-ICE 2021 Workshop on Intelligent Computing in Engineering, Berlin, Germany, 30 June–2 July 2021, Technical University of Berlin, Berlin, Germany, pp. 291–300 (2021)
8. Pauwels, P., Strobbe, T., Eloy, S., De Meyer, R.: Shape grammars for architectural design: the need for reframing. In: Celani, G., Sperling, D., Franco, J. (eds.) Computer-Aided Architectural Design Futures. The Next City - New Technologies and the Future of the Built Environment. CAAD Futures 2015. Communications in Computer and Information Science, vol. 527, pp. 507–526. Springer, Heidelberg (2015). https://doi.org/10.1007/978-3-662-47386-3_28

# Group-Based Collaborative Environments for Coastal Areas Monitoring

Sandra Sendra$^{(\boxtimes)}$ ⓘ, Alberto Ivars-Palomares, Miguel Zaragoza-Esquerdo, and Jaime Lloret ⓘ

Instituto de Investigación para la Gestión Integrada de Zonas Costeras (IGIC), Universitat Politècnica de València, Paraninf 1, 46730 Grao de Gandia (Valencia), Spain
sansenco@upv.es, {aivapal,mizaes2}@epsg.upv.es,
jlloret@dcom.upv.es

**Abstract.** Monitoring natural environments has become increasingly important, leading to research focused on improving their performance. This paper introduces a system for communication among nodes in an environment. Specifically, we propose a novel approach called group-based collaborative environments for coastal area monitoring. This approach utilizes a hierarchical network architecture, organizing nodes into groups. Multiple environments within a coastal area are monitored using group-based wireless sensor networks (WSNs). We have developed a mathematical model to estimate the energy consumption of this network configuration. Simulation results demonstrate energy savings of approximately 45% can be achieved using this approach.

**Keywords:** Collaborative Networks · Group-Based Topologies · Coastal Monitoring · Energy Efficiency · Environmental Monitoring

## 1 Introduction

One of the main concerns regarding the oceans is the temperature change that is a cause of climate change. It has been shown that temperature variation can affect the organisms that inhabit the oceans [1]. In Spain, specifically in the Region of Murcia, it is considered one of the central monitoring infrastructures where they monitor the Mar Menor Lagoon in the Mediterranean to observe how climate change affects this sea [2]. Monitoring can also serve to review the quality of other media, such as air, being able to measure the amount of pollutants it has to make the best decisions [3].

Monitoring natural environments is one of the most important applications of Wireless Sensor Networks (WSNs) [4]. They have become a powerful tool for monitoring marine and coastal ecosystems. Sensor networks consist of a set of electronic devices called sensors, which are strategically distributed at different points in the area to be monitored. These sensors can process information and transmit the data to other devices wirelessly [5].

Wireless sensor networks are decentralized and self-configuring networks where the nodes can gather data from the environment and forward it to the neighbors to reach

Y. Luo (Ed.): CDVE 2023, LNCS 14166, pp. 202–213, 2023.
https://doi.org/10.1007/978-3-031-43815-8_20

the gateway and transfer it to the main network [6]. In addition, these types of networks have a multidisciplinary application since they can be used in different sectors such as defense, scientific research, statistics, monitoring of areas where natural disasters have occurred, and monitoring of places where armed conflicts exist [7].

The sensor nodes are made of microcontrollers and are equipped with physical sensors. In WSNs, sensor nodes collaborate on one or more common tasks. They use wireless communication to transmit and forward data between the nodes, and it is used as a gateway that allows sending the data to the Internet. In this case, as we want to monitor different areas of the coastal zone [8], we will use sensor networks based on groups where sensor networks will measure specific coastal areas, such as a port or a fish farm. Sensor networks will be used together by a local network that will connect the data between the different sensor networks of the coast.

The problem with the conventional network is that when all the sensors are connected and data are sent, being in the same broadcast domain, all the nodes receive the information. However, in group-based networks, this broadcast is only sent to the group till it reaches the gateway of the group. Therefore, a data frame is discarded if it is not for that network, and a considerable amount of energy is saved in the nodes of that group [9]. Collaborative systems integrate all the technology used in the network in a single task. And thus, all the nodes of the network work with the same equipment, both software and hardware [10].

Considering the aforementioned issues, this paper presents a new approach to efficiently communicating nodes in a WSN. Specifically, we propose the concept of group-based collaborative environments where the different critical measurements collected in an environment are shared with the rest of the scenarios to finally make more accurate decisions that benefit the global sustainability of all environments. We propose a mathematical model to determine the total consumed energy in the network, as well as how the different environments would transmit its information. Finally, the proposal is simulated and compared with conventional WSN.

The rest of the paper is structured as follows. Section 2 presents some previous and related works. Section 3 presents an overall description of our proposal and the network architecture for our proposed group-based collaborative environment. Section 4 explains the mathematical model that describes the energy consumption of our entire network. This section also contains the simulation results. Finally, Sect. 5 explains the conclusion and future works.

## 2 Related Work

This section shows some works related to collaborative systems for environmental monitoring with WSNs and different issues related to the improvements in WSNs.

Collaborative sensor networks for environmental monitoring have experienced significant advances in recent years. These networks have become a crucial tool for real-time data collection and understanding ecosystems, enabling more accurate and efficient monitoring of the environmental surroundings.

There are several issues related to how to organize the network. For example, one of the main differentiating facts is how to create the network. i.e., collaborative sensor networks are based on the collaboration and coordination of multiple sensors distributed over a large geographical area. One of the most investigated topics in WSNs is the design of energy-efficient routing protocols. For example, Alghamdi [11] presents an optimized cluster head selection model, which considers various factors such as node proximity, residual energy, and communication cost. The authors also highlight the benefits of the model, including reduced energy consumption and increased network efficiency. The proposed protocol is evaluated through simulations and compared with other existing protocols. The results demonstrate that the optimized cluster head selection model outperforms the other protocols in terms of energy efficiency and network lifespan. Lilhore et al. [12] also present an energy-efficient routing protocol, but in this case, it is designed specifically for underwater wireless sensor networks (UWSNs). For this proposal, authors take advantage of the correlation between node depth and energy consumption, utilizing a depth-aware routing strategy.

In addition to the issues related to the communication process in WSNs, the quality and accuracy of data collected by sensors are fundamental for effective environmental monitoring. Data fusion techniques have been developed to combine information from multiple sensors and improve the quality of the collected data. Related to this, Muzammal et al. [13] introduce an ensemble approach for analyzing and integrating medical data collected from body sensor networks (BSNs) using multi-sensor data fusion techniques. The proposed approach is evaluated using real-world medical datasets collected from BSNs. The results demonstrate the effectiveness of the ensemble approach in improving the accuracy of medical data analysis compared to individual models or traditional single-sensor approaches.

As an improvement of traditional sensor networks, there has been an increasing integration of multiple data sources in collaborative sensor networks. The integration of these heterogeneous data sources allows for a more comprehensive and real-time view of the environmental surroundings. In this sense, Kim et al. [14], explore the integration of WSNs with big data systems. It discusses the challenges and opportunities that arise when combining these two technologies. The paper discusses various techniques and approaches to address these challenges. It covers topics such as data collection and aggregation in WSNs, data storage and processing in big data systems, and data analytics and visualization for extracting meaningful insights. Furthermore, the authors explore the potential applications and benefits of combining WSNs with big data systems in various domains, including environmental monitoring, healthcare, and smart cities. They provide examples of real-world deployments and case studies to demonstrate the practicality and effectiveness of this integration.

Finally, the use of machine learning and data analysis techniques in WSNs enables the extraction of patterns, identification of anomalies, prediction of events, and informed decision-making based on the collected data.

As far as we know, there are several proposals to improve the performance of WSNs. Additionally, some authors have already used the concept of collaborative networks. However, the idea of combining the information of environments which present a minimum relation between them is completely new.

# 3   Proposed Group-Based Collaborative Environments

This section presents the proposed group-based collaborative environments. Firstly, the section introduces the different environments it is possible to have in a coastal area and its main features, as well as, the typical parameters measured on them. Secondly, the group-based collaborative environments topology is presented. Finally, the section exposes the main advantages to work with a topology of those characteristics. When talking about environments, we refer to the physical space where a wsn deployed in this area is periodically measuring different parameters in the scenario.

## 3.1   Environments in Coastal Areas Scenarios

Marine and coastal environments are vital ecosystems that host a great diversity of life and play a fundamental role in the health of the planet. These regions are home to a wide variety of marine species, as well as human communities that depend on marine resources for their livelihoods. However, these environments are increasingly threatened due to various factors such as climate change, pollution, and overexploitation of resources. In this context, monitoring marine and coastal environments has become essential to understanding and effectively managing these ecosystems. Monitoring involves the systematic collection of data and relevant information about oceans, seas, and coastal areas, as well as the analysis and interpretation of this data to gain a clear understanding of their current state and long-term trends. Inside this complex scenario (see Fig. 1), it is possible to define different environments. Most of them are directly related to human activity and for this reason, having a picture of the state of each one is extremely important.

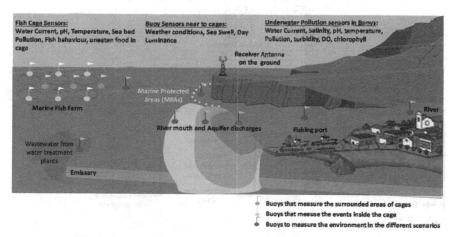

**Fig. 1.**  Example of a marine coastal collaborative environment.

In many of these environments, it is possible to monitor common parameters that provide a clear view of water quality, such as temperature, dissolved oxygen, salinity, pH, and other elements such as ammonia, nitrite, and nitrate. Additionally, measurements of fish farming activity such as fish weight and size (for performing the biomass estimation), the fish behavior, and or feed consumption, among others, can help to assess various parameters related to the water quality in surrounding areas, fish health, and overall farm performance.

Another essential scenario that should be carefully monitored is the marine protected area (MPA) which is focused on preserving and conserving marine ecosystems and biodiversity. But in some cases, those MPAs are affected by uncontrolled discharges or industry activities caused, for example, for fishing port areas, the discharges of emissaries in the sea, or the contribution of nutrients and freshwater from the river mouth and aquifer discharges. In all those cases, regular monitoring enables the identification of emerging issues, the evaluation of management measures' effectiveness, and the promotion of sustainable practices for the long-term viability of these areas.

As shown in Fig. 2, the combined use of all the mentioned parameters allows us to merge information from different network groups responsible for monitoring each mentioned environment. This enables us to extract more efficient decisions. The implementation of an intelligent system with predictive capability can be achieved through the combined use of artificial intelligence techniques, machine learning, and data fusion algorithms.

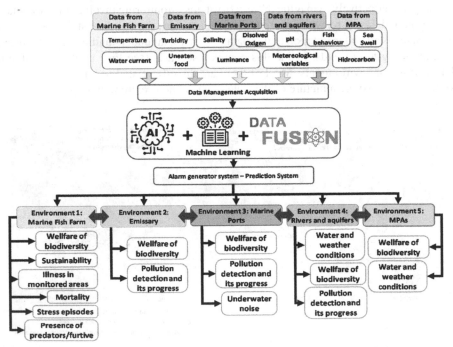

**Fig. 2.** Predictive system for taking efficient decisions in a coastal marine collaborative environment.

The use of artificial intelligence, and concretely deep learning algorithms over the received data to improve the real-time monitoring process improve the alarm systems, and predict undesired situations, at the time of enhancing the knowledge of the whole system. Collaborative monitoring by combining the information obtained from each environment of a complex scenario would improve the marine ecosystems management and monitoring process.

## 3.2 Group-Based Collaborative Environments

The main idea of Group-based Collaborative Environments is that a real environment is composed of different scenarios with certain characteristics. These characteristics can be related to the type of measured parameter or the type of event to be detected, among others. In this article, we start from the hypothesis that if we can share sensitive information among different environments in a network, it will be possible to make more precise decisions, even to develop a predictive system capable of anticipating an event or reducing the impact on an ecosystem due to a problem occurring in one environment.

Additionally, one of the main characteristic aspects of this proposal is its hierarchical structure of layers where each layer has a set of elements in charge of performing specific tasks.

Figure 3 shows the network architecture of our group-based collaborative environments. Our network architecture consists of 3 layers named the perception layer, the control layer, and the core layer. The functions and composition of each layer are described below:

**Perception Layer:** This layer is responsible for gathering and processing data from sensors placed in the environment. It consists of sensors, detectors, or any other means of capturing relevant information. The main function of the perception layer is to collect data and convert it into a format that can be understood and utilized by the network. This layer plays a crucial role in acquiring input signals and transmitting them to higher layers for further processing and decision-making. In our case, each environment is composed of several sensors joined by groups. These groups can be formed based on different criteria, including the type of parameter or parameters they measure. These groups have two types of communication: (1) intra-group communication, which establishes links between nodes within the same group, and (2) inter-group communication, which establishes links between different groups. Using information from each environment makes it possible to predict an event in another environment.

**Control Layer:** It hosts the sink nodes of each environment. Through this layer, the different environments can transmit their information from the sink nodes of each group. Likewise, these nodes will be responsible for sending the information to the upper layer. The control layer plays an important role since it permits the sharing of relevant data collected in a determined environment. For example, if a group in the Port environment detects the presence of fuels on the water, apart from generating the corresponding alarms to mitigate and limit its spread, this information will be communicated to other relevant environments, such as the one hosting the marine farm. This allows the facility managers to take measures to mitigate potential damage to the facilities and the animals contained within them.

**Core Layer:** The core layer is the highest one and it contains the different gateways of each group-based collaborative environment which is in charge of monitoring a complex scenario as the one described in this paper.

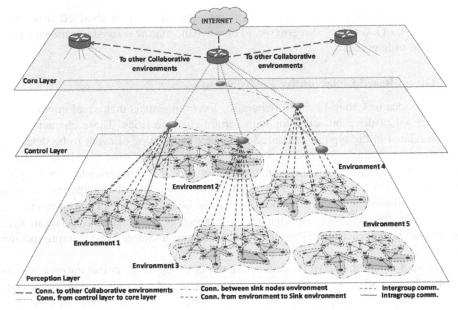

**Fig. 3.** Hierarchical architecture for our group-based collaborative environment.

## 4  Proposal of the Energy Efficient Model for a Group-Based Collaborative Environment

In this section, the mathematical model used for estimating energy consumption for group-based collaborative environments is presented. To do this, we will use as a starting point a previous work [9] by the same authors.

### 4.1  Energy Consumption in the Network

In order to estimate the energy consumption of a collaborative network of environments, we must take into account how collaborative group-based environments are formed. As explained in the previous section, each environment is composed of several groups.

On one hand, as explained in the previous section, each environment is formed by groups of nodes (see Fig. 4).

These groups contain nodes of three different types which can acquire a role or another depending on the network conditions. The different nodes are:

- Group Sink node: It is the most important node in the group and is responsible for sending information to the environment's sink nodes. It also can measure.
- Adjacent Nodes: These nodes are responsible for establishing adjacencies with other nearby groups. They also can measure.
- Normal Nodes: They only work within the group and their sole capability is to collect data from the environment and transmit their information.
- Finally, each collaborative environment has an environment sink node whose function is to send data to the cloud.

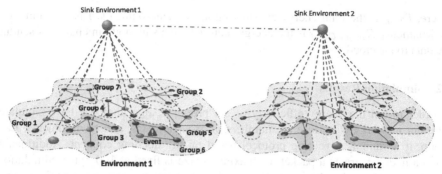

**Fig. 4.** A figure caption is always placed below the illustration. Short captions are centered, while long ones are justified. The macro button chooses the correct format automatically.

On the other hand, within each environment, it is possible to have nodes that, due to their position or characteristics, have not been able to establish a connection or cooperation within a group. This node should also have the ability to send its data to the sink environment. The work presented by M. Garcia et al. [15] demonstrated how to estimate the energy consumption of a collaborative WSN (Wireless Sensor Network) based on groups of nodes. Starting from the base of this work, we can establish that the energy consumption inside a group-based WSN would be (See Eq. 1):

$$E_{group} = E_{Sink\_Node} + \left(E_{Adj\_Node} * n_{adj}\right) + \left(E_{Normal\_Node} \cdot \left(N_{Nodes\_group} - n_{adj} - 1\right)\right) \tag{1}$$

where, $E_{group}$ is the energy of a group, $E_{Sink\_Node}$ is the energy consumed by a Group Sink node, $E_{Adj\_Node}$ is the energy consumed by a node in charge of creating adjacencies with other groups, $E_{Normal\_Node}$ represents the energy of a normal node, $n_{adj}$ is the number of adjacencies that a group establishes and, finally $N_{Nodes\_group}$ is the average number total nodes in a group.

Additionally, if we consider that a collaborative environment can be formed by several groups ($N_{groups}$) and that there may be nodes that, due to their characteristics or geographical position, for example, have not been able to establish adjacencies with a group, the total energy consumed by a collaborative environment would be (See Eq. 2):

$$E_{collab\_env} = N_{groups} \cdot \left(E_{Sink\_Node} + \left(E_{Adj\_Node} * n_{adj}\right) + \left(E_{Normal\_Node} \cdot \left(N_{Nodes\_group} - n_{adj} - 1\right)\right)\right)$$
$$+ \left(E_{Sink\_Node} \cdot \left(N_{Total\_nodes} - N_{Nodes\_group}\right)\right) \tag{2}$$

where, $E_{collab\_env}$ is the energy of a collaborative group-based environment and, $N_{Total\_nodes}$ is the total number of node in the entire network, considering all the groups in an environment.

Finally, it is considered that our complex network is composed of diverse environments that collaborate to each other to make more efficient decisions. In this case, the total energy of the network would be expressed by the Eq. 3:

$$E_{Total} = j \cdot E_{SN\_to\_Cloud} + \sum_{1}^{j} E_{collab\_env_j} \tag{3}$$

where, $E_{Total}$ is the total energy considering all the environments, $j$ is the number of environments, $E_{SN\_to\_Cloud}$ is the energy required for a sink node in charge of sending the data to the cloud.

### 4.2 Simulation Results

In order to test the energy efficiency of our proposed algorithm, we have simulated different networks with different numbers of groups, nodes, and environments. Each group, it is running a routing protocol based on the flooding concept. Additionally, when a node generates a packet, its maximum size is fixed at 100 bytes. Simulations have been performed with 6 sizes of the number of groups per environment ($N_{groups}$) and 18 different values of nodes per group ($N_{Nodes\_group}$). The maximum number of nodes in the entire network ranges between 25 and 500 nodes. We have also considered that a sink node consumes 3 mW, an adjacent node in charge of creating links with other neighbors' groups consumes 2 mW and finally, the rest of the nodes in the group would consume 1.5 mW. These energy costs are provided by a real sensor node called Waspmote [16].

In Fig. 5, the total energy consumption of a conventional network without implementing our proposal is shown. As we can observe, the growth is linear, meaning that the higher the number of nodes, the higher the overall consumption in the network.

In Fig. 6, we can see that total energy in an environment as a function of the number of nodes per group increases with the number of groups. The slope also increases as the environment grows in the number of groups of sensors when the number of nodes in the group increases. However, the tendency is still quantitative higher in traditional networks.

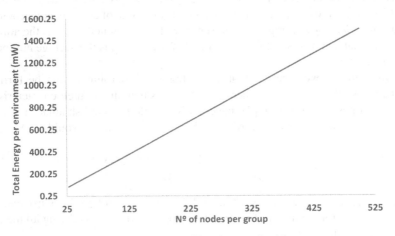

**Fig. 5.** Total energy in a traditional network without groups.

Finally, Fig. 7 shows the percentage of energy savings that would result from the implementation of our proposal in a large network like the one described in Sect. 3. In the figure, we can see that the energy savings vary logarithmically, reaching a minimum energy savings value of 25% for an environment with 5 groups, each with an

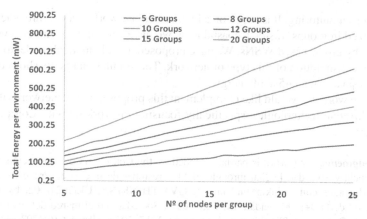

**Fig. 6.** Total Energy in a Group-based collaborative environment network.

average number of nodes per group of 5. It is also observed that the energy savings value approaches a stable value of 45% for large networks.

If we pay attention to this figure, we can observe that in general, the networks with a bigger number of groups present a slight improvement in energy usage.

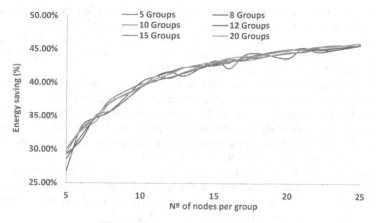

**Fig. 7.** Percentage of energy saving

## 5 Conclusion and Future Work

Monitoring natural environments is currently a topic that has gained special attention. For this reason, research related to improving its performance has become crucial. In this regard, in this paper, we have proposed a system to communicate the different nodes present in an environment. Specifically, this paper proposes a new mode of organizing and communicating sensor nodes called group-based collaborative environments for coastal areas monitoring. It is based on a hierarchical network architecture where nodes are organized in groups. Inside a coastal area, we have several environments which are monitored by group-based WSNs. We have proposed a mathematical model to estimate the energy consumption of this type of network. The simulation results showed that we are able to save around 45% of energy.

In future work, we would like to implement this proposal on real networks that operate with different technologies, specifically focusing on working with LoRa multihop technology.

**Acknowledgments.** This work is partially funded by the Conselleria de Innovación, Universidades, Ciencia y Sociedad Digital through the "Expresiones de Interés de Proyectos de Investigación Alineados con Thinkinazul" project GVA-THINKINAZUL/2021/002, by the "Programa Estatal de I+D+i Orientada a los Retos de la Sociedad, en el marco del Plan Estatal de Investigación Científica y Técnica y de Innovación 2017–2020" (Project PID2020-114467RR-C33/AEI/10.13039/501100011033), by "Proyectos Estratégicos Orientados a la Transición Ecológica y a la Transición Digital" (Project TED2021-131040B-C31), and by the "Generalitat Valenciana" through the "Programa Investigo", (Project INVEST/2022/467).

# References

1. Jessop, B.M.: Oceanic water temperatures less than 20 °C may largely adjust for underestimation of European elver otolith ages. Fish. Oceanogr. **31**(3), 353–367 (2022)
2. Pérez, C.A., Valles, F.S., Sánchez, R.T., Buendía, M.J., López-Castejón, F., Cervera, J.G.: Design and deployment of a wireless sensor network for the mar menor coastal observation system. IEEE J. Ocean. Eng. **42**(4), 966–976 (2017)
3. Brienza, S., Galli, A., Anastasi, G., Bruschi, P.: A low-cost sensing system for cooperative air quality monitoring in urban areas. Sensors **15**(6), 12242–12259 (2015)
4. Wu, M., Tan, L., Xiong, N.: Data prediction, compression, and recovery in clustered wireless sensor networks for environmental monitoring applications. Inf. Sci. **329**, 800–818 (2016)
5. Bello, A.D., Lamba, O.S.: Energy efficient for data aggregation in wireless sensor networks. Int. J. Eng. Res. Technol. (IJERT) **9**(1), 110–120 (2020)
6. Chaudhary, S., Singh, N., Pathak, A., Vatsa, A.K.: Energy efficient techniques for data aggregation and collection in WSN. Int. J. Comput. Sci. Eng. Appl. (IJCSEA) **2** (2012)
7. Garcia, M., Bri, D., Sendra, S., Lloret, J.: Practical deployments of wireless sensor networks: a survey. Int. J. Adv. Netw. Serv. **3**(12), 170–185 (2010)
8. Seah, W.K., Eu, Z.A., Tan, H.P.: Wireless sensor networks powered by ambient energy harvesting (WSN-HEAP)-survey and challenges. In: 2009 1st International Conference on Wireless Communication, Vehicular Technology, Information Theory and Aerospace and Electronic Systems Technology. 17–20 May 2009, Aalborg, Denmark (2009)
9. Garcia, M., Sendra, S., Lloret, J., Canovas, A.: Saving energy and improving communications using cooperative group-based wireless sensor networks. Telecommun. Syst. **52**, 2489–2502 (2013)
10. Yahia, N.B., Eljaoued, W., Saoud, N.B.B., Colomo-Palacios, R.: Towards sustainable collaborative networks for smart cities co-governance. Int. J. Inf. Manag. **56**, 102037 (2021)
11. Alghamdi, T.A.: Energy efficient protocol in wireless sensor network: optimized cluster head selection model. Telecommun. Syst. **74**(3), 331–345 (2020). https://doi.org/10.1007/s11235-020-00659-9

12. Lilhore, U.K., Khalaf, O.I., Simaiya, S., Tavera Romero, C.A., Ab-dulsahib, G.M., Kumar, D.: A depth-controlled and energy-efficient routing protocol for underwater wireless sensor networks. Int. J. Distrib. Sens. Netw. **18**(9), 15501329221117118 (2022)
13. Muzammal, M., Talat, R., Sodhro, A.H., Pirbhulal, S.: A multi-sensor data fusion enabled ensemble approach for medical data from body sensor networks. Inf. Fusion **53**, 155–164 (2020)
14. Kim, B.S., Kim, K.I., Shah, B., Chow, F., Kim, K.H.: Wire-less sensor networks for big data systems. Sensors **19**(7), 1565 (2019)
15. Garcia, M., Sendra, S., Lloret, J., Lacuesta, R.: Saving energy with cooperative group-based wireless sensor networks. In: Luo, Y. (ed.) CDVE 2010. LNCS, vol. 6240, pp. 73–76. Springer, Heidelberg (2010). https://doi.org/10.1007/978-3-642-16066-0_11
16. Waspmote. http://www.libelium.com/products/waspmote. Accessed 24 May 2023

# Turning Human into 2D Virtual Character Using Real-Time Motion Capture

Ky Trung Nguyen[1]($\boxtimes$), Linh Xuan Vu[1], and Thi Thanh Quynh Nguyen[2]($\boxtimes$)

[1] School of Computer Science and Engineering, International University - Vietnam National University, Ho Chi Minh City 700000, Viet Nam
ntky@hcmiu.edu.vn
[2] The University of Da Nang - University of Science and Technology,
Da Nang City 50000, Viet Nam
nttquynh@dut.udn.vn

**Abstract.** As technologies are advancing, people are also more interested in virtual reality experiences where not only virtual characters are intriguing but also how they are created and used. This paper proposes a way to apply motion capture using computer vision-based techniques to generate a 2D virtual character that can simulate human performance in real-time. Our proposed method is divided into two key phases in order to achieve a fully functional result: (1) the first phase consists of collecting virtual character data, and (2) the second phase constructs systems to detect and track the human upper body movements. In order to give the virtual character the capability to imitate human actions, which mainly includes the upper body motion-tracking system. The experiment demonstrates that the system is able to capture human upper body and facial expression which naturally simulate realistic 2D virtual characters in real-time. Ultimately, this technique provides a simpler, cheaper, and more efficient way of creating virtual humans in a digital environment, as well as proposes the potential applications of virtual humans in a variety of applications, such as identity security, the entertainment industry, education, and other areas that are related to human interaction with computers.

**Keywords:** motion capture · virtual character · face expression detection · movement detection · computer vision · visualization

## 1 Introduction

The concept of generating and animating virtual characters is a fascinating subject that is currently being explored with the emergence of a variety of virtual characters working in various professions ranging from AI virtual assistants [1] to virtual streamers [2,3] are becoming more and more popular on online entertainment in East Asia, especially in China and Japan. Furthermore, numerous

Y. Luo (Ed.): CDVE 2023, LNCS 14166, pp. 214–224, 2023.
https://doi.org/10.1007/978-3-031-43815-8_21

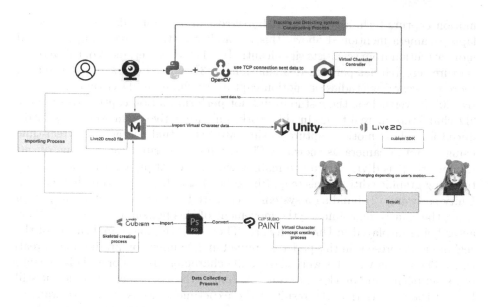

**Fig. 1.** Illustration of generating and simulating of 2D virtual character using motion capture

other applications can be derived from it such as identity security [4] or anti-cyberbully [5]. More recently, advances in motion capture are allowed virtual character animation and its appearance in a lot of movies, cartoons, and other potential applications such as in interaction with computers, connection with the virtual environment, virtual humans, video music, etc. For instance, Minato Aqua is an example of such an immersive virtual character and is shown to be lovable, and cheerful with rich facial expressions [2]. However, how to make 2D or 3D virtual character animation vividly and naturally in real-time is still a challenge as mentioned in [3]. The difficulty occurs when the traditional method of motion capture involves the use of special sensors such as data gloves [6], magnetic sensors [7,8], mechanical exoskeletons [9]; or optical markers [10], which are used to collect and analyze motion data from the performer's body parts based on the angle and position of the markers as they relate to the sensors. Moreover, the expense and complex nature of this equipment, including the personnel required and the physical environment needed to make it happen, is not affordable for an average person and for many of the desired applications.

To solve the problem, computer vision-based techniques provide an intriguing potential option due to the fact that they only require images from one or multiple cameras to be implemented. Utilizing these practical and economical techniques in motion capture, the need to invest heavily in expensive and specialized equipment is not required anymore as many personal computers today have cameras that can be used to record human motion, which vastly increases the range of possible applications. With the advantages of computer vision-based motion capture techniques along with low-cost and popular devices such as the laptop camera mentioned above, this research direction is receiving more and more attention from scientists significantly [11–17]. However, most of this motion capture research has performed simulations of 3D virtual characters. Currently, there are very few studies on motion capture to simulate 2D virtual characters [18–20]. Nevertheless, these studies did not perform motion capture to simulate 2D characters in real-time. In this work, an interactive framework was introduced for robust motion capture to simulate 2D virtual characters in real-time using a laptop camera as shown in Fig. 1, which describes the pipeline of our framework. It is divided into two main stages: (1) creating a 2D virtual character using graphic editing tools (e.g., Photoshop) and displaying this character on Unity software; (2) building a system to capture the movement of a real person using the camera and simulate the movement of this person on the virtual character being displayed in Unity software. Therefore, the main application of the technique we present in this paper is applied in 2D animation production in real-time. The reason why this work chose a 2D character instead of a 3D is because of its simplicity and quick setup time. Although the 2D model is simpler, it still has all the aspects that the result of the experiment needs. What we want to note in this paper is that motion capture is very well studied in computer vision and our aim here is not to develop a new motion capture method. The novelty of this paper is using this technique to make a 2D model animation in real-time, which is still a challenging problem so far. Furthermore, the objective of this paper is to concentrate on implementing the interaction and connection in virtual space by accurately imitating human arm movements in a two-dimensional avatar in real-time using a simpler, cheaper, less complicated method that anyone can access to explore the utilization of the virtual characters in many other potential applications across different fields.

## 2  Related Work

Most of the research to date on motion capture has been done on 3D animated models [11,12]. The main goal of these research directions is to reconstruct human shapes and simulate human behaviors in real-time in the form of 3D characters, which brings a lot of applications in different fields of science and technology and life such as computer games and the special effects industry. However, until now there have been very few studies on motion tracking for 2D model animation. An approach in [18] was developed for tracking movement from traditional cartoons. Using input from a traditional cartoon, their method was able to create new animations based on a combination of affine transformation and key-shape interpolation. The main principle of this method is based on extracting and mapping feature parameters (e.g., motion and deformation), hence it is difficult to simulate accurately human performance. In [19] presents a method to animate photos of 2D characters using 3D motion capture data. Given a single 2D image of a person, their method reconstructs a projective camera model and a 3D model pose which matches best the given 2D image.

Another approach was proposed in [20] a sketch-based 2D animation technique that effectively creates 2D character animation. Their method was divided into two stages: (1) given an input image of the character, their method produces new frames that sketch skeletons for subsequent key-frames; (2) the 2D motion capture method is used to track the movement of the character's joints. In comparison with the approaches mentioned above, our proposed method has many differences where it is based on two main stages from the initial stage of building 2D virtual character models using image editing tools such as Photoshop, then displaying this virtual character on Unity software. In the final stage, our method captures user movements from the camera in real-time such as head, face, eye, mouth, and arms movements, then the motion data captured by the camera is transmitted to Unity using TCP protocols to simulate 2D virtual character motion on Unity. Therefore, the approach we introduce in this paper allows the 2D virtual character to simulate the movement of the user in real-time. In the next section, we will explain this method in detail.

## 3    Method

### 3.1    Collecting Two-Dimensional Data

**Designing-Creating the Character Concept Design:** The character concept design will determine the virtual character's look and personality, in other words, this is where the character's soul is created. As a first step in creating a Virtual Model, it is necessary to use a drawing application with the capability of converting the digital artwork into a Photoshop file since the Live2D cubism editor only accepts PSD files as input sources. In the experiment, we use a full-body model designed in a 5000*8000px canvas with 900 dpi resolution using the Clip Studio Paint application. Each body part (including shadow) of the model's upper body is separated into different layers and folders as shown in Figs. 2 and 3.

**Rigging–Creating the Character Skeletal Animation:** The process of adding bones and joints to a virtual model is called Rigging, allowing them to move as shown in Fig. 4. In order to move these bones using Inverse Kinematics (IK), they are linked and follow a standard human skeletal structure. Blend shapes and facial expressions are usually the most challenging aspects of rigging. In the experiment, a 2D virtual character will be rigged using the Live2D Cubism Editor application. After the character design is ready to rig, import the PSD file to the Live 2D Cubism Editor application to start rigging. The important part of this process is to focus on the future movement of the virtual character. Each movement will depend on each parameter, different parameters will correspond to different movements (e.g., ArmL4A is a parameter of the left forearm that varies from 0.0 to 10.0, with 0.0 being completely closed to the hip and 10.0 being completely open). For each parameter, different body parts can be linked together and be affected by each other (e.g., ArmL4A can be connected

**Fig. 2.** An example of separating layers and folders in Clip Studio Paint application

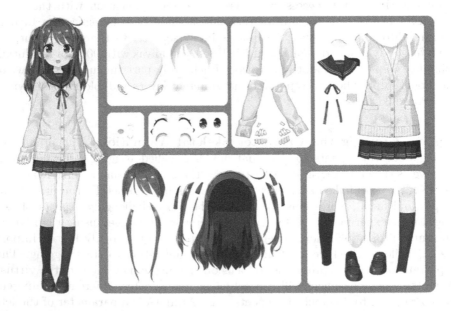

**Fig. 3.** An example of Hiyori Live2D model on how to separate a character design into animation-ready layers

**Fig. 4.** Parameters associated with different parts of the Live2D model for Rigging

to the left upper arm). After that, the left forearm can be determined what it looks like when the left upper arm is moving. The exact configuration of the virtual character is defined by these specific values of a parameter, which are called key forms. Therefore, when we adjust the parameter values between the key forms, then the part of the virtual model (e.g., left forearm) associated with the parameter (e.g., Arm L4A) will be moved to correspond to the adjusting values.

## 3.2   Constructing Tracking and Detecting Systems

After the first phase of creating the virtual character, we have also implemented effective algorithms to capture the user actions in front of the camera. The joints of user performances are extracted by the camera as inputs, and then we apply the motion tracking using the computer vision technique to simulate the virtual character. As we can see from Fig. 1, our system detects the participant's presence using a camera by capturing each frame from the camera, and with this information, different parts of the user can be detected by processing each frame. From that, the upper-body motion-tracking system is designed to accurately detect the position of the upper body, including head, facial expression, and arms are mainly implemented on the OpenCV and Mediapipe Library. The system consists of 3 stages. In the first and second stages, the system will detect the user's presence, then draw a landmark representation of the face and the upper body of the person it identified, in order to finally estimate the upper-body pose of the user in the final step. Next, the third stage is separated into three smaller parts: head, facial expression, and arms detection. In the first and second parts

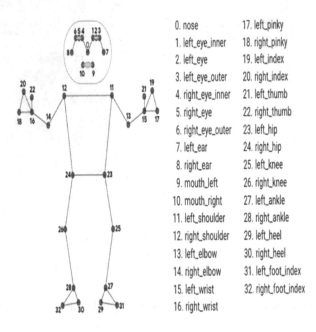

**Fig. 5.** The definition of human poses landmarks

- head poses estimation and facial expression detection respectively, our system was inspired and mainly re-implemented using the following GitHub[1].

The third part is the arms posture tracking, which is also our main contribution. To do this, our system detects the arms' position using the eight landmarks whose indices are 24 (right hip), 12 (right shoulder), 14 (right elbow), 16 (right wrist), 23 (left hip), 11 (left shoulder), 13 (left elbow), 15 (left wrist) as shown in Fig. 5. After that, these 3D landmarks of the left shoulder, left elbow, and left wrist are extracted to create two vectors $(v_{se}, v_{ew})$ with the same origin at the central left elbow landmark, where $v_{se}$ is the vector computed from left shoulder to left elbow landmark, and $v_{ew}$ is the vector calculated from elbow to wrist landmark. Next, we use Eq. (1) to compute the angle elbow value $\theta_e$ between these two vectors, and we estimated the left forearm pose $\rho_{L4Arm}$ using Eq. (2) derived from Eq. (1), where $\alpha \in (0,1)$ is a coefficient value to adjust the error estimation. In order to estimate the left upper arm pose three landmarks: left hip, left shoulder, and left elbow are extracted, and two vectors $(v_{hs}, v_{se})$ are created with the same origin at the central left shoulder landmark, where $v_{hs}$ is the vector computed from the left hip to left shoulder, and $v_{se}$ is the vector calculated from the left shoulder to left elbow landmark. The angle shoulder value $\theta_s$ is computed based on Eq. (3). Then, the left upper arm poses $\rho_{LUArm}$ were estimated using Eq. (4).

---

[1] https://github.com/mmmmmm44/VTuber-Python-Unity.

$$\theta_e = \arccos\left(\frac{v_{se}.v_{ew}}{||v_{se}||||v_{ew}||}\right) \tag{1}$$

$$\rho_{L4Arm} = \alpha * \left(\frac{180 - \theta_e}{10}\right) \tag{2}$$

$$\theta_s = \arccos\left(\frac{v_{hs}.v_{se}}{||v_{hs}||||v_{se}||}\right) \tag{3}$$

$$\rho_{LUArm} = \alpha * \left(\frac{\theta_s}{10}\right) \tag{4}$$

After that, these values $\rho_{L4Arm}$ and $\rho_{LUArm}$ were passed through to a stream data was connected with Unity using TCP protocol to adjust the parameters of the left forearm (ArmL4A) and left upper arm (ArmLA) of the virtual character, which is determined by character controller and make the virtual left arms move according to these adjusting values.

Similarly, the right arm posture tracking is also calculated as the same approach as the left arm posture tracking using these 3D landmarks right hip, right shoulder, right elbow, and right wrist.

## 4 Experimental Results

We evaluate our method on the task of a single human and simulate the left and right arms movement when new motion frames are received. In this experiment, we conducted our method with the different values of the parameter error estimation in the range $\alpha \in (0, 1)$, and we conclude that $\alpha = 0.6$ produces the best result in simulating performance. Table 1 illustrates animation results on the left and right arms of the virtual character, where the upper body of the human was represented with eight different poses, and the upper body of the virtual character is simulated corresponding to the eight poses. From the experiment, the results indicate that our method is capable to simulate accurately the left arm and right arm motion of the virtual character by capturing the two human arms motion using the camera.

**Table 1.** Animation results of the left and right arms with error estimation $\alpha = 0.6$.

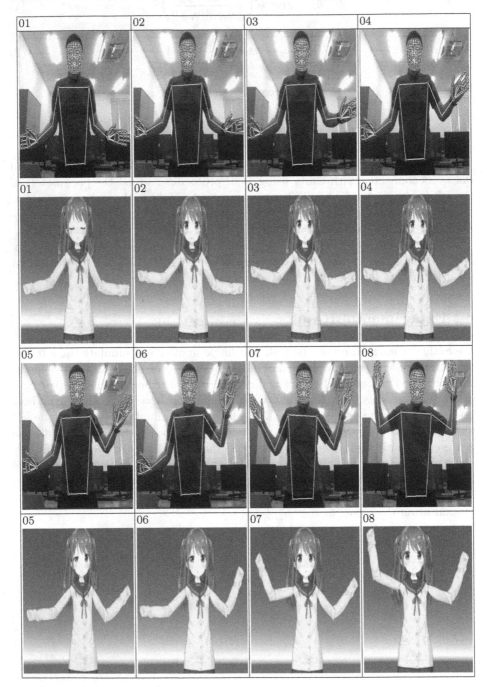

# 5   Conclusion and Future Work

In this paper, we implement a real-time framework that is able to capture and record the movement of humans in real-time and produce virtual character animation using a single camera. To achieve this, a combination of complex computer vision algorithms is used to build an upper body motion tracking system to track and detect human movements, capture their movements then send all that motion data to the virtual character. The animation results demonstrate that the virtual character has the ability to make head, arm movements and express emotions in the virtual environment. However, our current method is not possible to simulate the full body of the virtual character. Therefore, in future work, we will investigate other methods to simulate different parts of the full body of the virtual character.

# References

1. Mekni, M., Baani, Z., Sulieman, D.: A smart virtual assistant for students. In: Petkov, N., Strisciuglio, N., Travieso-González, C.M. (eds.) APPIS 2020: 3rd International Conference on Applications of Intelligent Systems, APPIS 2020, Las Palmas de Gran Canaria Spain, 7–9 January 2020, pp. 15:1–15:6. ACM (2020)
2. Lu, Z., Shen, C., Li, J., Shen, H., Wigdor, D.: More kawaii than a real-person live streamer: understanding how the otaku community engages with and perceives virtual youtubers. In: Kitamura, Y., Quigley, A., Isbister, K., Igarashi, T., Bjørn, P., Drucker, S.M. (eds.) CHI 2021: CHI Conference on Human Factors in Computing Systems, Virtual Event / Yokohama, Japan, May 8–13, 2021, pp. 137:1–137:14. ACM (2021)
3. Tang, M.T., Zhu, V.L., Popescu, V.: Altcrecho: loose avatar-streamer coupling for expressive vtubing. In: IEEE International Symposium on Mixed and Augmented Reality, ISMAR 2021, Bari, Italy, October 4–8, 2021, pp. 128–137. IEEE (2021)
4. Lin, J., Latoschik, M.E.: Digital body, identity and privacy in social virtual reality: a systematic review. Front. Virtual Real. **3**, 974652 (2022)
5. Yaar, N.M., Grossman, E., Kimchi, N., Nash, O., Hatan, S., Erel, H.: Tobe: a virtual keyboard and an animated character for individual and educational cyberbullying intervention. In: Barbosa, S.D.J., Lampe, C., Appert, C., Shamma, D.A. (eds.) CHI 2022: CHI Conference on Human Factors in Computing Systems, New Orleans, LA, USA, 29 April 2022–5 May 2022, Extended Abstracts, pp. 351:1–351:6. ACM (2022)
6. Liu, Q., Qian, G., Meng, W., Ai, Q., Yin, C., Fang, Z.: A new IMMU-based data glove for hand motion capture with optimized sensor layout. Int. J. Intell. Robotics Appl. **3**(1), 19–32 (2019)
7. Lee, Y., Kim, M., Kim, H., Lee, D., You, B.: CHICAP: low-cost hand motion capture device using 3D magnetic sensors for manipulation of virtual objects. In: Special Interest Group on Computer Graphics and Interactive Techniques Conference, SIGGRAPH 2018, Vancouver, BC, Canada, August 12–16, 2018, Emerging Technologies, pp. 4:1–4:2. ACM (2018)

8. Laidig, D., Lehmann, D., Bégin, M., Seel, T.: Magnetometer-free realtime inertial motion tracking by exploitation of kinematic constraints in 2-DoF joints. In: 41st Annual International Conference of the IEEE Engineering in Medicine and Biology Society, EMBC 2019, Berlin, Germany, July 23–27, 2019, pp. 1233–1238. IEEE (2019)

9. Gu, X., Zhang, Y., Sun, W., Bian, Y., Zhou, D., Kristensson, P.O.: Dexmo: an inexpensive and lightweight mechanical exoskeleton for motion capture and force feedback in VR. In: Kaye, J., Druin, A., Lampe, C., Morris, D., Hourcade, J.P. (eds.) Proceedings of the 2016 CHI Conference on Human Factors in Computing Systems, San Jose, CA, USA, May 7–12, 2016, pp. 1991–1995. ACM (2016)

10. Ghorbani, N., Black, M.J.: SOMA: solving optical marker-based mocap automatically. In: 2021 IEEE/CVF International Conference on Computer Vision, ICCV 2021, Montreal, QC, Canada, October 10–17, 2021, pp. 11097–11106. IEEE (2021)

11. Mehta, D., et al.: VNect: real-time 3D human pose estimation with a single RGB camera. ACM Trans. Graph. **36**(4), 44:1-44:14 (2017)

12. Kang, N., Bai, J., Pan, J., Qin, H.: Interactive animation generation of virtual characters using single RGB-D camera. Vis. Comput. **35**(6–8), 849–860 (2019)

13. Xu, W., et al.: Mo$^2$Cap$^2$: real-time mobile 3D motion capture with a cap-mounted fisheye camera. IEEE Trans. Vis. Comput. Graph. **25**, 2093–2101 (2019)

14. Yiannakides, A., Aristidou, A., Chrysanthou, Y.: Real-time 3D human pose and motion reconstruction from monocular RGB videos. Comput. Animat. Virtual Worlds **30**(3–4), 1–12 (2019)

15. Malleson, C., Collomosse, J.P., Hilton, A.: Real-time multi-person motion capture from multi-view video and IMUs. Int. J. Comput. Vis. **128**(6), 1594–1611 (2020)

16. Zhang, Y., An, L., Yu, T., Li, X., Li, K., Liu, Y.: 4D association graph for realtime multi-person motion capture using multiple video cameras. In: 2020 IEEE/CVF Conference on Computer Vision and Pattern Recognition, CVPR 2020, Seattle, WA, USA, June 13–19, 2020, pp. 1321–1330. Computer Vision Foundation / IEEE (2020)

17. Mehta, D.: XNect: real-time multi-person 3D motion capture with a single RGB camera. ACM Trans. Graph. **39**(4), 82 (2020)

18. Bregler, C., Loeb, L., Chuang, E., Deshpande, H.: Turning to the masters: motion capturing cartoons. ACM Trans. Graph. **21**(3), 399–407 (2002)

19. Hornung, A., Dekkers, E., Kobbelt, L.: Character animation from 2D pictures and 3D motion data. ACM Trans. Graph. **26**(1), 1 (2007)

20. Pan, J., Zhang, J.J.: Sketch-based skeleton-driven 2D animation and motion capture. Trans. Edutainment **6**, 164–181 (2011)

# Partnerships as a Means to Improve the Conditions for Achieving Sustainability in SMEs

Esben Skov Laursen(✉) , Christina Koch Pedersen , and René Bennyson

University College of Northern Denmark, 9200 Aalborg, Denmark
{esl,kpc,reb}@ucn.dk

**Abstract.** Environmental sustainability is a global challenge that requires urgent action. Companies, including small and medium-sized enterprises (SMEs), play a crucial role in achieving a sustainable future. However, SMEs often face challenges due to limited resources making it difficult to initiate sustainability efforts independently. One way to overcome these challenges is through partnerships. However, only limited knowledge exists on establishing partnerships in practice to improve the conditions for achieving sustainability. Hence, this article highlights the significance of establishing a partnership to improve sustainability conditions in an SME. The topic is investigated through a single case study at a Danish SME. The case study shows several practical aspects to consider when setting up a partnership to improve the conditions for achieving sustainability in an SME. E.g., an attractive value proposition for the chosen stakeholder(s) and a real opportunity to gain insight into sustainability factors. The results of this study are limited and should only be regarded as preliminary.

**Keywords:** Circular economy · Eco-design · Stakeholder Collaboration

## 1 Introduction

Sustainability has emerged as a global priority, demanding urgent action addressing the environmental challenges.

Companies play a crucial role in ensuring a sustainable future due to their significant influence and impact on various aspects of our society. Thus, companies must integrate sustainable practices into their core operations, products, strategies, and business models [1]. Larger companies typically have the needed resources, financial capacity, and influence to initiate and facilitate sustainability efforts. Small and medium-sized companies (SMEs), however, often face challenges due to the scale of operation. This results in, e.g., limited resources and financial capacity, as well as limited impact on suppliers and customers, making it difficult to initiate and facilitate sustainability [2, 3]. However, SMEs play a crucial role in the global transition to a sustainable future [2, 3]. SMEs constitute 99% of all companies in the EU, employ around 100 million people, and account for more than half of the EU's gross domestic product (GDP) [4]. There is, therefore, a

Y. Luo (Ed.): CDVE 2023, LNCS 14166, pp. 225–230, 2023.
https://doi.org/10.1007/978-3-031-43815-8_22

significant need and potential in focusing on the conditions for achieving sustainability in SMEs.

The literature widely recognizes that achieving sustainability requires collaboration between multiple stakeholders across the entire value chain [1, 2]. One way is through partnerships between stakeholders in the value chain [2]. In the literature, partnerships are described as an approach for SMEs to overcome some of the main barriers, e.g., lack of time, resources, awareness, and skills, when wanting to become more sustainable [2]. However, only limited knowledge exists on establishing partnerships in practice in SMEs to improve the conditions for achieving sustainability [2]. Hence, this article investigates the significance of partnerships as a means of collaboration between SMEs and their stakeholders. More specifically, this article emphasizes and explores the practical establishment of a partnership in an SME through a single case study. This study is the first step in a greater research effort toward this topic; hence the results are only to be regarded as preliminary and limited.

The rest of the article is structured as follows; first, the role of partnership in improving the conditions for sustainability in SMEs is discussed. This is followed by the case study as an empirical example of the first initial steps in an SME on how to establish a partnership. Finally, the main characteristic of establishing a partnership in practice when focusing on sustainability is summarized.

## 2   Partnerships as a Means for Improving the Conditions for Sustainability

Addressing environmental sustainability is complex and requires collaboration between SMEs and multiple stakeholders, e.g., suppliers, customers, public organizations, and NGOs [2]. The integrated nature of sustainability and the limited resources available makes it necessary to address the challenge as a collaborative effort across the entire value chain [3]. This is also to avoid suboptimization.

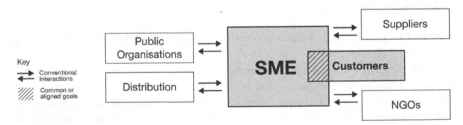

**Fig. 1.** Partnerships can occur among multiple stakeholders. In this study, the focus is on customer collaboration.

Facilitating a collaborative platform, partnerships are widely regarded as a practical and valuable approach to addressing the complexity of sustainability [2, 5]. A partnership can be described as a working arrangement or collaboration between two or more organizations collaborating to achieve a common or aligned goal that goes beyond the individual organizations' capabilities [6] (Fig. 1). Through partnerships, SMEs can extend their sustainability activities beyond their abilities, e.g., by sharing knowledge, resources, and technology with their partners [2, 6].

Moreover, partnerships provide a valuable opportunity to gain insights about, e.g., the use context and the use of the products. This insight helps companies understand the broader sustainability context and apply more informed initiatives, hence strengthening the companies' ability to achieve sustainability [6]. It also allows SMEs to better align sustainability goals with their stakeholders for more impactful outcomes [2]. Overall, partnerships potentially enhance SMEs' ability to achieve sustainability by providing insight into the context, ensuring collaboration, sharing resources, and creating alignment between goals. Partnerships thus have the capacity to play a key role when SMEs work towards achieving environmental sustainability.

However, the idea of partnerships as a means to achieve sustainability is not new [6]. The area has been widely researched from different perspectives over the years. E.g., focusing on sustainability governance [7], multi-stakeholder partnerships [8], barriers [9], and outcomes [10]. Hence, the importance of stakeholder collaboration in the form of partnerships is widely investigated and accepted in academia.

Although the role of partnerships is widely recognized in the literature, only limited knowledge exists on operationalizing partnerships in practice [2, 5]. Thus, there is a need to investigate this in further detail. Moreover, any empirical examples (e.g., case studies) could potentially serve as inspirational cases for other SMEs, making sustainability and partnerships more accessible.

## 3 Establishing a Partnership: A Single Case Study

In this case study, the company is an SME located in Northern Denmark, supplying healthcare equipment. The customers are primarily various national municipalities but also private end-consumers.

For years, the company has had a (partly informal) strategic focus on aspects associated with CSR (Corporate Social Responsibility). The company has recently started focusing on environmental sustainability. This emerged focus on environmental sustainability is mainly driven by an internal motivation fostered by the company's overall focus on CSR and the Sustainable Development Goals (SDGs) [11]. However, their focus on environmental sustainability is also driven by increased pressure from governmental institutions, which seems to continue to rise. Moreover, the company considers environmental sustainability a competitive element in future business, hence a strategic focus.

The data was collected based on an interview with the company's CTO. The interview was conducted as a semi-structured interview based on an interview guide and took approximately one hour. The interview was conducted in Danish and recorded for documentation purposes.

The company chose to focus on the customers (primary multiplicities) among the stakeholders when establishing the partnership. It should be noted that they could have chosen to focus on other stakeholders in their value chain, e.g., their suppliers. However, the customer focus was chosen because it was believed to bring the most added value in improving the conditions for achieving sustainability. In other words, further insights into the market were considered more valuable, as they already had close cooperation with suppliers and a deep insight into the processes and materials used. Moreover, as will later become apparent, the company saw some immediate benefits, including monetary ones, by focusing on the customer. Furthermore, the resources in an SME are typically limited. Therefore, SME activities are often required to support more than one area or have multiple and immediate (monetary) benefits to the company.

Being an SME without the ability to impose a partnership on its customers, the company needed a 'value proposition' to make it attractive for customers to engage in a partnership. At the same time, the partnership also needed to bring value to the company beyond getting sustainability insights. Hence, the company proposed to its customers that they take over responsibility for the customers' inventory (only of the company's products). In practice, that meant approximately one monthly visit to the customers, allow for regular interaction. This created a natural opportunity for further sales or, at least, maintaining the customers' awareness of the company and its products. Moreover, the company would bring back any broken- or worn-down products that no longer had value to the customers.

Hence, with this partnership (inventory-management agreement), the company offered their customers a service product to the benefit of both parties.

Although the partnership initially represented a cost to the company, it also had some benefits. The obsolete products provided insights into their usage and potentially uncovered areas of vulnerability of the products. Hence, this gave valuable insights to the R&D department in general, and it also strengthened the sustainability aspect of the products. This was done e.g., by improving the durability and longevity of the product, both vital to ensuring a sustainable future [12]. Moreover, the obsolete products were taken apart at the company, and any fit parts were refurbished, if needed, and reused to produce new products. Any parts not fit or useable for producing new products were disposed of for recycling, in some cases giving a small monetary output. Reuse, refurbishment, and recycling are also known as part of the R-strategies within circular strategies [13].

Besides giving valuable insight, which could be used to improve the sustainability of the products, the partnership also led to an immediate improvement in sustainability as obsolete products were reused or recycled rather than being stored, bringing no value, and awaiting recovery (also known as *Presource* [12]).

As the company continues to increase its efforts toward environmental sustainability, new insights and understandings are emerging. However, the emphasis on partnerships as a means to strengthen the company's effort to achieve environmental sustainability has proven to be a promising initial step. This is particularly because it serves multiple purposes and is not merely an isolated action.

In summary, the partnership, in this case, provides an opportunity for; additional sales, general input to the R&D department on the use of the products, and a small monetary benefit. However, the partnership also provides an opportunity for sustainable, related input to the R&D department and an immediate improvement of environmental aspects, e.g., by reusing and recycling parts and materials and lowering the amount of presource.

## 4  Summary

A sustainable future requires collaboration. Companies cannot achieve sustainability alone, especially SMEs. While larger companies often have the resources to initiate and facilitate sustainability efforts, SMEs rely on the motivation of their stakeholders to achieve sustainability. Hence, partnerships, valuable to all the actors in a partnership, have the potential to play a crucial role for SMEs aiming to improve their conditions for achieving sustainability.

However, several aspects are to be considered when setting up a partnership in practice to improve the conditions for achieving sustainability in an SME.

- An attractive value proposition for the chosen stakeholder(s) (in this case study, the customers) and the company itself is regarded as one of the main aspects of a successful partnership.
- Ensuring a real opportunity to gain insight into sustainability factors, e.g., the real-life use of the product, is another central aspect of the partnership. This requires the company to analyze the situation to understand where the most impact can be achieved (this initial analysis has not been covered in this study and is regarded as a prerequisite).
- The partnership also needs to bring value to the company beyond getting sustainability insights. Due to limited resources, the activities in an SME are often required to have several immediate benefits.
- Finally, the opportunity to immediately improve sustainability factors through the partnership makes it even more attractive. In this case study, e.g., reusing parts and materials from obsolete products.

In this case study, the focus has been on establishing a partnership with the customers of the SME. However, similar partnerships should be considered with other stakeholders in the value chain to achieve the full potential of this approach. This could be e.g., establishing partnerships with similar businesses (non-competitors), sharing experience, knowledge, or resources relevant to achieving sustainability, or partnerships with NGOs, consultants, or suppliers. The possibilities are many.

However, further research, including more case examples, is needed to explore the topic further. Additional case examples will potentially make sustainability more accessible to other SMEs, as the cases could serve as inspiration.

## References

1. Dzhengiz, T.: A literature review of inter-organizational sustainability learning. Sustainability **12**(12), 4876 (2020)
2. Journeault, M., Perron, A., Vallières, L.: The collaborative roles of stakeholders in supporting the adoption of sustainability in SMEs. J. Environ. Manag. **287**, 112349 (2021)
3. Rizos, V., et al.: Implementation of circular economy business models by small and medium-sized enterprises (SMEs): barriers and enablers. Sustainability **8**(11), 1212 (2016)
4. EUROPEAN COMMISSION Homepage. https://single-market-economy.ec.europa.eu/smes_en. Accessed 19 May 2023

5. Fobbe, L.: Analysing organisational collaboration practices for sustainability. Sustainability **12**(6), 2466 (2020)
6. Van Huijstee, M.M., Francken, M., Leroy, P.: Partnerships for sustainable development: a review of current literature. Environ. Sci. **4**(2), 75–89 (2007)
7. McAllister, R.R.J., Taylor, B.M.: Partnerships for sustainability governance: a synthesis of key themes. Curr. Opinion Environ. Sustain. **12**, 86–90 (2015)
8. Bäckstrand, K.: Multi-stakeholder partnerships for sustainable development: rethinking legitimacy, accountability and effectiveness. Eur. Environ. **16**(5), 290–306 (2006)
9. Frame, B., Taylor, R.: Partnerships for sustainability: effective practice? Local Environ. **10**(3), 275–298 (2005)
10. Hartman, C.L., Hofman, P.S., Stafford, E.R.: Partnerships: a path to sustainability. Bus. Strat. Environ. **8**(5), 255–266 (1999)
11. UNITED NATIONS Homepage. https://www.undp.org/sustainable-development-goals#: ~:text=The%20Sustainable%20Development%20Goals%20(SDGs)%2C%20also%20k nown%20as%20the,people%20enjoy%20peace%20and%20prosperity. Accessed 19 May 2023
12. Den Hollander, M.C., Bakker, C.A., Hultink, E.J.: Product design in a circular economy: development of a typology of key concepts and terms. J. Ind. Ecol. **21**(3), 517–525 (2017)
13. Kirchherr, J., Reike, D., Hekkert, M.: Conceptualizing the circular economy: an analysis of 114 definitions. Resour. Conserv. Recycl. **127**, 221–232 (2017)

# SmartOTP Solution for Small and Medium-Sized Businesses

Le Viet Thang and Phan Duy Hung<sup>(✉)</sup>

FPT University, Hanoi, Vietnam
Thang19MSE13041@fsb.edu.vn, HungPD2@fe.edu.vn

**Abstract.** With the rise of Web 2.0 and Web 3.0, personal information and identity have become a primary part of our lives, along with it, the security of said information. Most of the websites allow us to have our own user account to represent ourselves online. But with hacking and identity theft having no sign of decreasing, it is getting harder to trust those user accounts. As a result, identity authentication solutions have become a focus of attention for some time. One of the more focused solutions is One-Time Password (OTP). There are currently many commercial OTP solutions from many identity providers such as Amazon Web Service, Microsoft Azure, and Google Cloud that are complete and flexible to be applied to almost any use case. However, some businesses may require a simple and scalable solution that can quickly adapt to their needs. The paper presents such a solution for small and medium sized businesses. The paper describes the architecture and technologies applied to the solution to be able to achieve that goal. The approaches and results of the paper are completely applicable to businesses of any size.

**Keywords:** OTP · Hash Algorithms · Elliptic curve cryptography · ECDH · OCRA Algorithm · Microservices · Container Orchestration

## 1 Introduction

Before any OTP or Multi-factor Authentication (MFA) solutions, user accounts only needed passwords to authenticate. This was fine for some time, until the packets can be sniffed through man-in-the-middle attack [1], made our passwords vulnerable. Not to mention, in the early days of internet, the passwords were quite simple, so they are susceptible to brute force attacks [2]. This resulted in SSL/TLS, which uses ECDH [3], to make our packets encrypted end-to-end, meaning only us and the target server can decrypt the packets, eliminating man-in-the-middle attacks. However, this also proved not to be enough, since the attacker might not need to understand the content inside and just need to replay the last packets sent from the victim [4], for example to imitate a login from another device. This raised many questions about passwords and their effectiveness. Many tech corporations are gearing towards password-less future [5, 6], by using other factors to authenticate alongside passwords, or even removing passwords entirely. This technique is called MFA [7], with the factors ranging from SMS, software

Y. Luo (Ed.): CDVE 2023, LNCS 14166, pp. 231–241, 2023.
https://doi.org/10.1007/978-3-031-43815-8_23

on our personal smartphones, to hardware such as keys or physical tokens. This technique uses a traded secret key and other variables on personal device to generate an OTP that can only be used once, eliminating replay attacks.

The current commercialized OTP solutions like Amazon Web Service, Microsoft Azure and Google Cloud usually charges by both number of monthly active users and number of authentications [8]. Therefore, there is a need for a simple and scalable OTP solution, which may only need to scale based on the number of requests.

This paper introduces the SmartOTP solution, a simple and scalable solution for software OTP. This solution can serve as a single point of identity authentication for many businesses to integrate with or can be hosted on premises separately for each business. SmartOTP uses microservice architecture and containerization that can be scaled out on demand. This solution incorporates software-token based OTP generation mechanism.

The remainder of the paper is organized as follows. Section 2 provides a high-level overview of the proposed system. Secret exchange and OTP calculation mechanism will be described in Sect. 3. The system design and implementation are presented in Sect. 4. Section 5 will demonstrate a sample deployment and results. Finally, conclusions and future works are made in Sect. 6.

## 2   System Architecture and Requirements

### 2.1   Architecture Overview

The SmartOTP solution is designed with two parts: client application and backend system (Fig. 1). The backend system has three main components:

- Provider: this is the main component for communicating with clients, handling registration flows and authentication flows.
- Secret DB: this component is used to store user secrets that will be used to calculate OTP and partner keys.
- Temp DB: this component is used to store temporary data, used for locking, rate limiting and OTP invalidation.

The solution also explores the Application component on smartphones, but it is not the focus of this paper.

### 2.2   System Actors

The system has two main actors:

- Partner: corresponds to a business, has partner key to be used in user registration and rate limiting
- User: corresponds to an end user of a business, has user id to be used in authentication requests

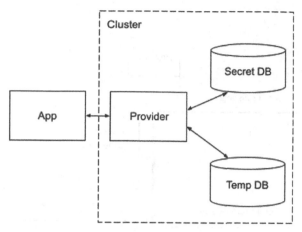

**Fig. 1.** Architecture overview

## 3 Secret Exchange and OTP Calculation Mechanism

The principle that the provider works on to generate and validate OTP has two main mechanisms. First is the secret exchange. The solution uses ECDH [9] to derive the shared secret key using only its own private key and the received public key. ECDH is a key-agreement protocol that allows two parties, each having an elliptic curve public-private key pair, to establish a shared secret over an insecure channel. This shared secret is used to derive another symmetric key. The ECDH protocol is a variant of the Diffie-Hellman protocol using elliptic curve cryptography. ECDH derives a shared secret value from a secret key owned by an Entity A and a public key owned by an Entity B when the keys share the same elliptic curve domain parameters. Entity A can be either the initiator of a key-agreement transaction, or the responder in a scheme. If two entities both correctly perform the same operations with corresponding keys as inputs, the same shared secret value is produced. After sharing and calculating shared secret, it will be stored securely.

The second mechanism, OTP calculation, is implemented following the OATH Challenge-Response Algorithm (OCRA) [10]. This is an extension to the previous HMAC-based One-Time Password Algorithm (HOTP) that generalizes OTP calculation with inputs other than just counter and secret key. The solution proposes two kinds of authentication: basic authentication where only timestep will be used in OTP calculation, and advanced authentication where besides timestep, a random challenge will be sent to be used in OTP calculation.

### 3.1 Partner Registration Flow

The partner registration flow is used the first time a partner wants to register to the system (Fig. 2). The partner will need to send a desired rate limit to the provider, then the provider will return a partner key that will be used to track users and rate limit.

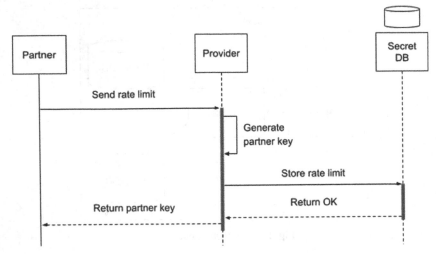

**Fig. 2.** Partner Registration Flow

## 3.2 User Registration Flow

After registering the partner key, the partner can use the key to register users (Fig. 3). First the client on user side needs to generate an EC key pair in the Prime256v1 domain (dA and dA*G). Then the partner uses the user generated public key (dA*G) to send to provider, where the provider will also generate its own EC key pair in the same Prime256v1 domain (dB and dB*G). After the provider has generated the key pair, it returns its public key (dB*G) back to the partner and to the user. When both the user and the provider have both private key and public key, they can use them to derive the shared secret key (dA*dB*G) and store it in secure storage.

## 3.3 Basic Authentication Flow

With the secret key shared between the two parts, they can now authenticate each other. In most cases, like logging in, viewing transaction history or transferring small amounts of money, the user will use basic authentication flow (Fig. 4). When the user needs to authenticate with the provider, the user calculates its OTP using the current timestep and the shared secret key. The timestep is chosen to have 30-s duration. The OTP is the result of HMAC SHA256 digest of the input. After calculating, the OTP is then sent to provider for validation. The provider also calculates OTP the same way then compares it to the received OTP, if it is the same, then the request is authenticated, otherwise it is invalid.

While this is happening, after the provider has received the request, the lock for the user will be initiated so the subsequent requests to the same user will be blocked. The provider will also keep track of the latest timestep that is used by the user to invalidate the duplicated OTP requests, mitigating the replay attacks. The rate limit for partners will also keep track of how many requests have been sent in a 1 s window. For example, if the partner has a rate limit of 100 limit per second, then in a 1 s window, only the

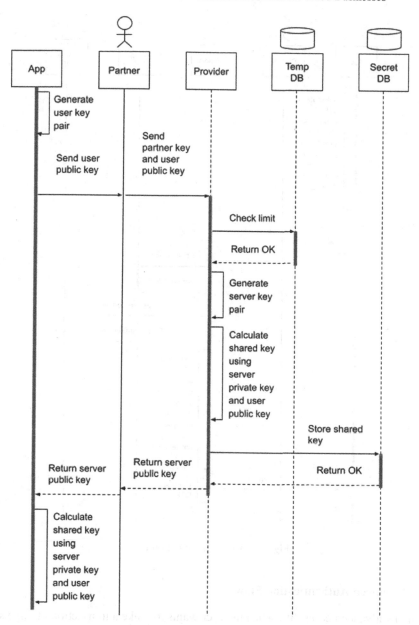

**Fig. 3.** User Registration Flow

first 100 requests are handled, others will be returned an error. This will help avoiding distributed denial-of-service attacks because in these kinds of attacks, we cannot just rely on the malicious IPs to keep track.

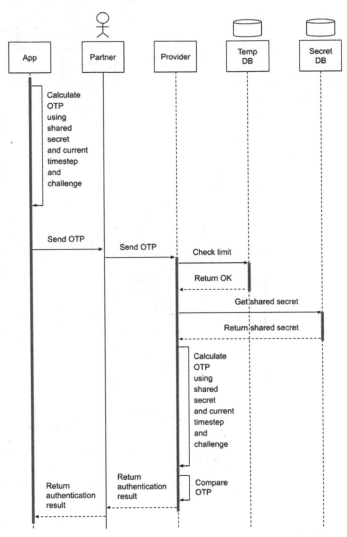

**Fig. 4.** Basic Authentication Flow

### 3.4 Advanced Authentication Flow

For more advanced cases, like when the user wants to make a transaction of large sums of money, the solution proposes the advanced authentication flow (Fig. 5). This works the same way as the basic authentication flow, but before the user generating OTP, the provider generates a random challenge sequence and sends it to the user. The user then uses this challenge, in addition to timestep and shared secret key. After any request using this challenge, the challenge will then be invalidated so it cannot be used in subsequent requests.

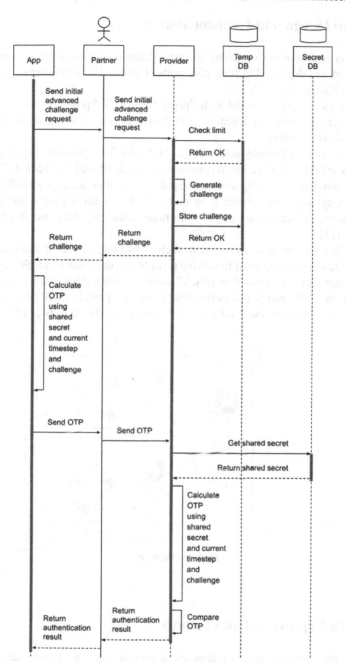

**Fig. 5.** Advanced Authentication Flow

## 4  System Design and Implementation

The solution is designed for scaling in mind. Each of the three main components is containerized and deployed in their own pods (Fig. 6). The container orchestration is managed in Kubernetes [11].

The provider is implemented with Spring Boot [12]. Spring Boot embeds a small but fast server. This also has a benefit of high startup time, making horizontal scale of provider pods responsive.

Main database technology is decided to be Redis. This provides high performance compared to other DBMS because it is an on-memory database [13]. Temp DB and Secret DB uses Redis Cluster configuration to apply techniques such as sharding, splitting data into many parts and storing it in many databases for higher write throughput, and replication, replicating a database into many read only databases for higher read throughput [14].

Temp DB only stores temporary data such as locking, rate limit and challenges, so this Redis Cluster does not need to survive restarts. On the other hand, Secret DB stores important data like user shared secrets. Therefore, Secret DB cluster is configured to use append-only-file, which makes it slower in comparison, but will be able to survive restarts, when it happens, the database will restore using the AOF file [15].

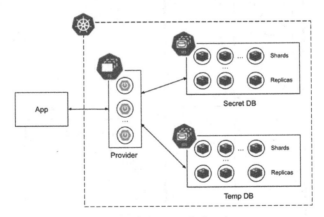

**Fig. 6.**  System design

## 5  Sample Deployment and Results

To measure the performance and scalability of the solution, we created a sample deployment. The sample deployment on Minikube [16] has a configuration of 3 pods for each of the components. Pods of Secret DB and Temp DB are all master nodes in Redis. As shown in the Fig. 7, pods are very light. Pods for provider each take about 250 MB after load tests have been run. The provider pod takes around 5 s to cold start, making it easy to horizontally scale.

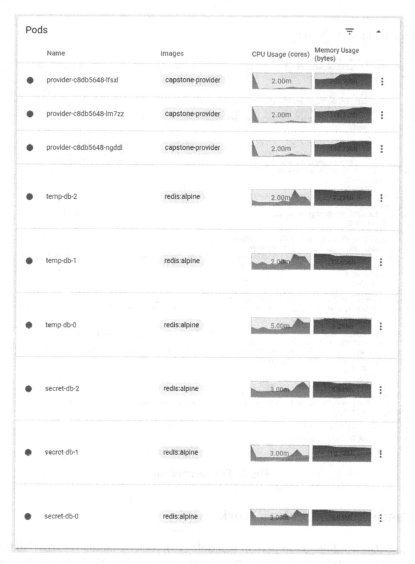

**Fig. 7.** Cluster Pods Metrics

Pods for Temp DB are the lightest, with only around 8 MB of memory usage and less than 1 s of cold start time. Pods for Secret DB are still light, but not as light as Temp DB, with around 15 MB, though the cold start time remains the same.

The request time is fast, around less than 5 ms per request, as shown in the Fig. 8 below. We could not make a real load test on the deployment because the Minikube load balancer was the bottleneck and could not forward enough concurrent requests. The solution has locking and invalidate used timesteps mechanisms to prevent replay attacks. Using rate limiting techniques, the solution is also able to mitigate distributed denial-of-service attacks, if somehow the partner key is leaked.

Logs from provider ▾ in provider-76df7… ▾

Handled basic challenge request: 2.333346ms
Partner key: 9zckTDQ2wBkH8lIOCIfgIKYezQF3XLO/Q7b3XzSntweTkts/06vtXusYuKz96J06woNz2XjSsBWgbl3X/bLWpw==
User id: LX6jxrZ6FC71AUVzsyNQrfZNS3oFcmUXhdsXgAGAtmo=
Server otp: 429934
User otp: 429934
Secret key: AL6Q8fOSmk/TkQzpKqpb95nctjd66f5ugL8fPX8q6ke4
Hash: 42c9f4paB1Tu4xdi2EY6JOsDkcLg1LH1yqdpQ1AS96U=
Message: TwBDAFIAQQAtADEAOgBIAE8AVABQAC0AUwBIAEEEAMgA1ADYALQA2ADoAVAAzADAAUwAAADUANgAwADkAMgA3ADMANwA=
Timestep: 56092737
Status: true
2023-04-29T15:28:37.842Z  INFO 1 --- [nio-8080-exec-6] c.provider.service.SpringService        : -----
Handled basic challenge request: 3.633861ms
Partner key: 9zckTDQ2wBkH8lIOCIfgIKYezQF3XLO/Q7b3XzSntweTkts/06vtXusYuKz96J06woNz2XjSsBWgbl3X/bLWpw==
User id: d0QTkUUZ//3pPnvxBUlcpKc+JRgG2xCzP/PtrQEFlvk=
Server otp: 626415
User otp: 626415
Secret key: FJQHiX0pbOOYfdtDdXUipY3PhjhrFk5uV3nbGrabUWA=
Hash: V9/QXdpOufXXTGzvFTPKBroEn8QDuOYjDTM1OpguQfg=
Message: TwBDAFIAQQAtADEAOgBIAE8AVABQAC0AUwBIAEEEAMgA1ADYALQA2ADoAVAAzADAAUwAAADUANgAwADkAMgA3ADMANwA=
Timestep: 56092737
Status: true
2023-04-29T15:28:37.857Z  INFO 1 --- [io-8080-exec-22] c.provider.service.SpringService        : -----
Handled basic challenge request: 3.996404ms
Partner key: 9zckTDQ2wBkH8lIOCIfgIKYezQF3XLO/Q7b3XzSntweTkts/06vtXusYuKz96J06woNz2XjSsBWgbl3X/bLWpw==
User id: MNcDPebEMzOcR9onXcqz0SMd4SfCeIZJhRiX0oQRCWY=
Server otp: 070540
User otp: 070540
Secret key: WgGHjEWdoYOSOHxZkDkJfZjdkRdfcjyCdu1JLtFzvvU=
Hash: 0ZdwBPhCLvm84wK32o/MgNYIsKJw08Gx+9Z97QJb1Ds=
Message: TwBDAFIAQQAtADEAOgBIAE8AVABQAC0AUwBIAEEEAMgA1ADYALQA2ADoAVAAzADAAUwAAADUANgAwADkAMgA3ADMANwA=
Timestep: 56092737
Status: true
2023-04-29T15:28:37.872Z  INFO 1 --- [io-8080-exec-10] c.provider.service.SpringService        : -----
Handled basic challenge request: 3.433815ms
Partner key: 0JcInr2ZgLNesTwtZAFq5Gx93Zq29ZCqndCKTwltAw1buArQjyBq3f+38kMG1AvY0ObedFIF4bHQ56EdzOKxLA==
User id: j2hsTfBPuSHuEL2apuL15L7Pjrq+9u96GOoFGEDDpXg=
Server otp: 507003
User otp: 507003
Secret key: bPG22mhAVZLFFZ+hFCOctpIDmC/RZzn8bepZtkZJaC8=
Hash: 4pzQS+gsuylzNWdWL4pXb0Os F4por4hwheZxWL7BvqM=
Message: TwBDAFIAQQAtADEAOgBIAE8AVABQAC0AUwBIAEEEAMgA1ADYALQA2ADoAVAAzADAAUwAAADUANgAwADkAMgA3ADMANwA=
Timestep: 56092737
Status: true
2023-04-29T15:28:37.887Z  INFO 1       [nio-8080-exec-1] c.provider.service.SpringService

Logs from Apr 29, 2023 to Apr 29, 2023 UTC

**Fig. 8.** Provider pod logs

# 6　Conclusion and Future Work

One-time Password are an important technology in today's online security landscape. In this paper, we described SmartOTP, a simple and scalable OTP solution that can be applied to small to medium sized businesses. We also demonstrated a sample deployment on Minikube to security test and load test. The solution being Kubernetes native makes it easy to incorporate into the current business infrastructure or create an independent service altogether. This also allows the businesses that are not yet using large third-party cloud infrastructure to avoid vendor lock-in. This solution is also a good reference for research directions of Software engineering, Information System, etc. [17–20].

In the future, we will investigate vulnerabilities on smartphone application side to minimize and mitigate attacks to provide a more secure solution. We will also investigate creating administrative functionality for the solution to help control and change the rate limits of partners.

# References

1. Jonker, H., Mauw, S., Trujillo-Rasua, R.: Man-in-the-middle attacks evolved... but our security models didn't. In: Anderson, J., Matyáš, V., Christianson, B., Stajano, F. (eds.) Security Protocols XXIV. Security Protocols 2016. LNCS, vol. 10368, pp. 26–34. Springer, Cham (2017). https://doi.org/10.1007/978-3-319-62033-6_4
2. Bošnjak, L., Sreš, J., Brumen, B.: Brute-force and dictionary attack on hashed real-world passwords. In: Proceedings of the 41st International Convention on Information and Communication Technology, Electronics and Microelectronics (MIPRO), Opatija, Croatia, pp. 1161–1166 (2018)
3. Why use Ephemeral Diffie-Hellman. https://mbed-tls.readthedocs.io/en/latest/kb/cryptography/ephemeral-diffie-hellman/#why-use-ephemeral-diffie-hellman. Accessed 29 Jan 2023
4. Singh, A.K., Misra, A.K.: Analysis of cryptographically replay attacks and its mitigation mechanism. In: Satapathy, S.C., Avadhani, P.S., Abraham, A. (eds.) INDIA 2012. AISC, vol. 132, pp. 787–794. Springer, Heidelberg (2012). https://doi.org/10.1007/978-3-642-27443-5_90
5. Jakkal, V.: The passwordless future is here for your Microsoft account. https://www.microsoft.com/en-us/security/blog/2021/09/15/the-passwordless-future-is-here-for-your-microsoft-account/. Accessed 29 Jan 2023
6. Srinivas, S.: One step closer to a passwordless future. https://blog.google/technology/safety-security/one-step-closer-to-a-passwordless-future/. Accessed 29 Jan 2023
7. Eldefrawy, M.H., Alghathbar, K., Khan, M.K.: OTP-based two-factor authentication using mobile phones. In: Proceedings of the 8th International Conference on Information Technology: New Generations, Las Vegas, NV, USA, pp. 327–331 (2011)
8. Identity Platform pricing. https://cloud.google.com/identity-platform/pricing. Accessed 29 Jan 2023
9. Naik, R.M., Sathyanarayana, S., Sowmya, T.: Key management using elliptic curve Diffie Hellman curve 25519. In: Proceedings of the third International Conference on Multimedia Processing, Communication & Information Technology (MPCIT), Shivamogga, India, pp. 33–39 (2020)
10. M'Raihi, D., Rydell, J., Bajaj, S., Machani, S., Naccache, D.: OCRA: OATH Challenge-Response Algorithm (2011). https://www.rfc-editor.org/rfc/pdfrfc/rfc6287.txt.pdf
11. https://kubernetes.io/. Accessed 29 Jan 2023
12. https://spring.io/. Accessed 29 Jan 2023
13. https://developer.redis.com/explore/what-is-redis/. Accessed 29 Jan 2023
14. https://redis.io/docs/management/scaling/. Accessed 29 Jan 2023
15. https://redis.io/docs/management/persistence/. Accessed 29 Jan 2023
16. https://minikube.sigs.k8s.io/docs/. Accessed 29 Jan 2023
17. Hai, M.M., Hung, P.D.: Centralized access point for information system integration problems in large enterprises. In: Luo, Y. (ed.) CDVE 2020. LNCS, vol. 12341, pp. 239–248. Springer, Cham (2020). https://doi.org/10.1007/978-3-030-60816-3_27
18. Tae, C.M., Hung, P.D.: A collaborative web application based on incident management framework for financial system. In: Luo, Y. (ed.) CDVE 2020. LNCS, vol. 12341, pp. 289–301. Springer, Cham (2020). https://doi.org/10.1007/978-3-030-60816-3_32
19. Chung, N.N., Hung, P.D.: Logging and monitoring system for streaming data. In: Luo, Y. (ed.) CDVE 2020. LNCS, vol. 12341, pp. 184–191. Springer, Cham (2020). https://doi.org/10.1007/978-3-030-60816-3_21
20. Nam, L.H., Hung, P.D., Vinh, B.T., Diep, V.T.: Practical fair queuing algorithm for message queue system. In: Joshi, A., Mahmud, M., Ragel, R.G. (eds.) ICTCS 2021. LNNS, vol. 400, pp. 421–429. Springer, Singapore (2023). https://doi.org/10.1007/978-981-19-0095-2_40

# Championing Electromobility with Co-engineered Services Based on Artificial Intelligence and Interdisciplinarity

Thomas Tamisier, German Castignani, and Laurence Johannsen[✉]

Luxembourg Institute of Science and Technology (LIST), 5, av. des Hauts-Fourneaux, 4362 Esch-Sur-Alzette, Grand Duchy of Luxembourg
{thomas.tamisier,laurence.johannsen}@list.lu

**Abstract.** While artificial intelligence is nowadays routinely and seamlessly part of our everyday life, a large potential of its impact is yet emerging on fundamental economic, environmental, and societal challenges such as developing alternative modes of driving, especially in urban areas. This article discusses a Luxembourgish Testing and Experimentation Facility specifically devoted to the expansion of electromobility, as part of the Digital Europe CitCom.ai project. The underlying approach combines cross-disciplinary expertise (in energy management, sustainability assessment, advanced computing, and secure communications) with powerful and trustworthy artificial intelligence for the collaborative design, implementation, and assessment of a range of innovative services answering the needs of Smart Cities and Communities for the benefit of citizens.

**Keywords:** scenarios and case studies of cooperative design for electromobility services · artificial intelligence for cooperative design and engineering · local digital twins and visualization

## 1 Introduction

Through the *Digital Europe Programme*, the European Commission promotes the development and adoption of trustworthy AI solutions by specifically relying on world-class *Testing and Experimentation Facilities* (TEF) in four areas: smart cities and communities, manufacturing, health, and agriculture. The TEFs must, on the one hand, foster innovation and competitiveness of European companies and, on the other hand, ensure ethics and responsibility of the AI solutions they have tested, as well as facilitate their uptake by communities and citizens.

With regards to the population, Luxembourg is a huge contributor of $CO_2$ emissions. This is due to the characteristics of its economy, notably the dependence on cross-borders commuters, and the crucial role of the logistics sector. The country is therefore deeply engaged into international policies towards lowering energy consumption while addressing multiple challenges: development of new urban areas, cohabitation with industry, fast growing population, heavy cross-border traffic, urban sharing of road and rail networks between passenger and cargos.

Y. Luo (Ed.): CDVE 2023, LNCS 14166, pp. 242–245, 2023.
https://doi.org/10.1007/978-3-031-43815-8_24

In CitCom.ai, Luxembourg TEF will be a testbed for the development of new innovative AI-enabled services and products in the field of electromobility over a period of 5 years starting in January 2023. The choice of electromobility is related to Luxembourg's 2030 goal to have a 49% share of electric vehicles. Within the project, electromobility is considered from an end-to-end perspective in the context of public transport, individual mobility, and logistics, and covers notably the aspects of electricity production (in particular from renewables), charging, and fleet management. More precisely, the objectives of Luxembourg engagement are as follows:

- set-up the TEF infrastructure (combining physical and virtual facilities, software, hardware, expertise & services) enabling the prototyping of trusted AI-enabled services and products in real conditions
- involve (local/non local) partners (SME, public/private organizations), in the collaborative design, test and experimentation of new AI-based services for the benefit of cities and local communities
- Promote the adoption of the resulting new services associated with electromobility across EU regions.

## 2  State-of-the-Art and Challenges

Bringing efficient response to customized needs depends on the ability to train AI models on relevant sets of data scattered among different networks, with timely and secure access to relevant time-space data streams, and to make essential breakthrough by fusing information coming from heterogeneous sources and usable for different usages. However, long lasting issues hinder the growth potential of AI and robotics solutions deployed for the public at large. They can be categorized as follows.

- Access to domain data. AI solutions need access to all relevant datasets from different stakeholders involved in the development of a complex real-word application. In the legacy situation they mainly work in silos, preventing the sharing of their data from technical and regulatory aspects. In particular, the format, management and meta-data are not harmonized between organizations and systems.
- Real-world testing. AI algorithms are used to predict phenomena and manage daily operations. To prove their accuracy and validate advanced AI based solutions before releasing them to the market, it is necessary to deploy them in real-world environments and check how they perform, which depends on the availability on both a model of the reality and real-scale datasets. As a response, significant Research and Development are nowadays invested to develop *test before invest* strategies. Yet, upscaling and developing AI algorithms from lower TRL levels to TRL 6–9 levels requires to invest significantly in capabilities and infrastructure (e.g. storage space, computing power, skills, and development tools).
- Private life and regulatory issues. Current EU and member state regulatory frameworks are often perceived as a brake to AI-based innovation. Moreover, risk of non-ethical use of data and lack of knowledge regarding complex regulatory frameworks lead hinder the adoption of innovative AI-based solutions both by decision makers and the public.

## 3 Testing Facility

The overarching goal of the Luxembourg TEF is the training and validation of solutions that can map, analyze, predict, and support the integration of electromobility in green cities and their communities. Complemented with the German, Belgian and French neighboring territories in the so-called Greater Region, Luxembourg offers indeed a vibrant area requiring enhanced mobility (as regards traditional use of cars, public buses, freight transport), enabling to drastically lower traffic congestion and $CO_2$ emissions and addressing specifically the fast expansion of cross-border traffic and logistics sector.

Multidisciplinary pilots considered for the TEF include the following:

- Impact assessment of EV-charging behaviour and PV production on the electrical grid,
- Energy potential simulation for Vehicle integrated PV,
- Performance of batteries enabled charging stations,
- Optimal location of the charging stations,
- Traceability of carbon-free electrons for EV-driving.

The TEF will manage acquisition and storage (in the shape of data lakes) of data from relevant sources across different domains such as: geodata in the Greater Region, real-time traffic information, mobility data providers, OEM connected car data integrators, energy grid management, PV generation, smart meters, citizen participation. This advanced data management will use and foster the development of Minimum Interoperability Mechanisms (MIMs) [1] and follow Open Standards to meet strict requirements in term of security, privacy, scalability, replication and explainability.

Operationally, the TEF will rely on LIST's AIDA (AI and Data Analytics), a powerful combination of hardware components, software layers, expertise, and engineering and services, proving researchers and practitioners with adequate infrastructure to make the most of the expansion of AI and support innovation roadmaps towards market readiness.

As an enabler of the Visual Analytics paradigm, AIDA includes notably the VisWall, a world-class interactive visualization facility (2 * 7 m and +50M pixels). Thanks to this unique mix of data visualization and analytics capacities, services will be offered that can check the outcome of the algorithms compared to the situation in the real world. To this end, the prototypes of new services will be tested in real-word environments and at scale, using Local Digital Twin models [2], to allow companies and final beneficiaries to get advance check of complicated and disruptive solutions enabled by artificial intelligence, and provide decision makers of cities and communities with accurate knowledge on real-scale scenarios to help the adoptions of concrete strategies. TEF will thus foster the co-engineering of solutions involving experts and stakeholders to consider complementary constraints and needs, such as those related to people, energy communities, public transportation, fleet management and professional logistics [3].

Figure 1 gives an overview of the TEF architecture of a pilot including visual dashboards.

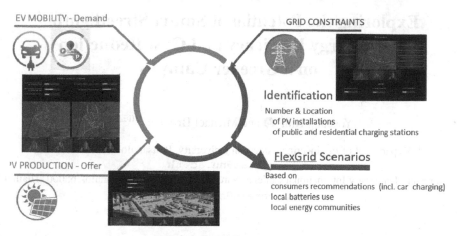

**Fig. 1.** TEF Pilot Scenario

## 4   Conclusion

The development of Smart Cities and Communities relies on digital and technological innovations which address long-standing issues towards the integration of all urban stakeholders in a sustainable city ecosystem. The article has reviewed the main challenges of the setting-up of a Luxembourg test bed and a living lab for training and validating algorithms that can map, analyze, predict, and foster the development of electromobility.

For the coming 4 years, this co-engineering infrastructure will specifically contribute to AI technology maturity assessment and fast integration of new AI technologies in sandboxed products targeting real world scenarios. Associated with this, Digital Twinning methodology will support upscaling and replication.

**Acknowledgements.** The project CitCom.ai is funded through the EU Digital Europe Programme, call "Cloud data & TEF, 2022".

## References

1. https://oascities.org/minimal-interoperability-mechanisms/
2. Sottet, J.-S., Brimont, P., Feltus, B., Gateau, B., Merche, J.-F.: Towards a lightweight model-driven smart-city digital twin. In: Proceedings of the 10th International Conference on Model-Driven Engineering and Software Development, January 2022 (2022). https://doi.org/10.5220/0010906100003119
3. Aggoune-Mtalaa, W., Habbas, Z., Ait Ouahmed, A., Khadraoui, D.: Solving new urban freight distribution problems involving modular electric vehicles. IET Intell. Transp. Syst. 9(6), 654–661 (2015). https://doi.org/10.1049/iet-its.2014.0212

# Exploring the Potential of Smart Streetlighting for Energy Efficiency and Cost Reduction on a Greener Campus

Yoseung Kim[1] and Michael Brückner[2]([⊠])

[1] Department of Engineering, Naresuan University, Phitsanulok 65000, Thailand
kingrise@nu.ac.th
[2] Naresuan University International College, Naresuan University, Phitsanulok 65000, Thailand
michaelb@nu.ac.th

**Abstract.** This paper presents the methods and preliminary results of a project investigating smart streetlighting, the Smart Street Lighting System (SSLS). The project came about because of a practical problem: reducing the electricity consumption, and, consequently, electricity costs, of a university in northern Thailand. We show simple and inexpensive ways to both monitor and reduce the power consumption of street lighting on a university campus. A cloud-based real-time database has been employed to support the administrative staff. The database is being used to manage and control streetlamps centrally. The data are displayed as an easy-to-use dashboard highlighting warnings and the general status of the streetlamps. Moreover, a smartphone app can control streetlamps locally, if necessary. The results show that during a period of five months power consumption of smart streetlamps could be reduced by about 55% compared to time-controlled streetlamps.

**Keywords:** smart street lighting system · Internet of Things (IoT) · power consumption reduction

## 1 Introduction

Streetlighting plays a vital role in ensuring the safety and security of people on the streets. Consequently, innovations in streetlighting have been sought after in recent years, especially when it comes to improvements in energy efficient streetlighting. Smart streetlighting is based on networks comprising sensors and actuators and is aimed to play a role in smart cities, where a wide range of components of the infrastructure is monitored and controlled via digital technology (Mahoor et al. 2000; Manyake and Mathaba 2022).

Many universities in Thailand struggle with scarce financial resources and therefore aim to use energy economically. Energy efficiency and cost reduction can also help campuses to achieve their sustainability goals. By reducing their energy consumption, campuses can lower their carbon emissions and help to protect the environment. One area where campuses can make significant improvements in energy efficiency is street lighting. Street lighting accounts for a significant portion of a campus's energy use. Smart street lighting systems can help improve energy efficiency by automatically dimming or brightening lights based on traffic or pedestrian activity. This can lead to significant energy savings, as well as improved safety and security (Dheena et al. 2017; Bhosale et al. 2017; Arjun et al. 2019). Umar et al. (2020), for example, claim a potential reduction of power consumption by up to 99% on roads with no or less traffic. In this study, we wanted to evaluate the actual reduction of power consumption on a university campus by using smart streetlighting with low-cost hardware (sensors, Internet) and software components (cloud-based real-time database, smartphone app) compared to a time-controlled streetlighting system.

Smart streetlighting is a rapidly evolving field, with new technologies and applications being developed all the time. In general, smart streetlights are equipped with sensors and other devices that allow them to collect data and communicate with other devices. This data can be used to improve energy efficiency, enhance safety and security, and collect information about traffic patterns and other environmental factors. There are two main types of smart streetlights: cellular-connected and wireless. Cellular-connected streetlights use cellular networks to communicate with a central control system. This allows for remote monitoring and control of the lights, as well as the collection and analysis of data. Wireless streetlights use a variety of wireless technologies, such as Wi-Fi, Bluetooth, or LoRaWAN, to communicate with a central control system. This allows for more localized control and data collection.

A challenge associated with smart streetlighting is the need for reliable internet connectivity. Smart streetlights rely on internet connectivity to communicate with a central control system and collect data. If internet connectivity is not reliable, it can disrupt the operation of the smart streetlighting system.

This paper is organized as follows. After the introduction, the smart streetlighting system is described and its hardware and software components are outlined. Then, the results are provided as the user interface, administrative dashboard, and smartphone app including data regarding users' attitude toward the app usage. Finally, conclusions are drawn and further work is indicated.

## 2 Methods and Tools

### 2.1 Hardware

Various data collected and connected to a sensor network is sent to a database via wireless communication technology. The collected information plays an important role in the world of IoT, and wireless communication technology allows for effective transmission of this information (Manyake and Mathaba 2022). The key elements of wireless communication technology include data rate, range, and power consumption (Lewandowski et al. 2022; Mahoor et al. 2000). Based on these elements, each technology has its own advantages and disadvantages. Wireless network technologies for IoT devices are as follows:

- Short Range Wireless Communication: WiFi, Bluetooth, Zigbee, NFC (Near-field communication)

- Licensed Lower Power Wide Area Network: EC (Extended coverage)-GSM IoT, NB (NarrowBand)-IoT, LTE-MTC (Machine Type Communication)
- Unlicensed Lower Power Wide Area Network: LoRa, Sigfox, MIOTY
- Cellular Communication: 2G, 3G, 4G/ LTE, 5G

In this study, we have used NB-IoT technology, because it has no significant impact on data rate, wireless communication range, or power consumption (Omar et al. 2022). In the next stage, we will apply wireless communication technologies suitable for external environments to conduct practical and more advanced research.

Two types of sensors are used for SSLS: motion sensors and light sensors. For this smart street light management system, Passive infrared motion sensors are suitable as it detects body heat to sense motion and can detect pedestrians and cars. They are also cost-effective, small in size, and consumes low power. As a suitable type of light sensors we apply photoresistor-based sensors. These sensors are passive components that change their resistance in response to the amount of light falling on them. They are also simple, low-cost, and can be easily integrated into the lighting system.

The sensors used in SSLS are the GL5516 LDR Photoresistor sensing ambient light (CdS based) and the motion sensor HC-SR501, which uses auto-senses motion and has an adjustable delay time between 0.3 s–200 s (See Fig. 1).

**Fig. 1.** Ambient light sensor (left) and motion sensor (right)

## 2.2 Software

**Sensor Data.** SSLS uses the sensor data in different modes. The ambient light sensor data applies a common threshold (W3C 2023) to control the luminance of the LED lamps (See Fig. 2). We use the WiPy WiFi module that is based on the MicroPython programming language. This makes it a good choice for projects using Python to control the sensors and send data to Firestore. The sensor data are transferred to a cloud-based Google Firestore Database, which has real-time capabilities.

**Cloud-Based Centralized Management System.** The SSLS database uses the following data points in Third Normal Form (3NF):

- Entities: Streetlights, Controllers, Sensors
- Relationships: A streetlight is connected to a controller, A controller is connected to one or more sensors
- Attributes:

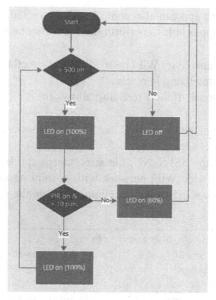

**Fig. 2.** Streetlamp algorithm (ambient light component)

- Streetlights: Streetlight ID (primary key), Location, Wattage, Installation date, Status (on/off/malfunctioning)
- Controllers: Controller ID (primary key), Location, Installation date, Status (on/off)
- Sensors: Sensor ID (primary key), Type, Location, Installation date, Status (on/off)
- Tables:
- Streetlights: Streetlight ID (primary key), Controller ID (foreign key), Location, Wattage, Installation date, Status
- Controllers: Controller ID (primary key), Location, Installation date, Status
- Sensors: Sensor ID (primary key), Controller ID (foreign key), Type, Location, Installation date, Status

To send data from your streetlamp sensors to the cloud database we used the following components and steps:

1. Streetlamp sensors to collect data such as light intensity and motion detection.
2. Microcontroller/IoT Devices that can interface with the streetlamp sensors and transmit the collected data to the cloud. These devices use the WiFi options to communicate with the cloud database.
3. Google Firestore Cloud Database to store the streetlamp sensor data.
4. API: Utilize the API provided by the cloud database service to establish a connection between your microcontroller/IoT device and the cloud database. This enables SSLS to send the collected sensor data securely to the cloud and to format and authenticate the data.
5. Data processing and storage: Once the data is received by the cloud database, SSLS processes, stores, and manages it. This involves structuring the data, creating collections and the tables.

**The App.** A smartphone app can also control SSLS streetlamps locally via the WiFi component WiPy. The app is able to perform the following tasks:

- Connect to the same university WiFi network as the streetlamp IoT device.
- Switch on and off a streetlamp in reach.
- Dim a streetlamp in reach, if the streetlamp allows for it.

The app has been developed with the React Native framework, which uses JavaScript to create Android and iOS apps.

After installing the app SSLS_NU, the streetlamps can be controlled directly by accessing the university-wide WiFi network with a valid password (See Fig. 3). The app can be used to monitor individual streetlamps within the range of the smartphone

```javascript
import React, { useState } from "react";
import AsyncStorage from "@react-native-commu-
nity/async-storage";
const App = () => {
    const [isConnected, setIsConnected] = us-
eState(false);
    const connectToWifi = async () => {
        const network = await AsyncStorage.getItem("net-
work");
        const password = await AsyncStorage.getItem("pass-
word");
        try {
            const wifiManager = RNWifiManager.sharedManager;
            await wifiManager.connect(network, password);
            setIsConnected(true);
        } catch (error) {
            console.log(error);
        }
    };
    return (
        <div>
            {isConnected ? (
                <h1>Connected to @NU-WiFi</h1>
            ) : (
                <button onClick={connectToWifi}>Connect to
@NU-WiFi</button>
            )}
        </div>
    );
};
export default App;
```

**Fig. 3.** Connecting the streetlamps to SSLS_NU WiFi network

(See Fig. 4). The app has been designed mainly in Thai language. The app shows the streetlamp IDs in the order of their signal strength, location, and status (On, Off, or Dim). Depending on their status, the lamps can be switched off or on and dimmed. The app only works when the WiFi connection of the phone is the same as that of the lamp, so external visitors who do not have access to the university's WiFi network cannot use the app (see the code snippet).

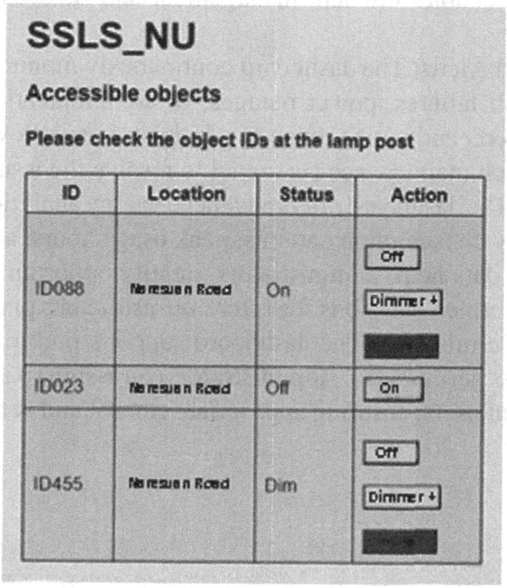

## SSLS_NU

**Accessible objects**

Please check the object IDs at the lamp post

| ID | Location | Status | Action |
|---|---|---|---|
| ID088 | Naresuan Road | On | Off<br>Dimmer + |
| ID023 | Naresuan Road | Off | On |
| ID455 | Naresuan Road | Dim | Off<br>Dimmer + |

**Fig. 4.** Connecting the streetlamps to SSLS_NU WiFi network

# 3   Results and Discussion

## 3.1   Data Visualization, or the Dashboard

The facility administrators use the SSLS dashboard in their everyday tasks monitoring and controlling the streetlighting network of the university. The dashboard for monitoring and controlling SSLS is a comprehensive tool that enables administrators to efficiently manage and optimize the entire lighting infrastructure. Designed with a user-friendly interface, the dashboard provides real-time insights, remote control capabilities, and advanced analytics for enhanced performance and energy efficiency. The dashboard comprises the following elements (See Fig. 5):

1. System Overview: The dashboard provides an at-a-glance overview of the entire smart street lighting system, including the number of connected lights, their operational status, and energy consumption metrics. Administrators can quickly identify any issues or anomalies and take appropriate action.

2. Real-time Monitoring: The dashboard displays real-time data on individual street-lights, such as their current status, brightness levels, and power consumption. It allows administrators to easily identify malfunctioning lights or areas with insufficient illumination and promptly address them.

3. Remote Control: Administrators can remotely control the streetlights through the dashboard. This includes turning lights on or off, adjusting brightness levels, and scheduling lighting profiles based on specific time periods or predefined conditions. This feature enables efficient management and reduces unnecessary energy consumption.

4. Fault Detection and Alerts: The dashboard continuously monitors the streetlights for faults, such as bulb failures, power outages, or communication issues (Fig. 5). It provides instant alerts and notifications to administrators, allowing them to quickly respond and dispatch maintenance personnel to resolve the issues promptly.

5. Energy Analytics: The dashboard offers advanced energy analytics, providing detailed insights into energy consumption patterns, peak usage hours, and potential areas for optimization. This data helps administrators identify opportunities to reduce energy costs and make informed decisions for future infrastructure planning.

6. User Access and Permissions: The dashboard supports multiple user accounts with customizable access permissions. Administrators can assign specific roles and responsibilities to different users, ensuring appropriate control and security measures are in place.

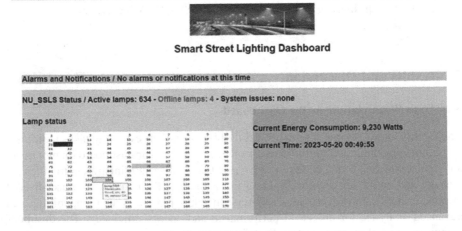

**Fig. 5.** The SSLS dashboard

The dashboard for SSLS provides administrators with a powerful tool to effectively monitor, control, and optimize the lighting infrastructure. With real-time insights, remote control capabilities, and advanced analytics, administrators can enhance energy efficiency, reduce maintenance costs, and improve overall facility operations.

The heat map of the streetlamp network on campus (See Fig. 6) uses the following color codes for backgrounds: white (normal function), grey as for lamp104 (unusual wattage), orange as for lamp76 and lamp77 (lamp malfunction), and black as for lamp22 (sensor malfunction). Administrators can click on suspicious elements (as shown for lamp104) and get additional information relating to the element: location of the lamp, on/off status, wattage of the bulb used (40 W), and sensor function.

**The Data.** Power consumption has decreased significantly with the use of the smart street lighting system so far (January to May 2023), as is shown in Table 2. The power consumption has been based on the same number and specifications of lamps for time controlled (_time) and sensor controlled (_smart) equipment. Each set of lamps consisted of 15 metal halide lamps (250 W) and LED warm white lamps (40 W).

The time-controlled lamps were turned on between 7 pm (January) and 6 pm (May), and they were turned off between 6 am (January) and 6.20 am (May). This caused a slight decrease of the power consumption of the time-controlled streetlights. The power consumption was significantly lower for the smart streetlights, which used ambient light and motion sensors to control the on/off periods. During an average night, around 40 to 60 movements of cars and/or pedestrians were monitored. Consequently, the cost of smart street lighting was reduced by about 55% during the period of observation (January to May 2023).

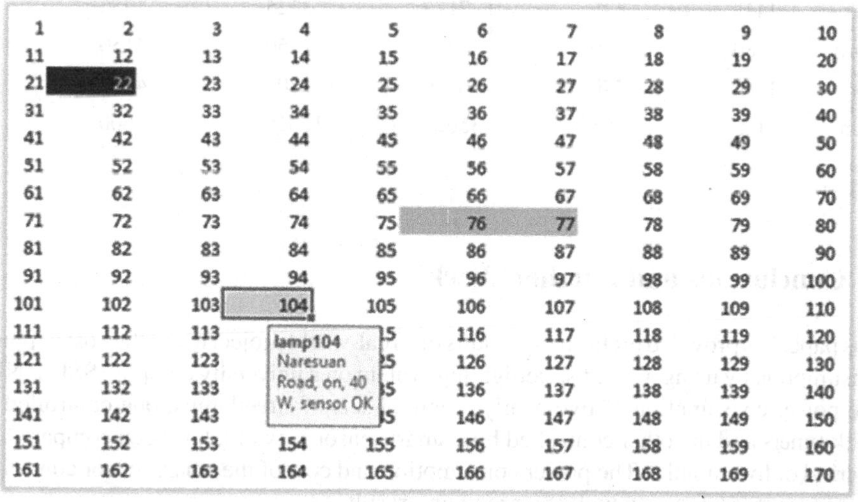

| 1 | 2 | 3 | 4 | 5 | 6 | 7 | 8 | 9 | 10 |
|---|---|---|---|---|---|---|---|---|---|
| 11 | 12 | 13 | 14 | 15 | 16 | 17 | 18 | 19 | 20 |
| 21 | 22 | 23 | 24 | 25 | 26 | 27 | 28 | 29 | 30 |
| 31 | 32 | 33 | 34 | 35 | 36 | 37 | 38 | 39 | 40 |
| 41 | 42 | 43 | 44 | 45 | 46 | 47 | 48 | 49 | 50 |
| 51 | 52 | 53 | 54 | 55 | 56 | 57 | 58 | 59 | 60 |
| 61 | 62 | 63 | 64 | 65 | 66 | 67 | 68 | 69 | 70 |
| 71 | 72 | 73 | 74 | 75 | 76 | 77 | 78 | 79 | 80 |
| 81 | 82 | 83 | 84 | 85 | 86 | 87 | 88 | 89 | 90 |
| 91 | 92 | 93 | 94 | 95 | 96 | 97 | 98 | 99 | 100 |
| 101 | 102 | 103 | 104 | 105 | 106 | 107 | 108 | 109 | 110 |
| 111 | 112 | 113 | lamp104 | 115 | 116 | 117 | 118 | 119 | 120 |
| 121 | 122 | 123 | Naresuan | 125 | 126 | 127 | 128 | 129 | 130 |
| 131 | 132 | 133 | Road, on, 40 | 135 | 136 | 137 | 138 | 139 | 140 |
| 141 | 142 | 143 | W, sensor OK | 145 | 146 | 147 | 148 | 149 | 150 |
| 151 | 152 | 153 | 154 | 155 | 156 | 157 | 158 | 159 | 160 |
| 161 | 162 | 163 | 164 | 165 | 166 | 167 | 168 | 169 | 170 |

**Fig. 6.** SSLS Heat map (Color figure online)

To test the app, 23 members of the university community (faculty and students) installed the SSLS_NU app and used it on a more or less regular basis. They used the app during roughly 60 days (about 2 months). They switched on and off streetlamps if necessary and also tried out the dimming capabilities. Then, we asked for their attitude towards usage of the app and applied a 5-point Likert scale. The results are shown in Table 1.

**Table 1.** Attitude towards the streetlamp management app SSLS_NU

|  | 1 | 2 | 3 | 4 | 5 |
|---|---|---|---|---|---|
| How easy to use is the app? |  |  | 3 | 9 | 11 |
| How helpful is the app to control streetlamps? |  |  | 4 | 10 | 9 |
| How likely is it that you will use the app in the future? |  | 2 | 2 | 8 | 9 |

The results show that the app is obviously easy to use and helpful. Nevertheless, potential users are somewhat hesitant to use the app in the future. This may be because the prototype app has not yet been designed in a visually appealing form. A second reason for the reluctance to use the app in the future may also be that the benefits are not really clear to users, since its usage makes only sense during nighttimes.

**Table 2.** Power consumption and cost of time controlled versus smart streetlights

|  | kW_time | kW_smart | Aaht_time | Baht_smart | Cost reduction |
|---|---|---|---|---|---|
| Jan. | 1500 | 740 | 7500 | 3700 | 3800 |
| Feb. | 1470 | 730 | 7350 | 3650 | 3700 |
| Mar. | 1435 | 645 | 7175 | 3225 | 3950 |
| April | 1380 | 550 | 6900 | 2750 | 4150 |
| May | 1340 | 540 | 6700 | 2700 | 4000 |
| Sum | 7125 | 3205 | 35625 | 16025 | 19600 |

## 4 Conclusions and Further Work

This paper has provided preliminary results of a real-world project to cut the cost of power consumption by using a smart streetlighting system on a university campus (SSLS_NU). The power consumption of two nearly identical sets of streetlamps, one controlled by clock timers and the other controlled by a smart sensor network, has been compared for a period of five months. The power consumption and cost of the smart sensor controlled lamps were 55% lower, which is a promising result.

The smartphone SSLS_NU, which was used by a group of 23 participants to control streetlamps locally, has been analyzed for its usefulness and the attitude toward future use by the participants. The app was found useful.

Regarding future work, it is desirable to connect the heat map of the streetlamps with a campus map to highlight and locate malfunctioning items more easily. Moreover, smart algorithms can analyze data from sensors and other sources to predict when maintenance will be required for street lighting systems. This can help reduce downtime and improve the overall performance and lifespan of components of the streetlighting system.

Another interesting application of the SSLS_NU is the inclusion of such further sensor applications as weather data and air condition (pollution status).

# References

1. Arjun, P., Stephenraj, S., Kumar, N.N., Kumar, K.N.: A study on IoT based smart street light systems. In 2019 IEEE International Conference on System, Computation, Automation and Networking (ICSCAN), pp. 1–7. IEEE (2019). https://doi.org/10.1109/ICSCAN.2019.8878770

2. Bhosale, S., Gaware, K., Phalke, P., Wadekar, D., Ahire, P.: IoT based dynamic control of street lights for smart city. Int. Res. J. Eng. Technol. (IRJET) 4(5), 1181–1183 (2017)

3. Dheena, P.P.F., Raj, G.S., Dutt, G., Jinny, S.V.: IOT based smart street light management system. In: 2017 IEEE International Conference on Circuits and Systems (ICCS), pp. 368–371. IEEE (2017). https://doi.org/10.1109/ICCS1.2017.8326023

4. Lewandowski, W., Wojewoda, A., Wojewoda, I.: Adaptive lighting systems and the method of implementing dynamically adjustable on-demand strategies – conclusions from research. Tech. Trans. 119, e2022014 (2022). https://doi.org/10.37705/TechTrans/e2022014

5. Mahoor, M., Hosseini, Z.S., Khodaei, A., Paaso, A., Kushner, D.: State-of-the-art in smart streetlight systems: a review. IET Smart Cities 2(1), 24–33 (2000)

6. Manyake, M.K., Mathaba, T.N.: An Internet of Things framework for control and monitoring of smart public lighting systems: a review. In: 2022 International Conference on Artificial Intelligence, Big Data, Computing and Data Communication Systems (icABCD), pp. 1–9. IEEE (2022)

7. Omar, A., et al.: Smart city: recent advances in intelligent street lighting systems based on IoT. J. Sens. 2022, 1–10 (2022)

8. Umar, M., Gill, S.H., Shaikh, R.A., Rizwan, M.: Cloud-based energy efficient smart street lighting system. Indian J. Sci. Technol. 13(23), 2311–2318 (2020). https://doi.org/10.17485/IJST/v13i23.636

9. W3C Homepage. https://www.w3.org/TR/ambient-light/#ambient-light-threshold-check algorithm. Accessed 5 May 2023

# The New Paradigm of Work from Home: An Exploratory Study in Thailand

Eugenia Arazo Boa(✉) ⓘ and Michael Brückner ⓘ

Naresuan University International College, Phitsanulok 65000, Thailand
{eugeniab,michaelb}@nu.ac.th

**Abstract.** The primary aim of this study is to investigate the challenges faced by employees in Thailand while working from home. It is a purely quantitative research endeavor, providing initial findings from a comprehensive study on work-from-home arrangements in the country. The study's sample size included 818 participants, with an equal representation of participants from each of the four regions: Northeastern, Northern, Central, and Southern. Single-cluster sampling was utilized as the sampling technique. The study's results revealed the most significant challenges experienced by Thai employees while working from home. These challenges include a lack of interaction with co-workers (56.5%), internet connection problems (51.3%), noise disturbances at home (49.5%), coping with hot weather (45.2%), and facing distractions leading to missed deadlines (40.1%). The work-from-home setup, shedding light on crucial factors affecting productivity and well-being during this mode of work.

**Keywords:** work from home · Thailand · work-home conflict · cooperative application

## 1 Introduction

The global workforce has changed drastically to work-from-home environments due to the pandemic. Consequently, addressing work–home issues are increasingly recognized as one of the main concerns of human resource development (HRD) more importantly during the pandemic. When Covid-19 started to spread in 2019 and relentlessly created havoc around the world, work from home (WFH) is the last resort for all organizations both public and private, including the self-employed. The World Health Organization (WHO) declared the outbreak of COVID-19 as a global health emergency in January 2020 [1]. Thailand is not an exception. In an effort of the Thai Government to control the disease several measures have been implemented, such as controlling international travel to high-risk countries, quarantine at home, working from home, social distancing, and prohibiting social gatherings [2].

The practice of WFH is not an unfamiliar concept to many employees. There have been previous studies on the subject. Studies posit that high home boundary permeability may be a double-edged sword as it was significantly associated with both greater work-to-home conflict and positive spillover [3–5]. Home boundary permeability refers to

© The Author(s), under exclusive license to Springer Nature Switzerland AG 2023
Y. Luo (Ed.): CDVE 2023, LNCS 14166, pp. 256–268, 2023.
https://doi.org/10.1007/978-3-031-43815-8_26

the extent to which one's home domain is interrupted by work-related matters [4–6]. Furthermore, Eddleston and Mulki [7] revealed that WFH results in the inability of workers to disengage from work. Additionally, it was identified in several studies the benefits of work from home including increased motivation of employees, increased gender diversity, reduced traveling time, no office politics, less absenteeism and turnover, and better productivity [8, 9]. Conversely, the drawbacks of WFH include paying higher electricity and interest cost [10] and the isolation of employees could result in lesser productivity according to Collins and Moschler [11].

It was reported in Thai Enquirer [12] that the myth that Thais cannot work remotely because they will not be motivated enough, and some might not know what they are doing is a fallacy. The WFH trend is going strong in Thailand in spite of the reopening of businesses, some companies turned WFH policies into the new normal. Furthermore, McKinsey Global Institute, reported that some companies are using a hybrid work model in which staff have the option of working from home or coming to the office for meetings or workshops. Hybrid models of work are likely to persist in the wake of the pandemic [13] which is true up to this day. According to the report, most Thai employees prefer working from home for at least two days a week. It was also reported that WFH has its own challenges as working from home can be very stressful, not to mention also other issues such as quality of work, productivity, motivation of employees, policies on vacations, cybersecurity, and employees' lack of cybersecurity awareness. However, it was found that more than half the workforce has little or no opportunity for remote work [8–14]. Some of their jobs require collaborating with others or using specialized machinery [13]. Indeed, remote work raises a vast array of issues and challenges for employees and employers. It shows that the potential for remote work varies across countries, a reflection of their sector, occupation, and activity mix. In an article by Lund, Madgavkar, Manyika, and Sven Smit [13], they stated that remote work potential is higher in advanced economies.

Some international organizations like the International Labor Organization [15] took center stage and came up with a guideline called, "An employers' guide on working from home in response to the outbreak of COVID-19." Its purpose is to provide practical guidance to member companies that have implemented "working from home" protocols for their staff in 2020 as an alternative temporary arrangement during the COVID-19 crisis.

Currently, there are few studies about WFH in Thailand. There is a current study in Thailand where the acceptance of online technology focuses mainly on Thai Generation Z during the outbreak of COVID-19 disease [16]. The researcher mainly focused on the Generation Z population as they are highly interested in technology. This study found that the employee's behavioral intention to use online technology during the pandemic is predicted by three key factors including performance expectancy, effort expectancy, and trust. Given the currency of WFH in Thailand as well as having no option left, but WFH, more study on the topic is needed. This study will fill in the gap in the literature and the management level and policymakers can use the findings in the planning of organizational strategies in the wake of the pandemic. Furthermore, given the prevalence of working from home, its impact on employee well-being, and vast challenges among employers and employees in Thailand, more research is needed to provide evidence-based advice for HRD professionals seeking to assist employees in achieving a healthy balance between work and home, explore and identify the challenges brought about by the new normal, hence, this study. This study is based on the home boundary permeability theory derived from the work of Kim & Holensbe [3] and the Work-Home Conflict theory by Greenhaus and Beutell [17] where work-home conflict is defined as a type of inter-role conflict in which the role demands stemming from one life domain are incompatible with role demands stemming from the other domain cited in the study of Delanoeije & Verbruggen [4].

This is descriptive research aimed at uncovering the challenges faced by individuals working from home (WFH). The primary focus is on identifying the potential relationship between the age and gender of the participants and the challenges they encounter while working remotely. The study specifically targets employees who have prior experience with or are currently engaged in remote work. It is essential to note that the results presented here are preliminary and part of an ongoing, broader investigation.

## 2  Literature Review

WFH is not new and has been brought to the attention of several schools of thought for many years. Cited in the study of Vyas and Butakhieo [18]. The WFH concept was initially mentioned by Nilles in 1988 dating back to 1973, known as "telecommuting" or "telework" [19]. Over the course of four decades, the concept of "working from home" (WFH) has been described and referred to using different terms, including remote work, flexible workplace, telework, telecommuting, and e-working. These terms encompass the capacity of employees to carry out their work duties in adaptable environments, with a particular emphasis on working from home, facilitated by the use of technology [20]. Telecommuting was defined as a flexible work setup where employees conduct tasks outside their primary or central workplaces, utilizing electronic communication to interact with colleagues both within and outside the organization. The researchers emphasized that the term "elsewhere" in this context specifically refers to the employees' homes [21]. These days, the most common work arrangement is the so-called hybrid work or hybrid model. Hybrid work, often referred to as a hybrid remote work model, entails a flexible work arrangement that integrates both remote work and on-site work [22]. Within this setup, employees are granted the freedom to work from their homes or other locations away from the central office for part of their work schedule, while also being required to attend the physical office for the remaining days. Typically, work-home practices consist of flexible work setups, such as home-based telework, and work-time adjustments, such as part-time employment according to Delanoeije & Verbruggen [4].

Based on the survey conducted by Global Workplace Analytics and Owl Labs in 2022 [23], it was observed that the work-at-home rate has increased to a certain percentage since 2009, with 18 percent of respondents reporting full-time remote work. Furthermore, in 2021, the Office of the National Economic and Social Development Council of Thailand (NESDC) [24] reported that 52% of companies permitted their employees to work from home for at least one day each week. Additionally, approximately 16% of these companies employed an entirely remote workforce.

According to the definition provided by Greenhaus and Beutell in 1985 [17], work-home conflict is characterized as a form of inter-role conflict, wherein the demands arising from one aspect of life (either work or home) clash with the demands arising from the other aspect.

Delanoeije and Verbruggen [4] conducted a study exploring how family life and work domains influence each other, leading to boundary violations. The researchers found that these boundary violations contributed to perceptions of work-family conflict both directly and indirectly, as they triggered cognitive appraisals of thwarted goals. In the work domain, boundary violations also elicited negative affective reactions. On the other hand, boundary violations were related to satisfaction through goal appraisal.

Moreover, it is worth mentioning that the significant wage differences observed in work-from-home arrangements have diminished according to White's study in 2019 [24]. Furthermore, the changes in variance imply that the reduced cost of monitoring employee effort has made it more feasible for companies to implement work-from-home policies. These findings align with agency theory, which proposes that changes in wages and wage structure for individuals working from home are influenced by considerations of agency costs and monitoring efficiency.

In the Australian study, it was discovered that the work-from-home arrangement yields positive effects. The research provided evidence indicating that remote work positively influences relationships and leads to a more balanced distribution of household responsibilities among couples with children [26].

This study utilized the work-home conflict theory to identify and examine the challenges associated with the work-from-home (WFH) arrangement.

# 3 Methodology

## 3.1 Population and Sampling

At the time of the study, the specific number of people working from home in Thailand was not determined.

For this study, a probability sampling technique known as single-cluster sampling was employed. The researchers divided the population of Thailand into multiple clusters based on the four-region system: northeastern, northern, central, and southern regions. The sample size for the study consisted of 818 participants, with an equal representation of 200 participants from each of the four regions. The focus of this research was on the administrative and statistical contexts of Thailand's four-region system as outlined in Wongboonsin, Keeratipongpaiboon, & Kua Wongboonsin's work from [27]. The sampling approach used was single-cluster sampling for selecting the sample.

Thailand is divided into four regions, each comprising different provinces. These regions are: Northeastern with 20 provinces, Northern with 17 provinces, Central Thailand with the highest number of provinces at 28, and Southern Thailand with 14 provinces [27, 28]. The researchers conducting this study are based in the Northern region of Thailand.

## 3.2 Research Tools

The questionnaire was formulated based on Greenhaus and Beutell's (1985) Work-Home Conflict theory, with a particular focus on the various challenges faced by employees while working from home. Following the questionnaire's development, three experts, each specialized in human resource management, business management, and statistics, were engaged to assess the questionnaire's face validity.

### 3.3 Data Analysis

The data analysis for this study was conducted using SPSS 18.0 software. Descriptive statistics, as well as tests to assess the reliability and validity of the sample, were performed. The gathered data was used to calculate frequencies and percentages to gain valuable insights.

## 4 Results and Discussion

### 4.1 Description of the Sample

As observed in Table 1, a significant proportion of participants fall within the 20–25 years age group, while the smallest number of participants belong to the 50–59 years age group. This can be attributed to the fact that the latter age group is approaching the early retirement age, which is 55 years old in Thailand. Hence, it is expected to have a lower number of participants in this age range.

Regarding the gender distribution of respondents, more than 50% are female. This could be attributed to the specific industries where the questionnaire was distributed, where there might be a higher representation of female employees.

**Table 1.** Participant's demographics ($n = 818$)

| Variables | Frequency | Percentage |
|---|---|---|
| 1) Age (years) | | |
| 20–25 | 321 | 39.2 |
| 26–30 | 185 | 22.6 |
| 31–35 | 108 | 13.2 |
| 36–40 | 66 | 8.1 |
| 41–45 | 60 | 7.3 |
| 46–50 | 41 | 5.0 |
| 51–55 | 25 | 3.1 |
| 56–59 | 12 | 1.5 |
| 2) Gender | | |
| Male | 270 | 33.0 |
| Female | 548 | 67.0 |

## 4.2 Challenges of Work from Home

In Table 2, the frequency and percentage of challenges faced by employees while working from home are presented. The most prevalent challenge reported by participants was the lack of interaction with co-workers, which accounted for 56.5% of respondents, surpassing more than 50% of the total participants. Interestingly, this finding aligns with a study conducted by Nandan and Madan [29] in India in 2022.

**Table 2.** Challenges of Work from Home ($n = 818$)

| Variables | Frequency | Percentage |
|---|---|---|
| **What is/are the biggest challenge/s you face when working from home?** | | |
| 1) Barking dog | 285 | 34.8 |
| 2) Toilet flush | 112 | 13.7 |
| 3) Child crying or screaming | 250 | 30.6 |
| 4) Distractions leading to missed deadlines | 328 | 40.1 |
| 5) TV noise | 205 | 25.1 |
| 6) Noise in the background | 405 | 49.5 |
| 7) The weather is too hot | 370 | 45.2 |
| 8) Internet stability | 420 | 51.3 |
| 9) Lack of interaction with co-workers | 462 | 56.5 |
| 10) Lack of socialization in the workplace | 287 | 35.1 |

Lack of interaction among employees while remotely working leads to communication barriers. Nevertheless, information technologies have successfully filled this void, enabling effective interaction, collaboration, and productivity in remote work environments. Numerous cooperative applications now exist, including virtual social events, virtual whiteboards and collaborations, online document collaboration, and virtual team-building activities, among others. These tools bridge the gap caused by physical distance, promoting better communication and efficient collaboration among remote employees.

Following closely, the second most common challenge was internet connection problems at home, reported by 51.3% of participants. Additionally, background noise during remote work was a significant issue for 49.5% of respondents. Working from home in Thailand also presented the challenge of coping with hot weather, affecting 45.2% of Thai employees. Notably, this problem led to an unexpected increase in expenses for those working from home.

Lastly, distractions at home emerged as a noteworthy concern, impacting 40.1% of participants. As with noise, distractions were considered unavoidable during remote work arrangements.

The findings from Table 2 highlight the prominent challenges faced by employees in the work-from-home setup, shedding light on crucial factors affecting productivity and well-being during this mode of work.

## 4.3  Relationship of Challenges of Work from Home to Age and Gender of Respondents

Table 3 illustrates the link between the identified challenges of working from home and the age and gender of the participants. The age group of participants was divided into five categories.

**Table 3.** Relationship of Challenges of Work from Home to Age and Gender of Respondents ($n = 818$)

| Demographics | 1. Barking dogs | | Chi-square | p-value |
|---|---|---|---|---|
| | Yes | No | | |
| Age (years) | | | 14.16 | 0.007 |
| 20–25 | 118 (14.4) | 203 (24.8) | | |
| 26–30 | 77 (9.4) | 108 (13.2) | | |
| 31–35 | 40 (4.9) | 68 (8.3) | | |
| 36–45 | 30 (3.7) | 96 (11.7) | | |
| 46–59 | 20 (2.4) | 58 (7.1) | | |
| Gender | | | 0.72 | 0.397 |
| Male | 100 (12.2) | 170 (20.8) | | |
| Female | 185 (22.6) | 363 (44.4) | | |
| Demographics | 2. Toilet flush | | Chi-square | p-value |
| | Yes | No | | |
| Age (years) | | | 35.59 | <0.001 |
| 20–25 | 39 (4.8) | 282 (34.5) | | |
| 26–30 | 47 (5.7) | 138 (16.9) | | |
| 31–35 | 16 (2.0) | 92 (11.2) | | |
| 36–45 | 6 (0.7) | 120 (14.7) | | |
| 46–59 | 4 (0.5) | 74 (9.0) | | |
| Gender | | | 9.88 | 0.002 |
| Male | 52 (6.4) | 218 (26.7) | | |
| Female | 60 (7.3) | 488 (59.7) | | |
| Demographics | 3. A child crying or screaming | | Chi-square | p-value |
| | Yes | No | | |
| Age (years) | | | 10.91 | 0.028 |
| 20–25 | 103 (12.6) | 218 (26.7) | | |
| 26–30 | 62 (7.6) | 123 (15.0) | | |

(*continued*)

**Table 3.** (*continued*)

| Demographics | 3. A child crying or screaming | | Chi-square | p-value |
|---|---|---|---|---|
| | Yes | No | | |
| 31–35 | 39 (4.8) | 69 (8.4) | | |
| 36–45 | 33 (4.0) | 93 (11.4) | | |
| 46–59 | 13 (1.6) | 65 (7.9) | | |
| Gender | | | 1.27 | 0.260 |
| Male | 90 (11.0) | 180 (22.0) | | |
| Female | 160 (19.6) | 388 (47.4) | | |
| Demographics | 4. Distractions leading to missed deadlines | | Chi-square | p-value |
| | Yes | No | | |
| Age (years) | | | 30.41 | <0.001 |
| 20–25 | 153 (18.7) | 168 (20.5) | | |
| 26–30 | 66 (8.1) | 119 (14.5) | | |
| 31–35 | 54 (6.6) | 54 (6.6) | | |
| 36–45 | 39 (4.8) | 87 (10.6) | | |
| 46–59 | 16 (2.0) | 62 (7.6) | | |
| Gender | | | 0.24 | 0.623 |
| Male | 112 (13.7) | 158 (19.3) | | |
| Female | 216 (26.4) | 332 (40.8) | | |
| Demographics | 5. TV Noise | | Chi-square | p-value |
| | Yes | No | | |
| Age (years) | | | 16.31 | 0.003 |
| 20–25 | 69 (8.4) | 252 (30.8) | | |
| 26–30 | 63 (7.7) | 122 (14.9) | | |
| 31–35 | 33 (4.0) | 75 (9.2) | | |
| 36–45 | 28 (3.4) | 98 (12.0) | | |
| 46–59 | 12 (1.5) | 66 (8.1) | | |
| Gender | | | 4.12 | 0.042 |
| Male | 80 (9.8) | 190 (23.2) | | |
| Female | 125 (15.3) | 423 (51.7) | | |

(*continued*)

**Table 3.** (*continued*)

| Demographics | 6. Noise in the background | | Chi-square | *p*-value |
|---|---|---|---|---|
| | Yes | No | | |
| Age (years) | | | 6.28 | 0.179 |
| 20–25 | 174 (21.3) | 147 (18.0) | | |
| 26–30 | 87 (10.6) | 98 (12.0) | | |
| 31–35 | 55 (6.7) | 53 (6.5) | | |
| 36–45 | 54 (6.6) | 72 (8.8) | | |
| 46–59 | 35 (4.3) | 43 (5.3) | | |
| Gender | | | 2.76 | 0.096 |
| Male | 122 (14.9) | 148 (18.1) | | |
| Female | 283 (34.6) | 265 (32.4) | | |
| Demographics | 7. Hot weather | | Chi-square | *p*-value |
| | Yes | No | | |
| Age (years) | | | 0.75 | 0.945 |
| 20–25 | 141 (17.2) | 180 (22.0) | | |
| 26–30 | 86 (10.5) | 99 (12.1) | | |
| 31–35 | 49 (6.0) | 59 (7.2) | | |
| 36–45 | 56 (6.8) | 70 (8.8) | | |
| 46–59 | 38 (4.6) | 40 (4.9) | | |
| Gender | | | 0.003 | 0.956 |
| Male | 123 (15.0) | 147 (18.0) | | |
| Female | 247 (30.2) | 301 (36.8) | | |
| Demographics | 8. Internet connection problem | | Chi-square | *p*-value |
| | Yes | No | | |
| Age (years) | | | 8.71 | 0.069 |
| 20–25 | 164 (20.0) | 157 (19.2) | | |
| 26–30 | 93 (11.4) | 92 (11.2) | | |
| 31–35 | 52 (6.4) | 56 (6.8) | | |
| 36–45 | 78 (9.5) | 48 (5.9) | | |
| 46–59 | 33 (4.0) | 45 (5.5) | | |
| Gender | | | 1.85 | 0.174 |

(*continued*)

**Table 3.** (*continued*)

| Demographics | 8. Internet connection problem | | Chi-square | p-value |
|---|---|---|---|---|
| | Yes | No | | |
| Male | 129 (15.8) | 141 (17.2) | | |
| Female | 291 (35.6) | 257 (31.4) | | |

| Demographics | 9. Lack of interaction with co-workers | | Chi-square | p-value |
|---|---|---|---|---|
| | Yes | No | | |
| Age (years) | | | 0.65 | 0.957 |
| 20–25 | 182 (22.2) | 139 (17.0) | | |
| 26–30 | 105 (12.8) | 80 (9.8) | | |
| 31–35 | 63 (7.7) | 45 (5.5) | | |
| 36–45 | 71 (8.7) | 55 (6.7) | | |
| 46–59 | 41 (5.0) | 37 (4.5) | | |
| Gender | | | 0.09 | 0.764 |
| Male | 155 (18.9) | 115 (14.1) | | |
| Female | 307 (37.5) | 241 (29.5) | | |

| Demographics | 10. Lack of socialization in the workplace | | Chi-square | p-value |
|---|---|---|---|---|
| | Yes | No | | |
| Age (years) | | | 9.70 | 0.046 |
| 20–25 | 123 (15.0) | 198 (24.2) | | |
| 26–30 | 68 (8.3) | 117 (14.3) | | |
| 31–35 | 34 (4.2) | 74 (9.0) | | |
| 36–45 | 46 (5.6) | 80 (9.8) | | |
| 46–59 | 16 (2.0) | 62 (7.6) | | |
| Gender | | | 1.87 | 0.172 |
| Male | 104 (12.7) | 166 (20.3) | | |
| Female | 183 (22.4) | 365 (44.6) | | |

The age of participants shows a significant relationship with several challenges, namely barking dogs ($p = 0.007$), toilet flush ($p < 0.001$), a child crying or screaming ($p = 0.028$), distractions leading to missed deadlines ($p < 0.001$), TV noise ($p = 0.003$), and lack of socialization in the workplace ($p = 0.046$). This indicates a statistically significant association between these challenges and the age of participants.

Regarding the gender of participants, challenges significantly related include toilet flush ($p = 0.002$) and TV noise ($p = 0.042$).

On the other hand, challenges of working from home that show no statistically significant relationship to participants include noise in the background, weather, internet connection problem, and lack of interaction among co-workers. These challenges do not display a meaningful statistical association with the age or gender of the participants.

## 5   Conclusion

In Thailand, the work-from-home arrangement was not commonly embraced until the pandemic forced employees to adapt to this new way of working. As a result, various challenges emerged within this arrangement, with the lack of interaction with co-workers being identified as the most prominent challenge faced by employees. Information technology significantly enhanced interaction and communication while working remotely.

Despite the challenges posed by remote work, it also presented unique opportunities for both employees and organizations. The shift to remote work opened doors to explore new possibilities and ways of conducting business and working efficiently in a remote setting.

## 6   Limitations of the Study

The study may not have considered all potential confounding variables, which could have influenced the observed relationships between the variables under investigation.

Additionally, the study's generalizability could be limited due to its relatively small sample size. Although the study includes representation from the four regions in Thailand, there are certain provinces with very few participants, potentially affecting the representativeness of the findings.

To gain deeper insights into the challenges of the work-from-home arrangement in Thailand, conducting interviews with participants could be a valuable approach. Interviews could provide a more comprehensive understanding of individual experiences and perspectives, complementing the quantitative data obtained in the study.

**Acknowledgment.** It is gratefully acknowledged the financial support provided by Naresuan University International College, Phitsanulok 65000 Thailand for this research project. The funding has been instrumental in the successful execution of this study.

## References

1. World Health Organization: Coronavirus Disease (COVID-19) Situation Report – 202 (2020). https://www.who.int/docs/default-source/coronaviruse/situationreports/2,02,00,809-covid-19-sitrep-202.pdf?sfvrsn=2c7459f6_2
2. Centers for Disease Control and Prevention: Interim guidance on management of coronavirus disease 2019 (COVI-19) in correctional and detention facilities (2020). https://www.cdc.gov/coronavirus/2019-ncov/downloads/guidance-correctional-detention.pdf

3. Kim, S., Hollensbe, E.: When work comes home: technology-related pressure and home support. Hum. Resour. Dev. Int. **21**(2), 91–106 (2018). https://doi.org/10.1080/13678868. 2017.1366177

4. Delanoeije, J., Verbruggen, M.: The use of work-home practices and work-home conflict: examining the role of volition and perceived pressure in a multi-method study. Front. Psychol. **10**, 2362 (2019). https://doi.org/10.3389/fpsyg.2019.02362

5. Hunter, E.M., Clark, M.A., Carlson, D.S.: Violating work-family boundaries: reactions to interruptions at work and home. J. Manag. **45**(3), 1284–1308 (2019). https://doi.org/10.1177/ 0149206317702221

6. Ashforth, B.E., Kreiner, G.E., Fugate, M.: All in a day's work: boundaries and micro role transitions. Acad. Manag. Rev. **25**(3), 472–491 (2000)

7. Eddleston, K.A., Mulki, J.: Toward understanding remote workers' management of work–family boundaries: the complexity of workplace embeddedness. Group Org. Manag. **42**(3), 346–387 (2017). https://doi.org/10.1177/1059601115619548

8. Mello, J.A.: Managing Telework Programs Effectively. Empl. Responsib. Rights J. **19**(4), 247–261 (2007). https://doi.org/10.1007/s10672-007-9051-1

9. Robertson, M.M., Maynard, W.S., McDevitt, J.R.: Telecommuting: managing the safety of workers in home office environments. Prof. Saf. **48**(4), 30–36 (2003)

10. Sutarto, A.P., Wardaningsih, S., Putri, W.H.: Work from home: Indonesian employees' mental well-being and productivity during the COVID-19 pandemic. Int. J. Workplace Health Manag. **14**(4), 386–408 (2021). https://doi.org/10.1108/IJWHM-08-2020-0152

11. Collins, J.H., Moschler, J.: The benefits and limitations of telecommuting. Defense A R J. **16**(1), 55 (2009)

12. Parpart, E.: Thai Enquirer. Working from home is here to stay while its hybrid model is becoming more popular, says experts, 9 September 2020. https://www.thaienquirer.com/ 18086/working-from-home-is-here-to-stay-while-its-hybrid-model-is-becoming-more-pop ular-says-experts/. Accessed 23 May 2023

13. Lund, S., Madgavkar, A., Manyika, J., Smit, S.: What's next for remote work: an analysis of 2,000 tasks, 800 jobs, and nine countries (2020). https://www.mckinsey.com/featured-ins ights/future-of-work/whats-next-for-remote-work-an-analysis-of-2000-tasks-800-jobs-and-nine-countries. Accessed 25 Jan 2023

14. O'Reardon, M.E., Rendar, M.: Managing security risk: how COVID-19 pandemic and work-from-home arrangements pose new security considerations. Empl. Relat. Law J. **46**(2), 62–67 (2020)

15. International Labor Organization: An employers' guide on working from home in response to the outbreak of COVID-19 (2020). https://www.ilo.org/wcmsp5/groups/public/---ed_dia logue/---act_emp/documents/publication/wcms_745024.pdf

16. Chayomchai, A.: The online technology acceptance model of generation-Z people in Thailand during COVID-19 crisis. Manag. Mark. Challenges Knowl. Soc. **15**(Special Issue), 496–513 (2020). https://doi.org/10.2478/mmcks-2020-0029

17. Greenhaus, J.H., Beutell, N.J.: Sources of conflict between work and family roles. Acad. Manag. Rev. **10**(1), 76–88 (1985). https://doi.org/10.5465/AMR.1985.4277352

18. Vyas, L., Butakhieo, N.: The impact of working from home during COVID-19 on work and life domains: an exploratory study on Hong Kong. Policy Des. Pract. **4**(1), 59–76 (2021)

19. Messenger, J.C., Gschwind, L.: Three generations of telework: new ICTs and the (R)evolution from home office to virtual office. New Technol. Work Employ. **31**(3), 195–208 (2016). https:// doi.org/10.1111/ntwe.12073

20. Grant, C.A., Wallace, L.M., Spurgeon, P.C., Tramontano, C., Charalampous, M.: Construction and initial validation of the E-Work Life Scale to measure remote e-working. Empl. Relat. **41**(1), 16–33 (2019). https://doi.org/10.1108/ER-09-2017-0229

21. Gajendran, R.S., Harrison, D.A.: The good, the bad, and the unknown about telecommuting: meta-analysis of psychological mediators and individual consequences. J. Appl. Psychol. **92**(6), 1524–1541 (2007)
22. Chellam, N., Divya, D.: A causal study on hybrid model and its impact on employee job performance. J. Pharm. Negative Results **13**, 866–873 (2022). https://doi.org/10.47750/pnr. 2022.13.S09.104
23. Global Workplace Analytics and Owl Labs. https://globalworkplaceanalytics.com/telecommu ting-statistics. Accessed 05 Feb 2023
24. Office of the National Economic and Social Development Council of Thailand (NESDC). https://www.nesdc.go.th/nesdb_en/ewt_dl_link.php?nid=4466&filename=social_ dev_report. Accessed 24 Mar 2023
25. White, D.R.: Agency theory and work from home. Labour: Rev. Labour Econ. Ind. Relat. **33**(1), 1–25 (2019). https://doi.org/10.1111/labr.12135
26. Dockery, A.M., Bawa, S.: When two worlds collude: working from home and family functioning in Australia. Int. Labour Rev. **157**(4), 609–630 (2018). https://doi.org/10.1111/ilr. 12119
27. Wongboonsin, P., Keeratipongpaiboon, T., Wongboonsin, K.: Changes in family composition and care relations in the Kingdom of Thailand. In: Care Relations in Southeast Asia. BRILL, Leiden, The Netherlands (2018). https://doi.org/10.1163/9789004384330_004
28. Ketkaew, C., Van Wouwe, M., Vichitthammaros, P., McMillan, D.: Exploring how an entrepreneur financially plans for retirement income: evidence from Thailand. Cogent Bus. Manag. **6**(1), 1–21 (2019). https://doi.org/10.1080/23311975.2019.1668676
29. Nandan, S., Madan, S.: Challenges and concerns of work from home during Covid-19 pandemic in India: an exploratory study. South Asian J. Manag. **29**(4), 108–130 (2022)

# Author Index

Y. Luo (Ed.): CDVE 2023, LNCS 14166, pp. 269–270, 2023.
https://doi.org/10.1007/978-3-031-43815-8

Printed in the United States
by Baker & Taylor Publisher Services